# DISTANCE EDUCATION
## A System under Stress

## About the Author

**Dr. S. Bhatnagar** was Director of Correspondence Courses and Professor of Political Science at the Panjab University, Chandigarh. Having been closely associated with the system of distance education ever since its inception in the country, he has profusely contributed to its development and growth in various different ways. Besides writing articles and research papers on its varied aspects, he participated in many national and international seminars and conferences, including the Eleventh and the Thirteenth World Meets of the International Council of Distance Education. He was also instrumental in establishing the first-ever country-wide forum of intensive deliberations and discussion on the problems of distance education, namely the National Council of Distance Education (an affiliate of the World Body). He presided over its Chandigarh Meet of 1994. With a view to further projecting the views and the research of the learned scholars, he instituted in his own Directorate the Indian Journal of Distance Education. Again being the first-ever such forum, its soon became a lively organ of academic debate and began to be enlisted among the first-rate international journals of distance education. In recognition of his manifold services to this discipline, the U.G.C. nominated him on a number of its decision-making bodies. This book is yet another venture towards the strengthening of this nascent discipline.

Besides distance education, political science is another area of his academic interest. Being primarily a student of this discipline and also having risen to the eminence of its professorship, he has widely lectured, researched and written on its various aspects. He has also authored and co-authored a number of books on such subjects as Political Theory, Local Government and Panchayati Raj. In addition, he has published numerous articles in various learned journals of international repute. Even after half a decade of his superannuation, he has been a pursuing his academic interests as actively as ever.

# DISTANCE EDUCATION
## A System under Stress
### (An in-depth Study of the Indian Institute of Correspondence Courses)

S. BHATNAGAR

CONCEPT PUBLISHING COMPANY, NEW DELHI - 110059

ISBN 81-7022-626-0

First Published 1997



*Published and Printed by*

Ashok Kumar Mittal
**Concept Publishing Company**
A/15-16, Commercial Block, Mohan Garden,
NEW DELHI - 110059 (INDIA)
Phones: 5554042, 5504042
Fax: (011) 5598898

# PREFACE

Distance education has been in existence in India for the last three decades. Vertical and horizontal expansion that it has made during these years has enabled it to establish its foothold in the realm of higher education of the country. In 1988-89, there were 5 Open Universities and 41 Institutes of Correspondence Courses which cater to the educational needs of over 5 lakh students who, in turn, constituted 1/8th of the total population of students in colleges and universities. This tremendous number apart, distance education has opened vast new avenues of higher education and skill development for those persons whom the rigours of the work-a-day world either have deprived of the opportunity of higher education or have tied them down to those occupations which ill-fit into their liking or potential competence.

Besides helping such individuals, distance education has established its profound societal relevance as well. It holds out an assurance to the nation to provide to it well-trained and competent cadres of the various types of technical personnel, thus sharing these responsibilities with the conventional system. Already a bold beginning has been made in this direction by a number of Open Universities and Institutes. They have also taken upon themselves the onerous task of helping people to redeploy themselves from one occupation to another which is the crying need of the time in view of the fast-mounting tide of liberalization of economy. Thus, distance education seeks to serve the nation as well as its citizens in various different ways.

While these years witnessed this system making an amazing progress, they have brought to the surface manifold problems that it suffers from. These problems, some of which are too subtle and deep-rooted, call for an urgent attention of the decision-makers at various levels. Unless an early solution to them is found and the working of the system is streamlined distance education would not be able to deliver the goods in as great a measure as expected of it.

There is no dearth of books on distance education in the country. But there are not many that may address themselves to the dynamics of the system in an exhaustive manner. Most of these books are either the compendia of disjointed and stray articles (generally born out of the seminars), or those that are sectoral in nature, dealing, though in depth, with one aspect of the system or another. In comparison to these books, this volume seeks not only to portray the system in its minutest detail but also to bring out, chapter by chapter, each and every problem (minor as well as major) that cripples its functioning. Efforts have also been made to offer, side by side, solutions to those problems. It may be underlined that neither the diagnosis of the ailments nor the solutions proposed thereof are abstract in nature or conjectural in substance. Instead, these are based on practical experience, relevant documentary evidence, field surveys and, above all, the learned literature. Thus, this book provides a vivid and detailed account of the system both in its micro and macro forms.

It may not be out of place to mention that distance education, as developed in this country, comprises broadly the Open Universities and the Institutes/Directorates of Correspondence Education (the latter being sponsored and run by the conventional universities). Though complimentary in nature, these two sub-systems have, by and large, failed to work in unison with each other. Their relationship is characterized more by mistrust and animosity for each other than by a spirit of co-operation and cordiality. This development is a big misfortune that has befallen this system. However we are sure that the recently-constituted Distance Education Council will help these sub-systems to close their ranks and make them march shoulder to shoulder with each other, in due course of time. We further hope that this book, even though focussing itself on the functioning and problems of the Institutes, too will help pave the way for their smooth functioning in close harmonious collaboration with each other, thereby enabling the system to fulfill its historic mission of lending its assistance to human resource development of a fast-modernizing nation of the size and stature of India.

To deal with a subject as vast as distance education one needs to interact with academics, having done some work in the field concerned. Such an interaction helps one not only to concretise one's thinking but also to chissel out the details of the work. In this respect, I have been privileged enough to have access to a number of such persons. It may be happily acknowledged that all of them have been good enought to lend to me their ungrudging support and assistance. To put on record my debt of gratitude to them individually is pretty difficult. However, I cannot help mentioning the names of Professor S.S. Mathur, Dr. Ravi K. Mahajan and Dr. Surinder K. Shukla. While the former two spent a number of long sessions with me discussing the various facets of the problem in hand, Dr. Shukla spared her valuable time in reading the manuscript from cover to cover and give her valuable suggestions.

The lack of any dependable and authentic source of information, reflecting the day-to-day functioning of the system, is one hurdle which an author of a book of this type has to grapple with. However, much of this deficiency has been made up by the two empirical studies that Professor Bakshish Singh and Principal Rudra Datt have brought out only recently. These were found highly useful and have been thus quoted extensively. Even then some gaps in information were left. In order to bridge them, I had to do some field work particularly in the neighbouring Directorates. In the course of this survey, my task was considerably facilitated by the help and cooperation received from Professor J.S. Anand, Head, Department of Correspondence Course, Punjabi University, Patiala, Principal Rudra Datt, Delhi School of Correspondence and Continuing Education, Mrs. Nisha Garg, Head, Department of Political Science, Directorate of Correspondence Courses, Kurukshetra University, Kurukshetra, Mr. S.R. Mehta, Deputy Registrar, HP University, Shimla, and above all, my highly valued friend and former colleague, Dr. S.S. Chib, Professor and Head, Department of Geography, Jammu University, Jammu. I feel highly grateful to all of them.

I must also put on record my deep sense of appreciation for Mr. Jagdish Gandhi and Mr. Bhuvan Singh for their having assisted me in the preparation of the computerised master copy of the manuscript. To transcribe an illegibly handwritten script into a flawless type-set version and, more irritatingly, to do the exercise repeatedly in order to incorporate the new data/information that poured in every time, is a task which exhausts the patience of even the highly patient persons. Both Mr. Gandhi and Mr. Singh bore with the author quite ungrudgingly.

I am equally grateful to Mr. Ashok Kumar Mittal of M/s Concept Publishing Company, New Delhi, for his painstaking efforts to bring out this book in a so beautiful get up.

In the end, I must also appreciate the steady and silent support from I received from my wife, Indra, in the course of the preparation of this book. The boredom, that she suffered, partly because of the immigration of our sons and grand-sons to a distant foreign land, and mainly because of silence imposed in the house by her husband, on the pretext of writing this book, cannot be compensated in any way. This devotion when viewed in the context of the fast crumbling citadel of male hegemony in Indian society is highly remarkable. I am beholden to her.

Incidentally, this book is being brought out in the centenary year of the birth of my father, late B.L. Kangriya. I dedicate it to his cherished memory.

2 October, 1996 S. Bhatnagar

# CONTENTS

CHAPTER 1

# THEORETICAL PERSPECTIVES

LITERALLY though it means providing education to people placed in non-contiguous situations, distance education is a comprehensive theoretical concept as well as a new unconventional mode of public instruction. Conceptually, it enunciates, first, that education is a life-long process and, second, that the educational system should not only help spread education among all but should also cater to the specific needs of each individual. Together with each other, these two theoretical constructs lend support to the theory of democracy and egalitarianism. Operationally, distance education seeks to modify the existing educational system in various different ways so as to translate the above stated theory into practice.

To dilate upon these conceptual postulates, ever since man has acquired consciousness, he feels that learning is an unending process, commencing at birth and terminating only at death. But in so far as the organised form of learning is concerned, it has been strictly confined to the children and the adolescents. Accordingly, our schools, colleges and universities prescribe a certain age limit for their students. They cannot remain on their rolls after having attained that age limit. Conversely, the conventional system does not make any provision for the education of those grown-up adults who may, for one reason or another, like to continue, or to renew, their studies. Another dimension of this theory is that education can be had only within the pricincts of the class room and nowhere else. The rationale of this theory is that man's mind is fresh and receptive during childhood and adolescence and hence this is the most appropriate age to receive education. Moreover, being too young to be tormented by the worldly affairs, one can devote himself to studies whole-heartedly and undistractingly.

Without rebutting any of these arguments, distances theorists seek to extend the purview of the formal system of education to the adult learners as well (Bonami , 1982). Their assertion is that when a person can learn things informally all through his life, why can't he grasp or even master the formal lesson given in a school/university ? Distance education theory is thus a vindication of the Platonic philosophy of life-long education.

The second theoretical postulate is `education for all' and `education for each'. Education is that rare asset of an individual, the possession of which makes one qualitatively different from those who are deprived of it. Besides equipping him with the knowledge of the three Rs, it makes a person not only conscious of the world around him but also articulate and assertive in his tone and tenor. If a vast majority of the people around the world have thus far suffered exploitation at the hands of a few of their compatriots, one important reason, among others, was their educational deprivation. The mounting tide of democracy has made people, by and large, conscious of this shortcoming on their part, with the result that massive efforts are under way almost every where to spread education among the masses. Hopefully, the day is not far when this laudable objective is attained.

The other facet of this theory is `education for each (Patricia Cross, 1978). The exigencies of modern life have kindled in the mind of every educated person an ambition for more and more of education. Some of them are bewitched of the desire to improve their educational qualifications in order to have a better status in life. Some seek it with a view to redeploy themselves from one occupation to another. Some others may be keen to keep themselves occupied during their leisure hours. There is yet another reason for the generation of this demand. Knowledge is expanding so fast that whatever we learn at school/university gets obsolescent rather too soon. The older idea that initial education gained during our childhood and adolescence would serve our purpose throughout the whole of our life is no longer tenable (Perry, p. 281).There is an imperative need to replenish our knowledge continuously all through our life, if we wish to discharge our professional obligations more faithfully and also want to lead our life more refreshingly.

Thus, the demand of the people for more and more of education, (more specifically continuing education) varies from individual to individual. One wants to shift, say, from engineering to medicine, another is tempted by music, yet another is fascinated by painting and wants to learn it, and so on. Why should such persons be tied down to a certain given rigid combination of subjects, or to a comprehensive course of studies, which happen to be a characteristic feature of the conventional system ? The educational system of a society should be such as may concede to the learner the requisite freedom and flexibility to pursue studies as per his needs and in a manner that suits his convenience. Precisely, this is what distance theorists propose. They are of the view that what, where, when and how to study are the issues which ought to be decided not by the university dons but by the adult learner himself. Keeping this fact in view, distance education may aptly be described as learner-oriented, as distinguished from the teacher-oriented system of conventional education. (Kegan, 1980). Thus, distance theorists make a case for the `deschooling' of education (to borrow the phrase from Ivan Illich, 1971) and want its benefits to reach everybody, irrespective of one's age, occupation or place of residence.

Incidentally, both these principles advance the cause of democracy. Hitherto, education was the guarded privilege of the wealthy few and they had a vested interest in "maintaining the cleft between the educated and the masses." (Gunnar Myrdal, 1971, p.195) In order to keep the common man out of the pail of education, they had made the educational system quite rigid by such contrivances as the venue of instruction, the minimum and the maximum age within which education can be received, entrance qualifications to schools, colleges and universities, fixed nature of the curricula of studies and meticulous care with which the schools/ universities administer it. Modernity permeated by the spirit of democracy and egalitarianism, does not make room for any such feudalistic notion as may help sustain, even remotely, the vestiges of the anachronistic social order. Education must become the fundamental right of every one, irrespective of one's birth or material worth. Coming in the wake of this mass-uprising and the assertion of the common man of his right for education, these principles of distance education not only reinforce the democratic demand for education but also break the mental barriers against the spread of education among all sections of society. Distance education would thus be a step further in the direction of equity and social justice which, in turn, would strengthen the roots of democracy.

Thus, distance education, conceptually, aims at opening the floodgates of education to people hailing from all sections of society and from all age-groups, thereby democratising the system in every possible way. Further espousing the cause of continuing education, it seeks to cater to the specific (as distinguished from the general) needs of the individual. Radical in approach as this new system is, it ushers into a new era of hope, equity and (consequently) of a perfect egalitarian socio-political order.

At the operational plane, distance theorists seek to pull down the narrow walls of the school/university. Instead of requiring the adult learners to come to the school and receive instruction regularly at the feet of their teacher, education should 'travel' to their homes and make itself freely available to all those who seek it. In support of this thesis, distance theorists argue that the age, maturity and ardent commitment of the adult learners to their studies amply qualify them to pursue their studies independently at their own homes and during their free time. By releasing the instructional system from the traditional hold of the conventionalists, distance theorists open the portals of education for those grown-ups who had thus far been deprived of the privilege of education on grounds of their age and inability to regularly commute to the school to receive instruction. The new system has thus laid open vast new avenues for the ambitious and enterprising individuals to fulfil their desire for education. No longer would their age, place of residence or occupational hazards come in their way. One would neither be debarred from education nor would he be forced for it. One may have as much of it as one wants or can absorb (Erdos, 1967).

The next important modification that distance theorists make in the conventional system in order to accommodate the adult learners in it relates to the methodology of instruction. Spatial separation of the teacher and the taught renders the traditional method of direct face-to-face interaction between the two totally redundant. In this changed perspective, the written lesson can alone prove to be the only viable medium of instruction. Of late, the audio and the video tapes, telephone, computer-mediated methods like video-conferencing and the like have also emerged as supplementary teaching aids. Together with the written lesson, they have gone a long way in making distance teaching effective by bridging the gap between the teacher and the taught.

Learning is a two-way process the teacher imparting instruction while the students reacting to them. In the conventional system, the teacher directly talks to his students and explains the lesson by the expression of his face and the gestures of his hands. On their part, the students give the feedback by nodding their head, winking their eyes and by many other gestures. In this process, they may interrupt him to seek more of elucidation and explanation, he may also admonish some and give a pat on the shoulders of the others. All this is not possible in distance teaching. Here the lessons of the teachers as well as the feedback of the students is mediated through correspondence. The students write their home assignments (response sheets) and mail them to the Institute where these are evaluated by the teachers. Not only do teachers assess them in terms of marks and grades but also point out the deficiencies in them and indicate how those deficiencies can be removed and further improvements can be made. Besides, the students can also get their difficulties ironed out at the hands of their teacher and can seek various other types of guidance on telephone. Video-conferencing which brings the teacher and the distance students electronically face-to-face with one another has further facilitated the interaction between the two. Thus, the two-way communication, whether built by means of the traditional method of correspondence or the newer electronic technologies, is by no means feeble. Being both 'real and simulated' (Holmberg, 1989), it is perhaps as potent and effective as obtains in the class-room setting. In fact, it is the essence of distance education (Garrison and Shale, 1990)

These two measures of reform (namely the demolition of the school walls and the delivery of the study materials at the homes of the students) are too inadequate either to suit the convenience of the adults to avail of the benefits of education or to translate the theory of distance education into practice. To make the existing system still more attractive for them, distance theorists induct into it an element of flexibility and openness.

Ronie Carr interprets flexibility and openness in terms "(a) the removal of barriers to participation which are inherent in the traditional system such as the timings and location of delivery, the pace of study and entry qualifications; (b) the giving of greater responsibility to learners to determine not only where and when they study, but also for example, what they learn, how they learn and how they are assessed." (I.C.D.E. Bulletin. No. 22, p. 48). In more specific terms distance education is flexible, first, in the duration of its study. The conventional system, for instance, binds down a person to a certain fixed duration of time within which one must complete a certain given course. If one fails to do so, he is debarred from its study. To illustrate, the Panjab University grants a maximum period of five years to complete the three-year bachelors course in arts, science and commerce. In case one does not do so within this prescribed duration, his candidature is scrapped. If one is still interested in that course, he will have to go through the whole process *de novo*; whatever number of examinations he has cleared earlier will no longer be of any avail to him. On the contrary, an Open University grants full freedom to a person to join a course whenever he likes. If at any stage, he finds it difficult to carry on with that course he may opt himself out of it. And if after a lapse of a few years, his interest in that course is revived, he can come back to it and claim the benefit of those credits which he had secured earlier. His claim is conceded without any loss whatsoever. Herein lies the superiority of this system and the secret of its immense popularity.

Second, the distance system does not restrict the choice of a candidate to a few pre-determined combination of subjects of a certain course. If, for instance, one wants to combine the study of music with political science, or chemistry with economics, one cannot possibly do so under the conventional system, whereas the distance system allows this freedom. Furtheron, one can go in for the study of even one single, stray subject, and not necessarily for the whole combination of subjects under the distance system. This feature is helpful particularly to those persons who, in the later years of their life, develop a taste in a certain new field/discipline which they had not studied earlier in their school/college days.

More important than all these facets of flexibility of the distance system is the freedom that it grants to the candidates to join a course even if one does not have any background of its study. To illustrate, no conventional university allows a person to join, say, the first degree course in arts or commerce unless he has passed the senior secondary (10+2) or the old pre-university examination of any university or board of school examinations. But in comparison to this, an Open University allows admission even to those who, not to speak of possessing that qualification , have not been to school at all. It would admit these persons after having given to them (and not necessarily requiring them to pass) a foundation course of a few weeks' duration and that too by means of correspondence. Infact, open universities do not prescribe any type of qualifications by way of a condition to admit candidates to a certain course.

Highlighting the concept of openness as practised by the Open University of Great Britain, its first Chancellor, Lord Geoffrey Crowther once remarked:, "We are open, first as to people... There are no limits on persons; We are open as to places... There are no boundaries of space; We are open to methods...There is no restriction on techniques; We are open, finally to ideas".(Hommadi.)

This type of openness may sound astounding to those who have been bred and brought up in the conventional system. But this is in tune with the philosophy of distance education. As hinted earlier, this system is based on the democratic philosophy that education should be thrown open and made accessible to all persons without any let or hindrance. Those of them who have the capability to acquire and absorb it may do so as much as they can, whereas those who cannot cope with it may not either come forward for it at all or may bow out of it whenever they so like.

Thus, flexibility is the corner-stone of the system of distance education and distance is the arch around which it revolves. These are the two major differences between this system and the conventional system.

Thus, distance education is a technique of teaching, an unconventional mode of instruction to a large mass of students. scattered far and wide on the length and breadth of the globe. So long as education was restricted to the narrow confines of the class-room, it gave the look of a village craft, typical of the medieval times when the village (school) master craftsman used to hammer his knowledge into the minds of his pupils, patiently and perseveringly, by means of his direct face-to-face interaction with them constantly throughout the course of the three hundred and sixty five days of the year. The advent of the theory of distance education and its synchronisation with the amazing advances in the field of communication technology, pulled out education from the level of a craft and converted it into a technology whereby education can be provided on a mass-scale to millions of people, not necessarily through the instrumentality of the traditional teacher. His place has been taken over partly by the printed word and partly by the new electronic-based communication technologies. Education has thus been suitably geared to meet the requirements of industrial and post-industrial societies It is an industrialised form of teaching and learning' as Otto Peters (1973), describes it.

## II

Distance education, as it has been shaped and modelled, both conceptually and operationally, presents a picture pretty different from the conventional system. Apart from the differences based on the spatial separation of the teacher and the taught, (emerging therefrom), the methodology of instruction, and flexibility and openness in the system , the two have drifted away from each other even with respect to the nature of the students that they cater. Those who come to the conventional system are children in their teens and the adolescents in their early twenties. Being premature in age, their conduct lacks somewhat the sense of responsibility, thus demanding of their teacher a role not only that of giving them instruction in a few academic subjects, but also that of helping them inculcate discipline, build their character and shape their personality. On the contrary, distance education system concentrates its attention on the grown-up adults who are advanced in age (generally in the range of the mid-twenties to early forties, quite a few of them may even be in the fifties and in the early sixties), employed (some of them may even be in high positions of authority and responsibility), married and having children. However, in India and perhaps in other developing countries, the number of the youngsters in their late teens and early twenties has also of late been on the increase, due to the fast-growing population of the school turn-outs and the comparatively smaller number of the conventional institutions to absorb them. All distance students, whether of the first category or of the second, are in the system more by their choice and far less on the compelling direction of their parents and family elders. Their age, motivation and the seriousness with which they pursue their studies combinedly constitute them into a class by themselves, having little in common with the class room based students of the conventional system.

Even though the two systems--distance and conventional--are different from each other in their philosophy, approach and methodology, they are not antagonistic to each other. Far from this, they are complementary in nature, one giving strength and support to the other. If the conventional system takes care of the education of the young, the distance system helps those adults who want more of education in their later life; who cannot go back to schools and colleges and pursue studies on a whole time basis because of responsibilities of the home and office. If the conventional system equips a person with the basic working knowledge of languages, humanities, science, commerce and the like, thereby enabling him to earn a living, the distance system helps him to further strengthen that knowledge and skills, perhaps to improve his station in life or to spend his leisure in a more meaningful manner. Thus, far from being rival, distance education takes over where the conventional system is compelled to leave. No nation can afford to pull on with either of the systems. In the present-day world where all societies have been badly overtaken by 'the revolution of rising expectations', everyone of them needs to have both these systems — the conventional system to groom the younger citizens in the art of living and the distance system to satiate the hunger of the elders for more of education and skill development.

The complementary nature of the two systems makes many a nation to integrate these two systems together in such a way that they may satisfy the demands and aspirations of both the young and the old in a harmonious manner. A number of conventional universities in Australia and Canada, for instance, which had for decades been giving traditional courses to the class-room based (what they call on-campus) students, have now thrown their gates open to the distance (off-campus) students as well. Those who teach courses to the former, also develop lessons on them for the use of the latter. The courses of study and the mode of evaluation are identical for both these categories of students. Why talk of Australia and Canada, even we in India have adopted this 'dual model'. As many as 41 universities of our country provide for correspondence studies alongwith the class-room based students. No less than 84 per cent of distance students studied through this dual mode in 1988-89.

Even the other model, namely Open Universities, makes a provision for some sort of traditional education in languages and humanities, more or less, on the lines of the conventional universities. They do so mainly with the objective of catering to the needs of higher education of those persons who fail to find accommodation in conventional institutions. The number of open universities is fast growing in all countries of the world, the reason being the escalating aspiration of the hitherto socially neglected sections of the population. Thus, both the systems grow side by side, one benefiting the other. Distance education puts much of its reliance on the scholarship that conventionalists have built up over the years. Most of the teachers associated with the development of study material, evaluation of response sheets, counselling and personal contact programmes and such other distance education aspects, hail from the conventional system. In the same manner, class-room teaching has also received a new orientation and impetus from the study material of the distance system. The audio-visual instructional material that the latter has developed is also being widely used by the conventional teachers, thereby establishing the mutuality and inter-dependence between the two systems.

## III

Historically, distance education marks the culmination of that process which found its humble beginning in the minds of those stray and isolated individuals who, motivated by the desire to have more of education, prosecuted their studies at their respective homes. As with the passage of time, the number of such individuals grew, some well-established institutions thought in terms of doing tangible help to them by means of written notes/lessons which were sent to them by post. It was in the U.S.A., Australia and Great Britain that such correspondence study programmes made a beginning in the 19th century. In the USA, for instance, correspondence courses were developed in the beginning of this century to "(a) allow young people who had finished elementary school in areas where secondary schools did not exist, to continue their studies, and (b) allow secondary school students to study subjects which their schools did not offer." (Daniel *1982* )

In no time, this mode of assisted postal instruction caught the imagination of both the educationists and the education-seekers the world over. The post-second world war period which heralded innumerable imperial colonies to independence, opened a vast new field for the system to scale new heights. Actuated by the long pent up ambition to develop their societies on the western model, as also by the heavy constraint of resources, these newly-freed countries discovered in this system a comparatively easier method to bring about educational development of their nationals. Sooner than later, almost everyone of them went the whole hog for this system and instituted correspondence study programmes on a large scale.

Meanwhile, the amazing progress that electronic technology had made, ushered in a new era of instructional technology. A vast range of electronic gadgetry was put at the disposal of the teachers, facilitating their task of communicating with their distance students both through their live voice and their moving and gesturing hands. Instead of depending upon postal coaching through the medium of the cold print, each individual student could now create in his own home the environments of a lively classroom. What he has to do is just to insert a cassette into his video machine and put the switch on. Audio Conferencing has made his task easier still.

Realising the revolutionary impact of the newer educational technologies on the instructional system, the doyans of this system of education rechristianed their global organisation from the International Council for Correspondence Education to the International Council for Distance Education in 1982. Since then, all such Institutes which make use of these technologies wear the dignified title of the Institutes of Distance Education and dub the others which continue to impart instruction through correspondence as the Institutes of Correspondence Education. It may not be an exaggeration to say that today distance education has come to be associated more with electronic technologies and less with the distant span of its sweep.

## IV

Despite its immense utilities and vast potentialities, the common man is not as well-aware of the system of distance education and whoever has some idea, generally carries a poor impression of it. Lamenting this fact,

Kegan says, "Even a cursory reading of educational literature shows that distance systems are usually ignored. It merits not a paragraph in most volumes of educational philosophy, in guides to administrative progress or in analysis of didactic strategy" (Quoted by G.Ram Reddy in B.N.Kaul, *et al.*, 1988, p.11). Another commentator makes a more pithy statement. He says "... distance education has, by and large, failed to project a good image of itself. Even though it provides a supplementary channel for higher education by absorbing the overflow from colleges and university departments, no respectable person likes to send his wards to a Directorate of Correspondence Courses. For, education that is imparted through them is considered second grade." (Editorial *Indian Journal of Distance Education* ).

Distance education could not make much of an impact on the general public partly for the reason that it is comparatively a new system. Many people and even some of the educationists are not quite aware of its development. But more importantly, it is the conventionalists who are responsible not only for side-tracking it but also for obstructing its progress. They perceive in its potentialities a challenge to their hitherto unshared monopolies. Their apprehension is that with the spread of this system, as Qtto Peters (1969) rightly puts it, "the Institutes of higher learning could lose much of their dignified academic exclusiveness, their secluded atmosphere and circumscribed forms and conventions. Their teaching processes could be open to public control" (Proceedings of the 8th ICCE Conference. p.100) The conventionalists have thus tended to ignore this system in their learned writings and also to slight it down in their day-to-day dealings. This fact manifests itself in the shabby treatment that the traditional universities meet out to this system especially when it is tied to their apron strings as most of the Institutes of Correspondence Courses in India are. Not only are the problems of these Institutes not sympathetically appreciated but even tangible hindrances are put in the way of their progress (This issue will be discussed in detail in the chapters to follow).

The entire blame cannot, of course, be laid at the door of the others. The system itself cannot be absolved of the charge that it has not worked hard to earn a good reputation for itself. At the initial stages of its inception, distance education was in the hands of the private persons who had a very limited objective in view. Thus hampered by poor vision, on the one hand, and narrow objectives, on the other, they failed to spread its message and ideology forcefully. Later on, it came to be tagged with the conventional system, which too did not make serious efforts to realise its full worth. It is at a much later stage that it came to acquire an independent pedestal of its own when it got freedom to work its way up. Even then not all the Institutes could make a mark because freedom alone was not a sufficient prerequisite for its progressive functioning . Many other inputs needed to be adequately taken care of if the goal of social credibility was to be achieved. Those Institutes which really worked hard could establish a good reputation, and came to be known far and wide. If distance education has any credit today, it is entirely due to the good work done by those few Institutes/Open Universities.

It may, however, be underlined that it is quite difficult for a new system to acquire roots, especially when it is locked against another system which is so well-entrenched. And if the potentialities of the new system are as weighty (if not more) as those of the existing one against which it is to compete, the challenge becomes all the more formidable. Although distance education was in no way antagonistic to the conventional system, yet the latter (as alluded above) perceived in it a challenge to its monopoly and power and thus created problems for it.

More significantly, the criteria of evaluation in the case of distance education, were more open and exposed to the public than those of the conventional system. This characteristic of the new system further created problems for it. To spell out the criteria of evaluation of an educational system. In the first place comes the quality of instruction. This is one of the major variables that determines the reputation of an educational institution. In the case of the conventional system, instruction are generally imparted orally, making/leaving nothing on record. How good or bad are the instructicn that a particular institution imparts, only those students know of them who are their recipients. The others cannot have even an inkling of them. But in so far as distance education is concerned, the whole process of instruction is non-oral in character. The study material that is given to distance students is generally in the form of either the written lesson scripts or the audio and the video cassettes. Both of these manifestations are on record and thus open to the public at large to read, listen or view it and pass their judgment freely on its quality. Thus, this system, being open and transparent, is more prone to public gaze and criticism than the conventional system. (Ralph E Smith, 1988 and Bakshish Singh. 1995 ). Without casting reflection on university teachers, it may be vouched that many well-known among them who enjoyed wide reputation as excellent class-room teachers, when approached, declined to write a lesson for distance students. Some of them were candid enough to tell this author that by putting their lesson in black and white, they would expose themselves to the criticism of the general public and thereby spoil their hard-earned reputation.

The second criterion of the reputation of an Institute of distance education is the efficiency of its delivery system. Whether or not its study materials reach its distance students as timely as they expect of it? Again, this is something which cannot be hidden from the public eye. Since the whole process of the preparation and production of the study material is so long-drawn and many a divergent individual and institution are engaged in its manipulation, it is very unlikely that the final step in the series of this multi-stage process may always be accomplished in accordance with the pre-determined schedule. Sometimes delay is bound to occur with the result that the reputation of the Institute would suffer a setback. But as far as the conventional system is concerned, there is no such slippery path for it to tread. Instruction are delivered by the teachers in the classroom. If anyone of them misses his pace some- times, he is conscious enough to make good that lapse sooner than later. The authorities as well as the students of the institution concerned are there to pull up the erring individual, if any . Thus, the incidence of lapse on the part of the teachers is nominal. But in the case of the distance system, the process is too complicated to be easily controlled by the institute's authorities.

Finally, the performance of students in the final terminal examination forms another criterion of an Institute's reputations. What is the pass percentage of the students, what is their drop-out rate, and how good is their performance in qualitative terms—are some of the traditional yard-sticks with the help of which the reputation of an educational institution is generally measured. However, this criterion is relevant only for the conventional system in view of the fact that in this case the whole instructional process is fully controlled. It is controlled in the sense that the number of students admitted to a class or an institution is limited; they always remain under the constant gaze and supervision of their teachers who receive a continuous feedback of their students and so on and so forth. It is therefore very appropriate that the performance of the conventional institutions is judged in terms of the number of those who take the final terminal examination, who drop out, and who bag top positions. On the contrary,the case of distance education is pretty different. The whole system is so open-ended and loose that those who impart instruction do not know what motivated their students to distance studies, whether or not the lessons that they send are studied by them, whether or not are they keen to complete the course and so on. It is, therefore, not very relevant to apply the criterion of performance in the terminal examination to judge either the quality of the instruction or the reputation of an Institute.

All these criteria are too harsh on distance education. Their application is bound to lower it in the estimations of the general public. But since the conventional system has so much clouded our vision that we cannot think of any other criterion (though there are many others) more suitable to this system. Hence, distance education does not cut much ice with the common man.

There is no gain-saying the fact that all these criteria are misplaced in so far as distance education is concerned. Nevertheless, we need to be vigilant on at least two of these three fronts, if public image is of any consideration to us. We must ensure by all means that the study material that we service to our students is by far the best and, further, that it is delivered to its users in some well-planned rhythmic order. It is needless to point out that if the Indira Gandhi National Open University (IGNOU) has been successful in establishing the reputation of a first-rate Institute of Distance Education in the country, the secret lies in the quality of its study material. Any compromise on this account will pull down an Institute to the level of a third-rate private coaching centre.

As for the new and more apt criteria to judge the reputation of an Institute of Distance Education, the first and the foremost is the type of courses of study that it offers. Most of the typical Institutes give the bachelors and the masters courses in art and humanities. Some of them proliferate to such disciplines as commerce, law, education, library science and the like. All these courses have thus become too common place. That Institute which deviates from this beaten track alone would qualify itself to be rated differently and would thus steal a march over the others in popularity and reputation. To cite the case of the IGNOU again. If today it has surpassed all other Institutes of Distance Education and Open Universities in India, one distinctive feature that accounts for its growing popularity is the non-conventional and need-based nature of most of its study programmes.

The second criterion is, how far an Institute and for that matter distance education system as a whole, serve the cause of the nation with respect to such of its needs as training and retraining of its technical man-power As mentioned above,every developing society not only suffers from a dearth of suitably trained technical man-power but also faces an urgent need of redeploying people from one employment to another. Distance education provides a ready and convenient mode to meet this challenge more effectively and at a comparatively far lesser cost. How far an Institute is conditioned and actually equipped for this task would further determine its worth and reputation. Obviously, those Institutes which provide in collaboration with the industrial and commercial houses of the country the training needs of their personnel would beat the others in both their relevance to the nation and popularity in general.

Finally, the reaction of those persons who have been the students of an Institute toward their alma mater, toward its instructional strategies and toward its services constitutes perhaps the biggest barometer of its success. Ralf. C Smith (1988) very aptly remarks, "They can lead or deter, others to follow in their footprints" ( In G.Ram Reddy p.248). Those who go out of an Institute become the ambassadors of its goodwill as well as of its evil reputation, depending upon their respective personal experience. Allied with this factor is the image that they project and the way their education, and more specifically the skill training that they have received from it, has an impact upon their employers in particular. In case the employers are impressed by the quality of the training an Institute imparts, it is but natural that its reputation would travel far and wide, attracting the attention and interest of many others. Reporting from Spain, for instance, Garcia Garrido (1988) says that the students of UNED (its open university) do not face any problem in having their credentials recognised. For, they have proved to possess important qualities such "as self-discipline, persistence, determination, self-esteem, all of which are highly appreciated by their employers." ( G.Ram Reddy)

In the end, it may be observed that distance education with all its weaknesses and strengths, has gained a strong foothold all over the world. It would not be an exaggeration to say that it provides the key to the future development of society, irrespective of the level of its development. For, we have already entered into an age "where education in general and higher education in particular is, at one and the same time, a necessary condition of a modern technological society and defence against its abuse" (British Open University Report). In such a radically changed perspective of society, such education, as Erling Ljosa (1990) emphasises, "cannot be provided by a return to the school room but has to be provided by non-traditional means through the old media of books and through the new media of electronic communications. . . . If distance education had not been invented a hundred years ago or more, the needs of the population would be inventing it now. Distance education is indeed a necessary part of life for the next generations".

## REFERENCES


Bakshish Singh, "Mechanics of Maintenance of Standards in Distance Education", in Bakshish Singh (Ed.) *New Horizons in Distance Education.* New Delhi, Uppal. 1995.

Bomani, Giampaolo, "Correspondence Teaching : second chance or second class" in Daniel, John S. Martha, A Stroud and John, R Thomson (Eds.), *Learning at a Distance: A World Perspective.* Edmonton Athabsca University, 1982.

Carr, Ronie. 'Open Learning: An Imprecise Term'. *I.C.D.E. Bulletin* No. 22.

Cross, Patricia K, 'For All and For Each', (1978), quoted in S.S. Mathur, 'Building A Philosophy of Distance Education'. *Indian Journal of Distance Education* (Chandigarh). Vol. I.

Crowther, Geoffray, quoted by Hommadi, A .H.*Open University, Retrospect and Prospect.* Delhi, Indian Bibliographies Bureau, 1989.

Daniel, Johns, in Daniel, John S. *et al. Op. Cit.*

Dodds, Jony. Quoted by Bakshish Singh, 'Distance Education, some definitions and teaching learning component', in Bakshish Singh (Ed.) *Op.Cit.*

Erdos, Renee F., *Teaching By Correspondence*, UNESCO, Source Book. London, Longman. 1967

Garrido, Garicia in G.Ram Reddy, *Open Universities, Ivory Towers Thrown Open.* Delhi, Sterling, 1988.

Garrison, D.R. and Shale, D.G. 'Filling At Windmills? Destroying Mythology in Distance Education: *I.C.D.E. Bulletin*, No.24. (September,1990)

Holmberg, Borje, *Theory and Practice of Distance Education*, London, Routledge. 1989.

Holmberg, Borje. 'A Paradigm Shift In Distance Education,' *I.C.D.E. Bulletin*, No.22. (January, 1990)

Illich, Ivan, *Deschooling Society*, Penguin Books, 1971.

Kegan, J.A. 'On Defining Distance Education' (1980) quoted by Daniel, John S. *et al. Op. Cit.*

Kegan, Din quoted by Daniel, John S. *et al., Op.Cit.*

Kegan, D. Quoted by G.Ram Reddy, 'Distance Education What, Why And How ?', in B.N.Koul, Bakshish Singh and M.M.Ansari, (Eds.) *Studies In Distances Education.* New Delhi, Association of Indian Universities And IGNOU. 1988.

Ljosa, Erling. '*Distance Education in Europe and Models for Organising Future Co-operation'.* *I.C.D.E. Bulletin.* No.25. (December, 1990)

Myrdal, Gunar, *The Challenge of World Poverty*, Penguin Books Series. 1971.

Peters, Otto, 'New Perspectives in Correspondence Study Programmes in Europe' in Qenee Erdos (Ed.) *Proceedings of the Eighth International Conference of The International Council on Correspondence Education.* UNESCO House Press, 1969.

Peters, Qtto, *The Didactical Structure of Distance Teaching: Investigations towards an industrialised form of teaching and learning.* 1973.

Smith, Ralph E .in G.Ram Reddy. *Open Universities Ivory Towers Thrown Open.* Delhi. Sterling. 1988.

Swamy, V.C. Kulandai, 'Communication Technology and Productivity in Distance Education in Bakshish Singh (Ed.). *Op.Cit.*

*Indian Journal of Distance Education* (Chandigarh) Vol.IV.

CHAPTER II

# THE INDIAN SCENARIO

## I

PRESENTLY, distance education in India is provided by 6 Open Universities and 41 conventional university-run institutes. Together, these three dozen institutions cater to the higher education needs of half a million students, which constitute 10.5 per cent of the total population of students in the universities and colleges of the country. It is expected that by the turn of the century, this system would absorb one quarter of the total number of 6.9 million higher education students. The study programmes that they offer range from the traditional degree courses in arts, humanities and commerce to the highly sophisticated and specialised studies in technology and computer sciences, from courses of the general nature to job-oriented training programmes, from certificate courses to research degree.

## II

Distance education is a recent development in this country, tracing its origin to the early 1960's. Anticipating the generation of an unprecedented demand for education as a result of the introduction of freedom, democracy and development, and also the comparative lack of state's resources to meet that demand, the Government of India thought it prudent in the late fifties to find out a suitable alternative which may be both academically sound and economically viable. It was this quest which led to the establishment of the School of Correspondence and Continuing Education at the University of Delhi in 1962. This maiden experiment in distance education in the country was launched with a view (as K.L.Shrimali, the then Minister for Education had put it while inaugurating that Institute) "(1) to provide an efficient and less expensive method of educational instruction at a higher level. (2) to provide facilities to pursue higher education to all qualified and willing persons who had failed to join higher university courses due to personal and economic reasons or because of their inability to get admission to a regular college, and (3) to provide opportunities of academic pursuits to educated citizens through correspondence instruction without disturbing their present employment."(Quoted by G.Ram Reddy in Koul. p.19).

This experiment proved to be a resounding success. A large number of persons who had for long been keenly looking forward to an opportunity to improve their qualifications found in this institution a God-sent opportunity. They seized it by its forelock. Impressed by its success, the Punjabi University, Patiala and the Meerut University set up Directorates of Correspondence Courses. In this way, a new dimension of extension education came to be added to the conventional universities. Hitherto the education seekers used to come to the universities and enrolled themselves with them on a whole-time basis. From now onward, the universities would go to the people, offering opportunities of higher education to them at their door-step. Equally significantly, the students would no longer tie themselves with their educational institutions, and instead they would now pursue their studies at their own time and pace and in the familiar environments of their home. Thus, the whole set-up and approach to education came to be revolutionised.

That distance education can be imparted at a comparatively less cost caused a glee to many a university in the country. For, this new system indirectly meant a lot of money which could help them tide over many of their financial difficulties. And in this bargain, they could also incidentally project the image of a true builder of the nation by helping thousands of socially and economically handicapped men and women to improve their educational qualifications. The grand success that the Delhi and the Patiala experiments achieved provided to the gleeful universities an additional spur to launch themselves in this field.

Impelled by the profit motive and also by the genuine missionary desire to open their portals to distance learners, many universities went ahead with the establishment of the Institutes of Correspondence Education. The seventies saw these Institutes coming up in the universities of Mysore (1970), Panjab, Madurai, Himachal and Bombay (1971), Andhra and Sri Venkateshwara (1972), C.I.E.F.L. Hyderabad (1973), Patna (1974), Bhopal and Utkal (1975), Kurukshetra, Kerala, Jammu , Kashmir and Rajasthan (1976), Osmania (1977), Allahabad (1978), Kolhapur, Annamalai, S.N.D.T.Bombay and Udaipur (1979). In this way, distance education came to be firmly rooted in the Indian soil by the end of the 1970's. Not only did it spread its network all over the country, but most of the Institutes which had hitherto confined their distance institutes to the under-graduate level upgraded their study programmes to the post-graduate level. A modest beginning in the job-oriented direction was also noticed.

The 1980's witnessed a further expansion of this system. More and more conventional universities set up these Institutes, providing therein a number of new study programmes of the non-conventional nature, of course, besides the beaten-track ones, thereby making this stream of education more relevant to the growing needs of the nation. However, the more significant development of that decade was the emergence of open universities in the country. A beginning in this direction was made by the State of Andhra Pradesh which set up in 1982 the first Open University of the country (Andhra Pradesh, now renamed Dr. B.R. Ambedkar Open University, Hyderabad). It was followed by the establishment of the Indira Gandhi National Open University (IGNOU) at New Delhi in 1985. Being a venture of the Central Government and having been launched with a lot of fanfare, the birth of the IGNOU was hailed by everyone as a very big leap forward in the direction of making distance education more open and flexible, thereby putting distance education to the service of the nation more effectively.

Anyway, the emergence of this university provided to this system, (as S.K. Aggarwal and M.M. Ansari very aptly put it) "the legitimacy it rightly deserves in the national educational system of the country" (Directory of Distance Education Institutions, Part I, India, p.3). Three more Open Universities came up in a rapid succession to each other, namely Kota Open University (1987) which the Rajasthan Government set up by merging together the Directorates of Correspondence Courses of Jaipur and Udaipur; Yashwant Rao Chavan Maharashtra Open University, Nasik (1989) and Nalanda Open University, Patna (1989). Another Open University (Raja Bhoj Open University) was set up at Bhopal in 1992.

The emergence of Open Universities particularly the IGNOU, inducted into the system of distance education an element of 'openness'. So long as this system was hinged with the conventional system, admission to it was rigidly rule-bound. Only those who had attained the prescribed minimum qualification could get admission to a course. But now the concept of the minimum qualification was done away by the Open Universities. They instituted foundation courses. Anyone could now enroll oneself with these universities even if one does not have any formal degree/diploma/certificate to one's credit. Emulating the example of the Open Universities, many other Institutes also followed suit. In this way, the system acquired the features of both openness and flexibility.

Thus, by the end of the 1980's there were 6 Open Universities and 41 Institutes of Correspondence Courses in the country. Of the latter, 4 provide extension education in agricultural technology to the farmers (Panjab Agricultural University, Ludhiana; G.B. Pant University of Agriculture and Technology, Pant Nagar; Jawaharlal Nehru Krishi Vishwa Vidyalaya, Jabalpur and Tamil Nadu Agricultural University, Coimbatore); and another 6 offer specialised degree level courses (one each) in such disciplines as education, engineering, adult education, English, Urdu and the like). The rest of the 31 Institutes are multi-discipline in nature, mostly confining themselves to the traditional type courses of study (Aggarwal and Ansari Directory and Bakshish Singh, *Research Report*).

## III

The Institutes imparting distance instruction in India are, broadly, of two types—Open Universities and the Institutes/Directorates of Correspondence Courses. Exclusively devoted to the cause of distance education, the Open Universities have been set up both by the Central and the State Governments. Deriving their powers and jurisdiction from their respective legislative/parliamentary statutes, these universities, like the conventional universities, are autonomous institutions, fully empowered to take their own decisions. Among them the IGNOU which has been accorded the status of a central university, enjoys a place of unique distinction. Besides imparting distance instruction like any other Open University/Institute, the IGNOU has been vested with the powers and responsibility of developing, controlling and co-ordinating the activities of the various other Open Universities and Institutes of Distance Education in the country. It is expected to play the role that the University Grants Commission performs vis-a-vis the other universities and higher education institutions in the country. It is, therefore, central to the orbit of distance education.

The other stream of distance education comprises those Institutes/ Directorates of Correspondence Courses (to be described as Institutes hereafter) which have been set up by the conventional universities. As alluded above, when the ideology of distance education began to sweep across the country, a number of conventional universities were tempted to constitute within their own existing structural frame, separate wings for imparting distance instruction in arts, humanities and commerce on the same lines as they had been giving to the class-room based students for a long time. These wings are mostly designated as the Institutes or Directorate of Correspondence Courses. Unlike the Open Universities, these Institutes are part and parcel of their parent universities and do not enjoy any autonomy whatsoever. The entire decision-making pertaining to the courses of study that they would offer and other day-to-day activities vests with the various decision making bodies of the university concerned. Similarly, the syllabi and courses of study, the mode of evaluation of the students' performance and the degrees/diplomas awarded to distance students, are identical with those of the conventional system. This dual mode is favourably comparable to the Deakin Model of Australia where the university concerned gives instruction to the 'off-campus' (distance) students alongwith the 'on-campus' (class-room based) students. This model, compared to the open university model has both its strengths and weaknesses.

## IV

Even though distance education has attained a country-wide recognition, its spatial spread has not been uniform. There are glaring regional imbalances. As Table 2.I shows there are states as (West Bengal and the Assam Hill States) which did not have until the end of the 1980's even one single Institute whereas there were the other's (Andhra Pradesh and Maharashtra) which had as many as 6 Institutes each. Further, Madhya Pradesh (area-wise the largest state of the country) had only two Institutes, one of which (Raja Bhoj Open University) was of too recent an origin whereas the other (Barkatula University Institute) had on its rolls as few as 2,100 students in 1988-89. Similarly, the situation in Uttar Pradesh was no better. Its two Institutes combined together provided in 1988-89 distance instruction to only 4,769 students which constituted 0.9 per cent of the total number of students of higher education in that State (Ruddar Datt 1991). In contrast to this, the tiny State of Himachal Pradesh catered to the higher education needs of 46.2 per cent through the distance mode.

As for the regional distribution of distance education, the Eastern region, covering as many as 10 states, had only 4 Institutes and, similarly, the Central region too had 4 Institutes, whereas the Southern region, containing only 4 states, had 15 Institutes and the northern region 11 Institutes. (It may be relevantly pointed out here that for purposes of this discussion we have excluded those Institutes which provided instruction

**TABLE 2.1: Region-wise Break-up of O.U's and Institutes**

| Region | State/U.T. | OU's/Institute | Total | |
|---|---|---|---|---|
| | | | State Wise | Region Wise |
| Northern | Chandigarh | Punjab | 1 | |
| | Punjab | Punjab (Patiala) | 1 | |
| | Himachal Pradesh | Shimla | 1 | |
| | Haryana | Kurukshetra, M.D.University | 2 | |
| | Delhi | IGNOU, Delhi | 2 | |
| | Rajasthan | Kota O.U. & Birla (Pilani) | 2 | |
| | Jammu & Kashmir | Jammu & Kashmir | 2 | 11 |
| Western | Gujarat | Gujarat Vidyapeeth | 1 | |
| | Maharashtra | Y.C.Maharashtra O.U., Bombay, Poona, SNDT Tilak Maharashtra Vidyapeeth, Shivaji (Kohlapur) | 6 | 7 |
| Southern | Andhra Pradesh | A.P.O.U.,Osmania, Andhra Pradesh, Venkateshwara, Kakatiya, J.L.Nehru Tech. Univ. | 6 | |
| | Tamil Nadu | Madras, Madurai Kamraj, Annamalai, Alagappa, Mother Teresa (Madras) | 5 | |
| | Kerala | Kerala (Trivandrum) Calicut | 2 | |
| | Karnataka | Bangalore and Mysore | 2 | 15 |
| Central | Uttar Pradesh | Allahabad and Meerut | 2 | |
| | Madhya Pradesh | Barkatula (Bhopal) Raja Bhoj O.U.Bhopal | 2 | 4 |
| Eastern | Bihar | Nalanda O.U. & Patna | 2 | |
| | Orissa | Utkal | 1 | |
| | West Bangal | — | — | |
| | Assam | — | — | |
| | Meghalaya | North Hill Univ. | 1 | |
| | Nagaland | — | — | |
| | Tripura | — | — | |
| | Manipur | — | — | |
| | Sikkim | — | — | |
| | Arunachal Pradesh | — | — | 4 |
| Grand Total | | | 41 | 41 |

*Note*: Those Institutes which impart distance instruction in agricultural sciences and languages, have been left out of this purview, for they are too small to be taken note.

*Sources*: Aggarwala and Ansari, Directory and Bakshish Singh Report

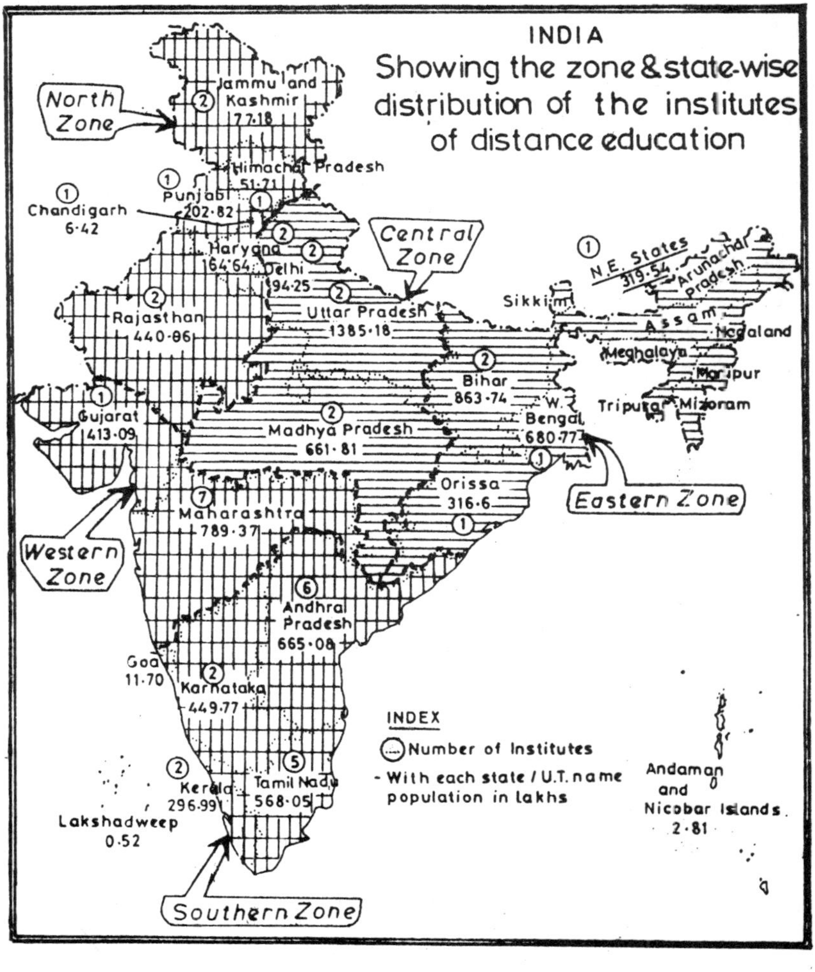
INDIA
Showing the zone & state-wise distribution of the institutes of distance education
North Zone
Jammu and Kashmir 77.18
Himachal Pradesh 51.71
Chandigarh 6.42
Punjab 202.82
Haryana 164.64
Delhi 94.25
Rajasthan 440.86
Central Zone
Uttar Pradesh 1385.18
N.E. States 319.54
Arunachal Pradesh
Sikkim
Assam
Nagaland
Meghalaya
Manipur
Tripura
Mizoram
Bihar 863.74
W. Bengal 680.77
Gujarat 413.09
Madhya Pradesh 661.81
Orissa 316.6
Eastern Zone
Maharashtra 789.37
Western Zone
Andhra Pradesh 665.08
Goa 11.70
Karnataka 449.77
INDEX
Number of Institutes
- With each state / U.T. name population in lakhs
Kerala 296.99
Tamil Nadu 568.05
Andaman and Nicobar Islands 2.81
Lakshadweep 0.52
Southern Zone

in one discipline only such as agricultural science/extension or any language (English or Urdu). We have taken into consideration only those Institutes/OU's which were multi-disciplined in nature. Their number was 41 in 1988-89.

Enrolment-wise, the spread too was quite uneven. The density of distance learners (Table 2.2) was perhaps the thickest in the Southern

**TABLE 2.2: Regionwise Enrolment of Distance Students in India (1989-90)**

| *Region* | | *Enrolment* | *Percentage* |
|---|---|---|---|
| **Northern Region** | | | |
| 1. | Punjab | 14,108 | 2.9 |
| 2. | Himachal Pradesh | 16,260 | 3.3 |
| 3. | Haryana | 18,960 | 3.9 |
| 4. | Delhi | 72,829 | 14.9 |
| 5. | Jammu & Kashmir | 1,885 | 0.4 |
| 6 | Rajasthan | 14,131 | 2.9 |
| | *Sub-total* | 1,38,171 | 28.3 |
| **Western Region** | | | |
| 7. | Gujarat | 129 | 0.03 |
| 8. | Maharashtra | 36,089 | 7.4 |
| · | *Sub Total* | 36.218 | 7.43 |
| **Southern Region** | | | |
| 9. | Andhra Pradesh | 65,782 | 13.4 |
| 10. | Tamil Nadu | 1,91,027 | 39.2 |
| 11. | Kerala | 7,848 | 1.6 |
| 12. | Karnataka | 22,532 | 13.5 |
| | *Sub Total* | 2,87,189 | 67.7 |
| **Central Region** | | | |
| 13. | Uttar Pradesh | 10,359 | 2.1 |
| 14. | Madhya Pradesh | 2,106 | 0.4 |
| | *Sub Total* | 12,465 | 2.5 |
| **Eastern Region** | | | |
| 15. | Bihar | 5,632 | 1.1 |
| 16. | Orissa | 7,674 | 1.6 |
| | *Sub Total* | 13,306 | 2.7 |
| | *Grand Total* | 4,87,349 | 100.0 |

Source: Ruddar Datt, *Indian Journal of Distance Education*, Vol. IV (1991).

region (67.7 per cent) and it was the thinnest in the Central and the Eastern regions (respectively 2.5 and 2.7 per cent). In other words, two-thirds of those who derived benefit from this system lived in the South of the Vindhya chain of mountains and another one-quarter of them (28.3 per cent) belonged to the northern region.

Viewed from another perspective, the share of the distance learners in the total enrolment in higher education (Table 2.3) was the highest in the southern region (23.0 per cent), to be followed by the northern region (16.8 per cent). It steeply declined to just 1.0 per cent in the case of the central and the eastern regions. The total picture that thus emerged in 1988-89 was that distance education found its maximum concentration in the belt running from the North to the South through the West (as the map shows) with respect to both the number of Institutes (33 out of the total of 41) and the extent of enrolment (95 per cent), whereas the central and the eastern regions constituted the arid zone. Incidentally, the area as well as the population of the latter is larger than the former.

**TABLE 2.3: Spatial Distribution of Enrolment in Higher Education (1988-89)**

| *Region/State* | *College/Uni. Department* | *Distance Education* | *Total* | *Share of D.E. to the total* |
|---|---|---|---|---|
| **Northern Region** | | | | |
| 1. Punjab | 1,46,574 | 16,303 | 1,62,877 | 10.00 |
| 2. Himachal Pradesh | 22,437 | 19,257 | 41,694 | 46.0 |
| 3. Haryana | 82,588 | 2,959 | 85,547 | 3.5 |
| 4. Delhi | 1,10,921 | 55,899 | 1,66,760 | 33.5 |
| 5. Jammu & Kashmir | 31,256 | 1,939 | 33,195 | 5.8 |
| 6. Rajasthan | 1,92,990 | 22,546 | 2,15,536 | 10 5 |
| *Sub Total* | 5,86,766 | 1.18.845 | 7,05.509 | 16.8 |
| **Western Region** | | | | |
| 7. Gujarat | 2,32,602 | 152 | 2,32,754 | 0.1 |
| 8. Maharashtra | 5,14,809 | 20,423 | 5,35,232 | 3.3 |
| *Sub Total* | 7,47,401 | 20,575 | 7,67,986 | 0.4 |
| **Southern Region** | | | | |
| 9. Andhra Pradesh | 2,99,213 | 76,075 | 3,75,988 | 20.2 |
| 10. Tamil Nadu | 2,83,854 | 1,98,284 | 4,82,138 | 41.1 |
| 11. Kerala | 1,53,753 | 10,194 | 1,63,947 | 6.2 |
| 12. Karnataka | 2,74,103 | 17,615 | 2,91,718 | 6.0 |
| *Sub Total* | 10,11,623 | 3,02,168 | 13,13,791 | 23.0 |

**TABLE 2.3 (Contd.)**

| | | | | | |
|---|---|---|---|---|---|
| **Central Region** | | | | | |
| 13. | Uttar Pradesh | 5,48,791 | 4,769 | 5,53,560 | 0.9 |
| 14. | Madhya Pradesh | 2,87,240 | 303 | 2,87,543 | 0.1 |
| | *Sub Total* | 8,36,031 | 5,072 | 8,41,103 | 1.0 |
| **Eastern Region** | | | | | |
| 15. | Bihar | 2,73,303 | 3,262 | 2,76,565 | 1.2 |
| 16. | Orissa | 78,771 | 4,323 | 83,094 | 5.2 |
| 17. | West Bengal/Tripura & Sikkim | 3,04,738 | — | 3,04,738 | — |
| 18. | Assam | 87,235 | — | 87,235 | — |
| 19. | Manipur | 11,941 | — | 11,941 | — |
| 20. | Maghalaya/Nagaland | 10,103 | — | 10,103 | — |
| | *Sub Total* | 7,66,091 | 7,585 | 7,73,676 | 1.0 |
| | *All India Total* | **39,47,922** | **4,54,243** | **44,02,165** | **10.3** |

*Source*: University Grants Commission.

This analysis leads us to the conclusion that there is an immense scope for the expansion of this system in the central and the eastern regions which are presently quite deprived of its advantages. Strenuous efforts are urgently called for if the national goal of drafting one-fifth of the higher education students of the nation to this stream by the turn of the century is to be achieved. It may be pointed out that this goal has so far been attained by Himachal Pradesh, Andhra Pradesh, Tamil Nadu and Delhi only, whereas all other States are far behind it. Therefore, it is not necessary that only the States of the eastern and the central India need to work hard in this direction but many others too. Madhya Pradesh has already set up an Open University while the States of West Bengal, Uttar Pradesh and Kerala are actively working on these lines. As for the Assam Hill States, the Shillong University has made a provision for off-campus studies. These are, indeed, healthy developments. Hopefully other States would also follow suit sooner than later.

## V

The study programmes that these Institutes offer are of a wide-ranging nature. Most of them having been sponsored by the conventional universities, more or less, as the extension wings of their instructional system, concentrate largely on the traditional type of B.A. and M.A. courses. As Table 2.4 highlights, 26 of these Institutes and 4 Open Universities provided (in 1994) for the bachelors degree programme in arts. But for the IGNOU, the courses and syllabi of all these Institutes/ Open Universities are by and large a replica of the degree programmes of their respective parent (conventional) universities. It is only the IGNOU programmes which show some deviations from the beaten track with respect to both the choice of the subjects and the syllabi thereof.

**TABLE 2.4: University-wise Break-up of Degree (Bachelor and Master) Course**

| Institute | B.A. | B.Com | B.Sc. | M.A. | M.Com | M.Sc. | B.Ed. | M.Ed. |
|---|---|---|---|---|---|---|---|---|
| 1. Allahabad | ✓ | ✓ | — | — | — | — | -- | — |
| 2. Andhra Uni. (Vishakhapatnam) | ✓ | ✓ | ✓ | ✓ | ✓ | — | ✓ | ✓ |
| 3. Bangalore | ✓ | ✓ | — | ✓ | ✓ | — | — | — |
| 4. Barkatula | ✓ | ✓ | — | — | — | — | ✓ | — |
| 5. Bombay | ✓ | ✓ | — | ✓ | ✓ | ✓ | — | — |
| 6. Calicut | ✓ | ✓ | — | ✓ | — | — | — | — |
| 7. Delhi | ✓ | ✓ | — | ✓ | ✓ | — | — | — |
| 8. Jammu | ✓ | ✓ | — | — | ✓ | — | ✓ | — |
| 9. Gujarat | — | — | — | — | — | — | — | — |
| 10. Kerala | ✓ | ✓ | — | ✓ | ✓ | — | — | — |
| 11. Kuruk-shetra | ✓ | ✓ | — | ✓ | ✓ | ✓ | ✓ | ✓ |
| 12. Madras* | ✓ | ✓ | ✓ | ✓ | ✓ | ✓ | — | ✓ |
| 13. Madurai Kamraj* | ✓ | ✓ | ✓ | ✓ | ✓ | ✓ | — | ✓ |
| 14. M.D.Rohtak | — | — | — | — | — | — | ✓ | — |
| 15. Mysore | ✓ | ✓ | — | ✓ | ✓ | ✓ | — | — |
| 16. Osmania | ✓ | ✓ | — | ✓ | ✓ | ✓ | ✓ | ✓ |
| 17. Patna | ✓ | ✓ | — | — | — | — | — | — |
| 18. Poona | ✓ | — | — | — | — | — | — | — |
| 19. Panjab (CHD) | ✓ | ✓ | — | ✓ | — | — | — | — |
| 20. Punjabi ( Patiala) | ✓ | — | — | ✓ | ✓ | — | ✓ | — |
| 21. SNDT | ✓ | ✓ | — | — | — | — | — | — |
| 22. Venkateshwara | ✓ | ✓ | — | ✓ | ✓ | ✓ | — | — |
| 23. Tilak Maharasht-tra (Poona) ** | ✓ | — | — | — | — | — | — | — |
| 24. Utkal | ✓ | ✓ | — | — | — | — | ✓ | — |
| 25.Annamalai* | ✓ | ✓ | ✓ | ✓ | ✓ | ✓ | ✓ | ✓ |
| 26. Himachal | ✓ | ✓ | — | ✓ | ✓ | ✓ | — | ✓ |
| 27. Kakatiya | -- | — | ✓ | ✓ | — | ✓ | ✓ | — |
| 28.Kashmir | ✓ | ✓ | ✓ | ✓ | ✓ | — | ✓ | — |
| 29.Meerut | ✓ | ✓ | — | ✓ | — | — | ✓ | — |
| 30. JLN Tech.Univ Hyderabad | —— | ✓ | — | — | — | — | — | |

*(Contd.)*

**TABLE 2.4 (Contd.)**

| Institute | B.A. | B.Com | B.Sc. | M.A. | M.Com | M.Sc. | B.Ed. | M.Ed. |
|---|---|---|---|---|---|---|---|---|
| 31. A.P.O.U | ✓ | ✓ | ✓ | — | — | — | — | — |
| 32. Kota O.U. | ✓ | ✓ | — | — | — | — | ✓ | — |
| 33. Y.C.Maharashtra O.U. | ✓ | ✓ | — | — | — | — | ✓ | — |
| 34. IGNOU | ✓ | ✓ | ✓ | — | — | — | — | — |
| **Total** | 30 | 28 | 7 | 19 | 15 | 10 | 14 | 7 |

* Provision for the foundation courses preparatory to B.A..
** B.A.(Visharad) only in Hindi Medium
*Source:* Aggarwal and Ansari, Directory of Distance Education Institution Bakshish Singh Report and IGNOU Information Folder.

The picture with regard to the M.A. courses is no different. These were offered by as many as 19 Institutes. As for the Open Universities, they do not make, for the present, a provision for them. They do, however, propose to introduce post-graduate courses in certain disciplines, as for instance, the IGNOU would go in for M.A. in Distance Education while the Dr. B.R. Ambedkar O.U. and Kota O.U. propose to institute M.A. courses in Political Science, Public Administration, History and English (Bakshish Singh *et al.*, Research Report.).

Again, most of these post-graduate study programmes, are traditional in nature. They relate mostly to Political Science, Economics, History (17 each), English Literature (14), Hindi, Sociology and Public Administration (9 each), Sanskrit (6), Philosophy (2) and the various regional languages (Table 2.5). All of them continue to be patterned on traditional lines.

As regards the popularity pattern of these post-graduate courses in arts and languages (as measured in terms of the number of students that they attract), History and Political Science which at one time used to be at the pinnacle of their glory are sliding down. On the other hand, Public Administration and Economics have stolen a march over everyone else. The third position is occupied by the English Language and Literature. Hindi too is not far behind them. The fluctuating nature of job potential of those courses appears to be the main cause of the changes in the popularity curve.

Next to the arts and social sciences, the other most widely prevalent group of study programmes relates to Commerce. In fact, this group of studies has of late begun to command an edge over the pure arts. In 1994

**TABLE 2.5: University-wise Break-up of M.A. Courses**

| | *Institute* | *Eng.* | *Hindi* | *Pol.Sc* | *Pub.Admn.* | *Eco.* | *Socio.* | *History* | *Sanskrit* | *Others* |
|---|---|---|---|---|---|---|---|---|---|---|
| 1. | Andhra | ✓ | ✓ | ✓ | ✓ | ✓ | ✓ | — | — | Telugu.Phil.Telu |
| 2. | Bangalore | ✓ | ✓ | ✓ | — | ✓ | ✓ | ✓ | ✓ | Hindi |
| 3. | Bombay | — | — | ✓ | — | ✓ | ✓ | ✓ | — | |
| 4. | Calicut | — | — | ✓ | — | — | ✓ | ✓ | — | — |
| 5. | Delhi | — | ✓ | ✓ | ✓ | — | — | ✓ | ✓ | |
| 6. | Kakatiya | ✓ | — | ✓ | ✓ | ✓ | — | ✓ | — | |
| 7. | Kerala | ✓ | — | ✓ | — | ✓ | ✓ | ✓ | — | Malayam |
| 8. | Kurukshetra | ✓ | ✓ | ✓ | — | ✓ | — | ✓ | ✓ | |
| 9. | Madras | ✓ | — | ✓ | ✓ | ✓ | ✓ | ✓ | — | |
| 10. | Madurai | ✓ | — | ✓ | ✓ | ✓ | — | ✓ | — | Tamil |
| 11. | Mysore | ✓ | ✓ | ✓ | — | ✓ | ✓ | ✓ | — | Kannada |
| 12. | Osmania | — | ✓ | ✓ | ✓ | ✓ | ✓ | ✓ | — | Phil. & Telugu |
| 13. | Punjab (CHD) | ✓ | ✓ | ✓ | ✓ | ✓ | — | ✓ | — | Punjabi |
| 14. | Punjabi Patiala | ✓ | — | ✓ | — | ✓ | — | — | — | Punjabi |
| 15. | Venkatesa-wara | ✓ | — | — | — | ✓ | — | — | — | Indian Culture |
| 16. | Annamalai | ✓ | — | — | ✓ | ✓ | — | ✓ | ✓ | Psychology |

(Contd.)

**TABLE 2.5 (Contd.)**

| | *Institute* | *Eng.* | *Hindi* | *Pol.Sc* | *Pub.Admn.* | *Eco.* | *Socio.* | *History* | *Sanskrit* | *Others* |
|---|---|---|---|---|---|---|---|---|---|---|
| 17. | Himachal Pradesh | ✓ | ✓ | ✓ | ✓ | ✓ | — | ✓ | ✓ | |
| 18. | Kashmir | — | — | ✓ | — | ✓ | — | ✓ | — | Urdu |
| 19. | Meerut | ✓ | ✓ | ✓ | — | ✓ | ✓ | ✓ | ✓ | — |
| | Total | 14 | 9 | 17 | 9 | 17 | 9 | 17 | 6 | |

Philosophy- 2; Psychology- 1; Telgu- 3; Kannada-2; Punjabi- 2; Urdu-3; Malayalam - 1; Defence Studies-1; Indian Cultural-1

*Source*: Aggarwal and Ansari.

the Bachelor programme in Commerce (B.Com) was given by 28 Institutes and Open Universities. As for the Master's programme, it is comparatively less common. (Given by 15 Institutes only). If the number of the latter is less, it is so not because of less demand for it but because of the niggardly attitude of those conventional teachers who preside over the Boards of Studies in Commerce. They are apprehensive that the entrustment of a course of this much higher nature to distance learning system would erode the standards which they have so painstakingly developed. Their fears are however quite illfounded for, it is not the mode of instruction which militates against the standards of a study programmes. If there is any thing which impinges upon its standards, it is the competence of the teachers who teach a course. If those who handle a course in the class-room are not upto the mark or do not take pains to teach it properly, they will spoil the show and rock bottom its standards. If, on the other hand, competent teachers come forward to develop good study material for distance learners and if a proper two-way communication is maintained between the teacher and the taught, there is no reason why a study programme does not cut ice with its scholars. Those Institutes which are already running the Masters course, have been doing it creditably as is manifest in the number of students that they attract, in the qualitative performance of the distance students vis-a-vis the class-room based students, and in the recognition that they earn at the hands of their employers. While allowing an Institute to give a certain study programme through the distance mode, we should be guided by the public demand for it and not by its nature or the academic level. The old myth about the suitability of the distance mode to only a few study programmes stands exploded long since.

One wonders why these degree level programmes in arts, humanities and commerce continue to attract distance students in large numbers, particularly when the job market for them has shrunk considerably. One can understand the logic of the youngsters who join the conventional system, opting for these courses of study. But it appears somewhat baffling when one looks at the popularity of these courses even by the distance mode. Craze of the common man for a university degree mainly accounts for their popularity. Despite the best of our intentions and pious wishes of our planners and educationists to make the university degree selective (to be attained by only those who deserve it), we could not delink it from employment. As a result, all those who have at the back of their mind the desire to go in for a white-collar job (which too is a wild goose pursuit) enroll themselves for these degree programmes. The general perception of the comparatively easier nature of the study of these disciplines further makes every Tom, Dick and Harry to pursue them. Another reason is that a university degree, more particularly an M.A.degree, is a status symbol, especially with those who receive education in their first generation. The vast multitude of the illiterate and the semi-literate persons who have acquired political consciousness only recently are too keen to see their sons going in for university education (may be through the distance mode if conventional institutions are not at hand.) and attain B.A. and M.A. degrees and then be in a position to rub shoulders with their erstwhile masters.

It is interesting to note that these graduate and post-graduate distance education programmes have, of late, become quite popular among the women and the superannuated persons. Again, the reason is the ready availability of these study programmes (unlike the position obtaining earlier) and that too without involving any physical or professional dislocation or inconvenience. As a result, many a house-wife and the retired person now think in terms of further adding to their qualifications. The parents of the young girls, particularly those hailing from remote rural areas, are a very happy lot today. For, with the availability of these facilities right at their doorstep, their daughters are now in a position to equip themselves with higher education, thereby elevating the social status of their families, on the one hand, and enhancing the prospects of their own marriage, on the other.

Yet another area of rich clientele for these courses is that of those youngmen and youngwomen who (in thousands) fail to get admission to the post-graduate courses in particular due to the paucity of seats in conventional colleges and universities. Until recently, these persons had to curb their ambition for all times to come. But now an opening is available to them as well. In sum, the study programmes of these Institutes and more particularly their post-graduate sections have everywhere been quite popular, brimming with the young and the old alike. Herein lies the secret why many Open Universities also propose to institute M.A. courses in conventional disciplines.

Compared to the arts, humanities and commerce, science programmes are given by these Institutes but very sparingly. Only 7 Institutes/Open Universities made a provision in 1994 for the bachelors degree (Table 2.4) and 10 for the masters degree (Table 2.6). The most favourite discipline in which all of them have instituted the M.Sc degree is Mathematics which, though a pure science, does not involve any laboratory work, hence more akin to the arts than to science in so far as its teaching is concerned. Only the Annamalai and the Osmania Institutes provided for the M.Sc degree in Chemistry, Physics, Botany and Zoology. The intake of students in these study programmes is, however, limited. The reason why the science courses have not struck roots in the Indian soil is, again, the inhibition of the conventionalists not to allow these Institutes to run the laboratory-based courses. Their phobia of the inability of the distance system to suitably handle these courses does not seem to have been shaken so far, even though a number of these Institutes have been managing them so wonderfully well. Some of them, as for instance the Birla Institute of Technology and Science, Pilani, or the Jawaharlal Nehru Technological University, Hyderabad, have ventured to institute the Masters level courses in technology, science and engineering by the distance mode. These technology courses are by far more difficult than ordinary M.Sc. courses, yet these universities provide for them. Anyway, we find that a beginning has been made to impart science education through this mode in our country as well. By and by, it would mitigate the conventionalists' phobia, on the one hand, and would catch the imagination of the people, on the other, in the same manner as has been the case elsewhere in the world.

**TABLE 2.6: University-wise Break up of M.Sc. Courses**

| | *Institute* | *Maths* | *Chemistry* | *Physics* | *Botany* | *Zoology* |
|---|---|---|---|---|---|---|
| 1. | Kurukshetra | ✓ | — | — | — | — |
| 2. | Annamalai | ✓ | ✓ | ✓ | ✓ | ✓ |
| 3. | Bombay | ✓ | — | — | — | — |
| 4. | Kakatiya | ✓ | — | — | — | — |
| 5. | Kamraj | ✓ | — | — | — | — |
| 6. | Osmania | ✓ | ✓ | — | — | — |
| 7. | Venkateshwara | ✓ | — | — | — | — |
| 8. | Madras | ✓ | — | — | — | — |
| 9. | Himachal Pradesh | ✓ | — | — | — | — |
| 10. | Meerut | ✓ | — | — | — | — |
| | Total | 10 | 2 | 1 | 1 | 1 |

*Sources*: Aggarwal and Ansari, Directory and Bakshish Singh Report

To conclude, our impression is that people are gradually veering round to the idea that they should care more for the job-oriented education than to the general education. The growing rigours of the day-to-day life have been pushing them to this harder truth. As a result an increasing number of Institutes are supplementing their existing study programmes with the job-oriented courses.

## VI

The range of the job-oriented courses too is very vast with the result that to classify them is quite a difficult task. However, we try to bracket them together into the following few categories. To begin with, we take up the teachers' training programmes. It hardly needs to be emphasised that we have already set up a very large number of schools all over the country and yet we would need more of them as our plans to provide education to all those sections of the population who have thus far remained deprived of this privilege, mature. To manage this tremendous number of institutions, we require teachers in hundreds of thousands. Realising this vast potential, good many Institutes of Distance Education have made a provision for teachers' training programmes. As Table 2.4 shows, 14 of these Institutes provided for a bachelor degree in education (B.Ed) and 7 for the masters degree (M.Ed.) in 1994. These programmes have been so popular that each one of these Institutes attracts students in thousands. It may not be irrelevant to mention here that too great a demand for this type of study programmes has been capitalised rather too unduly by many an Institute. Finding in them a huge mine of money, a number of universities have instituted them to ward off the fiscal deficit of their respective Institutes of Distance Education or to improve their own financial position. This too undue lust for money, further coupled with the poor quality of their instruction, has brought a bad name to the distance system as a whole. The situation at one time deteriorated so much that the UGC was compelled to put an embargo on the proliferation of this type of study programmes. But too inadequately empowered as the UGC is, this directive utterly failed to curb the greed of these Institutes. More and more universities go on instituting such programmes with impunity. The newly constituted National Council for Teachers Training is reported to have banned the first training degree (B.Ed.) through correspondence.

Next to the teachers training came the technology-based amorphous group of study programmes. The fast-growing impact of science and technology on our day-to-day life has unleashed a great demand for a variety of technically trained personnel whom we need to manipulate a multitude of technological operations of our trade and industry. Distance education provides an economically viable method to suitably meet the needs of this type of personnel. Our Institutes of Distance Education have already assumed responsibility in this behalf.

Defying all types of inhibitions and propaganda, a number of universities and Institutes have come forward to provide science and technical education in various disciplines through the distance mode. Table 2.7 shows that until 1994 the Birla Institute of Technology, Pilani, had instituted the M. S. degree (Master in Science) in Computers, Electronics, Systems Information, Software Systems, Technical Operations and Pharmacy, and the Bachelor Degree in Pharmacy. Similarly, the Jawaharlal Nehru Technological University, Hyderabad, provided for the M. Tech degree (Master in Technology) in Advanced Electronics, Environmental Engineering, Electrical Power Systems, Industrial Engineering, Production Engineering and B.Tech in Civil, Electrical, Electronics and Mechanical Engineering. These two very bold and elaborate experiments apart, the Indian Institute of Technology, Madras, and the Indian Institute of Science, Bangalore, had gone in for master courses in Science and Technology.

Besides these degree level programmes, there were a number of Institutes and Open Universities which provided for Diploma and Certificates courses in various trades. The IGNOU, for instance made a provision for three types of diploma courses, namely Post-Graduate Diploma (Computer Application), Advanced Diploma in (Construction Management and Water Resources Engineering) and Diploma (in Computers in Office Management.)

Among the various courses, those relating to Computers (Application, Programming and Language) had attracted the attention of many an Institute. Apart from the IGNOU, these were administered by the Alagappa, Mother Teressa, Kurukshetra and Venkateshwar Institutes and the Kota Open University. While all others provided for diploma level distance instruction only, the latter two also made an additional provision for a certificate course. Besides, the Kota Open University gave a diploma as well as a certificate course in Applied Electronics.

Thus we find that but for the Birla Institute of Technology (Pilani) and the Jawaharlal Nehru Technological University (Hyderabad) none of the Institutes/Open Universities spanned a wide range of technology-based study programmes. By and large, they cover two or three trades only. In other words, they have not been able to exploit the full potential of this field. However, it is encouraging to note that the Institutes of Distance Education have at long last set their foot on a domain which the

**TABLE 2.7: Institute-wise Breaking of the Technology-based Study Programmes**

| Level of the study Programme | Alagappa | I.I.S. Banga-lore | BITS Pilani | Jadavpur | IGNOU | JLN Tech. Wing Hyderabad | Mother Teressa Madras | IIT Madras | Kuruk setra | Kota OU | YCM OU | Venkate-shwara | Anna-malai |
|---|---|---|---|---|---|---|---|---|---|---|---|---|---|
| 1. Master | — | Sc. | M.S. in<br>a) Comp.<br>b) Electr.<br>c) Sys. infor.<br>d) Soft . syst.<br>e) Tech.<br>f) Pharm | — | — | M.Tech. in<br>a) Advanced Elect.<br>b) Envir. Eng.<br>c) Elec. Power Systems<br>d) Indust. Eng.<br>e) Prod. Engg. | — | Teachy | — | — | — | — | — |
| 2. Bachelors | — | — | Pharm. | — | — | a) Civil Engg.<br>b) Elect. Engg.<br>c) Electro. Engg.<br>d) Mech. Engg. | — | — | — | — | — | — | — |
| 3. Diploma | | | | | | | | | | | | | |
| a) Post-Grad. | — | — | — | — | *Comp appl* | — | — | — | — | — | — | — | — |
| b) Advanced | — | — | — | — | a) Const. Mgt.<br>b) Water Res. Engg. | — | — | | | | | | |

*(Contd.)*

**TABLE 2.7 (Contd.)**

| Level of the study Programme | Alagappa | I.I.S. Banga-lore | BITS Pilani | Jadavpur | IGNOU | JLN Tech. Wing Hyderabad | Mother Teressa Madras | IIT Madras | Kuruk setra | Kota OU | YCM OU | Venkate-shwara | Anna-malai |
|---|---|---|---|---|---|---|---|---|---|---|---|---|---|
| c) Ordinary | Comp. Appl. | — | — | Med. Lab. | a) Comp.<br>b) office mgt. | —<br>— | Computer App. | Comp, | Elect. Prog. | Compu- | | | a) Concrete Tech<br>b) Const. Marg.<br>c) Chemical process<br>d) Instrum-entation |
| Certificate | — | — | — | — | — | — | a) Comp.<br>b) App. Elect. | —<br>— | a) Comp.<br>b) App. Elect. | Elect.<br>— | Comp.<br>— | — | |

*Sources:* Agriculture and Ansari. Directors Bakshish Singh Report and IGNOU information folder.

conventionalists had thus far put them out of bounds for them. Hopefully, they would soon tie up with the industry and try to provide to it trained personnel as per its requirements.

Commerce-based group of study programmes constituted another category which was very popular both with the Institutes and the students thereof. The IGNOU courses have blazed a trail in the realm of management studies. Its Management Programmes, more specifically its MBA stream, has caught the imagination of the working people far and wide. Besides this study programme, it provided in 1994 for Post-Graduate Diplomas in Financial Management and the Operations Management. It may be underlined that the study material that it provides to its students and the level at which it maintains its instruction have surpassed the teaching standards of many a department of the conventional universities, thereby exploding the myth that standard education cannot be given in such disciplines through distance mode.

Apart from the IGNOU, there were a number of other Institutes and Open Universities which made a provision for a wide range of commerce-based study programmes (Table 2.8). The Annamalai University offered as many as 8 such diploma courses, to be followed by the Punjabi University (Patiala), the Madurai Kamraj and the Kota Open Universities with 5 courses each. Trade-wise, the most common courses related to management: personnel management (Madurai Kamraj, Annamalai, Shimla and Kota), hotel management (Kurukshetra, Madurai Kamraj, Shimla and Kota), financial management (Bombay, Annamalai and IGNOU), bank management (Punjabi, Annamalai and Kota), business management (Annamalai and IGNOU), and material management (Punjabi and Annamalai). The next important group consisted of such courses as diplomas in industrial relations (Madurai Kamraj, Punjabi, Kota and Venkateshwara), taxation (Madurai Kamraj and Madras), insurance (Madras and Annamalai) and marketing (Punjabi and IGNOU).

Compared to the technology-based courses, the range that commerce based courses cover is quite wide, though there are many more areas which need to be brought into the purview of this system. But what is of greater concern is that out of 41 Institutes and Open Universities only 12 made a provision for these courses. This venture is too inadequate particularly in view of the growing demand for managers, accountants and the other trade personnel that our fast developing industry needs. It is high time that other Institutes which have not so far proliferated their academic programmes in this direction should pay their attention to this side.

**TABLE 2.8: Institute-wise Breakup of Commerce-based Study Programmes**

| *Course* | *Bombay* | *Kuruk-shtra* | *Madurai-Kamraj* | *Madras* | *Punjabi Patiala* | *Punjab (Chd)* | *Anna-malai* | *Shimla* | *IGNOU* | *APOU Kota* | *Venkt.* |
|---|---|---|---|---|---|---|---|---|---|---|---|
| *Management* | | | | | | | | | | | |
| i Business | — | — | — | — | — | — | ✓ | — | ✓ | — | — |
| ii Financial | ✓ | — | — | — | — | — | ✓ | — | ✓ | — | — |
| iii Personal | — | — | ✓ | — | — | — | ✓ | ✓ | — | — | — |
| iv Bank | — | — | — | — | ✓ | — | ✓ | — | — | — | — |
| v Office | — | ✓ | ✓ | — | — | ✓ | — | — | — | — | — |
| vi Hotel | — | ✓ | ✓ | — | — | — | — | ✓ | — | — | — |
| vii Material | — | — | — | — | ✓ | — | ✓ | — | — | — | — |
| viii Project | — | — | — | — | — | — | — | — | — | — | — |
| ix Cooperative | — | — | — | — | — | — | — | — | — | — | — |
| x Operation | — | — | — | — | — | — | — | — | ✓ | — | — |
| xi Production | — | — | — | — | — | — | — | — | — | — | — |
| xii Industrial | — | — | — | — | — | — | — | — | — | — | — |
| Taxation | — | — | ✓ | ✓ | — | — | — | — | — | — | — |
| Insurance | — | — | — | ✓ | — | — | — | — | — | — | — |
| Marketing | — | — | — | — | ✓ | — | ✓ | — | — | — | — |
| Accountancy | — | — | — | — | — | — | — | — | — | ✓ | — |
| Indus Relation | — | — | ✓ | — | ✓ | — | ✓ | — | — | — | ✓ |
| Operation Research | ✓ | ✓ | — | — | — | — | — | — | — | — | — |

*Sources*: Aggarwal and Ansari Directory, Bakshish Singh Report and IGNOU Information forder.

The law-based courses constituted yet another very popular category of study programmes. Good many people like to learn the law in general or the law of a certain sector of life in particular, perhaps for the reason that law governs the conduct of both the individuals and the institutions at every step of their life. To meet their demand five Institutes (Jammu, Madurai Kamraj, Kashmir, Shimla and Annamalai) made a provision for a degree course in law (LL.B/B.G.L.). However, the duration of their course was limited to two years, instead of three years. The Bar Council of India does not allow these Institutes to go in for the third practising year. This restriction notwithstanding, the degree that these Institutes award is quite sufficient to fetch to its holders good many jobs. Moreover they can also set up their own practice after doing the third year course which every university normally allows.

Besides the degree course, these Institutes provide for a number of diploma level study programmes (Table 2.9). The Annamalai and the Madras Institutes, for instance, provided for, respectively, 7 and 6 such study programmes, the most common among them being the Labour and the Taxation Laws. The former was given by 5 Institutes/Open Universities (namely Madurai Kamraj, Madras, Annamalai, Shimla Institutes and the Kota Open University), whereas the latter by 3 Institutes (Madurai Kamraj, Annamalai and Madras). The other favourite courses related to Criminal Law or Criminology (2 Institutes), Insurance Law (2), Mercantile, Indian Constitutional, Administrative, Company and Banking laws (one Institute each).

A number of Institutes also paid their attention toward the education of the women in such vital areas of their concern as women studies in general, child care, nutrition, diet therapy, interior decoration as also population growth awareness in particular. The Mother Teressa University provided for an M.A.degree in Women Studies through the distance mode, while the SNDT (Bombay) made a provision for only a certificate course in Women and Law. As for the Nursing Course, the IGNOU maintained it at the degree level and the Shivaji University (Kolhapur) at the diploma level. The IGNOU provided for three types of courses in Nutrition, namely Diploma in Nutrition and Health Education, Certificates Courses in Food and Nutrition, and a non-credit course in Nutrition for the Community. The SNDT made a provision for a Diploma Course in basics of Diet Therapy. In this way, we find that the IGNOU, the SNDT and the Shivaji universities are doing a lot of service to enlighten the women as also the others about those things which closely impinge upon their everyday life.

**TABLE 2.9**: **Institute-wise Break up of Law-based Study Programmes**

| | *Study Programme* | *Anna-malai* | *Jammu* | *Kashmir* | *Kota* | *Madras OU* | *Madurai-Kamraj* | *Shimla* |
|---|---|---|---|---|---|---|---|---|
| 1. | L.M.M./BGL | ✓ | ✓ | ✓ | — | — | ✓ | ✓ |
| 2. | Labour Law | ✓ | — | — | ✓ | ✓ | ✓ | ✓ |
| 3. | Taxation law | ✓ | — | — | — | ✓ | ✓ | — |
| 4. | Criminal law/ Criminology | ✓ | — | — | — | ✓ | — | — |
| 5. | Mercantile law | — | — | — | — | ✓ | — | — |
| 6. | Indian Lang. Law | — | — | — | — | ✓ | — | — |
| 7. | Administrative Law | — | — | — | — | — | ✓ | — |
| 8. | Company law | ✓ | — | — | — | — | — | — |
| 9. | Industrial law | — | — | — | ✓ | ✓ | — | — |
| 10. | Insurance law | ✓ | — | — | ✓ | — | — | — |
| 11. | Banking Law | ✓ | — | — | — | — | — | — |
| | Total | 7 | 1 | 1 | 3 | 6 | 4 | 2 |

*Sources*: Aggarwal and Ansari. Directory Bakshish Singh Report.

Finally comes the assorted lot of a number of study programmes. The range of disciplines that they cover as also their being given by one or two stray Institutes, renders any systematic classification difficult, hence they are being mentioned individually. They are, first the Library and Information Science. This course was being given at four different levels: Masters (Madras), Bachelor's (IGNOU, Dr.B.R.Ambedkar and Madurai Kamraj), Diploma (Punjabi) and Certificate (Jammu and Madurai Kamraj). Similar is the case with Journalism and Mass Communication. The Madurai Kamraj Institute maintained it at the Master's level; the Dr.B.R.Ambedkar Open University at the bachelor's level, while Madurai Kamraj Institute at the Diploma level and the Mysore Institute at the Certificate level. There is yet another discipline where distance instruction were given, again. at different levels. This is Distance/Higher Education. In this case, there is only one Open University, namely the IGNOU which alone provided for courses in this field. These courses are Master of Arts in Distance Education, Post-Graduate Diploma in Distance Education and Post-graduate Diploma in Higher Education. Further, the IGNOU is the only university which made a provision for such other courses as Diploma in Creative Writing (English and Hindi) and Certificate in Rural Development and in Guidance. A number of Institutes/Open Universities also give diploma and certificate level courses in the learning of such languages as English (Andhra, Jammu, Mysore and the SNDT), Urdu (Jamia Milia), Kannada (Mysore), Hindi (Mysore), Punjabi (Punjabi), Sanskrit (Mysore).

Besides these certificate, diploma and graduate level courses, research oriented programmes were given by certain universities. The number of the Institutes as also the range of these courses was however, not very large. These courses are confined either to science and technology or social sciences and languages. Keeping in view the requirement of M.Phil. degree as the minimum entrance qualification for university/ college lectureship (stands modified long since), the Punjabi University (Patiala) ran an M.Phil course in Punjabi, English, Political Science and Economics. The Jawaharlal Nehru Technological University (Hyderabad) also gave a two semester M.Phil course in technology and also prepared students for Ph.D. The Indian Institute of Science (Bangalore) and the Indian Institute of Technology (Madras) made an identical provision. Thus, the facilities for research by distance mode are highly limited in nature and as a matter of fact they should remain limited to those Institutes which have the requisite infra-structure for the same.

## VII

The scenario of distance education, as portrayed in the foregoing pages, depicts a few good as well as bad features. It is indeed encouraging to find that the rate of growth of distance education has been quite impressive in respect of the number of both the Institutes and the enrollment of students thereof. That the number of Institutes should multiply from just 3 (in 1968) to 47 (by the end of the 1980's) is no mean an achievement. More significant is the manner how the concept of open universities has caught the imagination and attention of the State Governments. The day does not seem to be far when a number of more open universities would come up, especially in the central and the eastern parts of the country where distance education has not so far made much of an impact thereby eradicating the phenomenon of regional imbalances.

In the same manner, the enrollment in the various Institutes and Open Universities has also marked a very impressive trend. Compared to 0.64 lakh enrollment in 1975-76, it has risen to 4.54 lakhs in 1988-89, thus showing a growth rate of 16.2 per cent. In relative terms, its share in total enrollment in higher education (both the conventional and the distance institutions) has gone up from 2.6 per cent (in 1975-76) to 10.5 per cent (in 1988-89) (Ruddar Datt, 1991) If this trend is maintained (infact, it is expected to get further strengthened quite considerably), the national goal of diverting at least 20 per cent of the total enrollment to this system, is bound to be attained.

Another laudable achievement of distance education is the remarkable beginning that it has made in the realm of job-oriented education. In 1988-89 there were 88,545 students on the rolls of the Institutes of Distance Education in the country for diploma and certificate courses in various job-related study programmes, whereas the number of students for the same courses in the conventional institutions was 55,271. Thus, more than 3/5 (or 61.6 per cent) of the total enrollment is in the distance mode as compared to less than 2/5 (38.4 per cent) in the conventional mode (Ruddar Datt, 1991.)

That distance education should far excel the conventional system is something for which distance educators should feel legitimately proud of. If this system further ties up with industry, it can serve the nation still more effectively. It need not be emphasised that this system which imparts education/training without dislocating its students from their places of residence or work, suits the industry and commerce more than the conventional system. It can also prove to be an ideal instrument for deploying people from one job to another. A beginning needs to be made in this respect too. Once it is made, the programme would acquire a momentum of its own.

However, the scenario is not so bright. There are a few shady spots in it as well. They need to be seriously taken care of if the future development of the system on systematic lines is to be ensured. To begin with, we may refer to the fact that in this country distance education has developed without any proper direction or policy perspective. Emphasising this fact, S.K.Gupta (1990) says, " There has hardly been any national and regional level planning in terms of requirements, aims and objects, and the infra-structure necessary to develop it on the right lines." He adds, "The show of distance education appears like a commercial performance dictated by the expediencies and exigencies of the traditional system. No wonder, some of the worst features of the latter got shamelessly transmitted to the system of distance education. This process has also resulted in the internalisation of certain complexes down to the student clientele. Further, the goals have neither been delineated in qualitative nor in quantitative terms; the left-overs of the traditional system have been our domain." (*ICDE Bulletin* No.23, p.30).

If there was any motivating factor for the conventional universities to start these Institutes it was the cost-efficient nature of this system (nay, its profit yielding potential). This factor had inspired a number of universities in the 1970's and 1980's to create their own respective extension wings for the imparting of distance instruction in some of the disciplines in arts, humanities and commerce. While setting up these Institutes, each one of them acted in complete isolation of the other without regard for any type of co-ordination or co-operation even with the neighbouring universities. This hap-hazard growth had led to the springing up of a number of Institutes in the northern and the southern regions of the country, thereby creating a situation of regional imbalances. Another equally serious outcome of this development was the overlapping of the study programmes. To cite a case, there is a 150 kilo metre long strip of land in the northern region. It has 4 Institutes, namely Shimla (Himachal Pradesh),Chandigarh (Union Territory), Patiala (Punjab) and Kurukshetra (Haryana). All of them provide, by and large, 7 identical type of study programmes (M.A. in Political Science, Economics, Public Administration, History, English, and Punjabi and Hindi) ; B.A.( in arts and humanities and B.Com). Not only are the study programmes identical in nature, but the syllabi of most of them are also same to a very large extent. Deploringly, each one of these Institutes drives its own lonely furrow, thus badly playing with the standards of their instruction. Instances of this types of unplanned and hap-hazard growth of the system can be cited in abundance.

The cut-throat competition that this type of growth has generated among these Institutes has led to yet another type of development. Within a few years of their having been set up many of these Institutes have become economically unviable. Ruddar Datt (1991) reveals that of the 41 Institutes (Open Universities not taken into consideration) 12 had in 1988-89 a total enrollment of less than 2,000 each. Another 10 ranged between 2,000 and 5,000. There were only 13 Institutes whose enrollment exceeded 10,000 each (Table 2.10). If an enrollment of 10,000 is considered to be optimum, as Ruddar Datt opines, then 70 per cent of these Institutes were totally unviable economically.

**TABLE 2.10: Frequency Distribution of Institutes on the basis of their Enrollment**

| *Enrollment* | *No. of Institutes* | *Percentage* |
|---|---|---|
| 0- 2,000 | 12 | 29 |
| 2,001- 5,000 | 10 | 24 |
| 5,001- 10,000 | 6 | 15 |
| 10,000- 20,000 | 6 | 15 |
| 20,001 and above | 7 | 17 |
| Total | 41 | 100 |

*Source:* Ruddar Datt, *Indian Journal of Distance Education*, Vol. IV, p. 64

The plight of the economically unviable Institutes is quite horrible. While, on the one hand, their economic conditions do not allow them to maintain reasonably high instructional standards (which, in turn further militate against good enrollment, thereby creating a vicious circle of bad chain effects), on the other hand, their parent universities do not look kindly upon them. Thus, they are just pulling on. In fact, they constitute the ill-scars on the face of the distance system.

It is high time that the parent universities of all these Institutes should rise above the narrow considerations and constraints of their functional autonomy and get together and consider these problems in a spirit of give and take. The only way that would bail them out of these problems is that of mutual net working among themselves. To begin with, this networking should cover only two aspects, that is the existing study programmes and long term perspective planning, for the future development of the system. It should also create a common consultation mechanism on a permanent basis with a view to sorting out their day-to-day problems. Above all, the institution of private appearance (wherever in vogue) should also be abolished. The U.G.C. has been persistently impressing upon the universities to stop this practice. In its latest communique, it says, "Private appearance at university examinations for which distance education courses are available, must be stopped as has already been suggested by the UGC" (Additional Secretary UGC letter). Bakshish Singh study (1994) reveals that the secret of high enrolment in the Madras Institute (which with 1,12,740 students in 1989-90 is the leading most Institute in India) lies in its parent university having completely stopped private appearance (p.58). All those who want to improve their educational qualifications should avail of the services of the distance system. There is hardly any sense to allow such people to take a university examination privately when facilities of guided studies are available through the distance mode. Such a step would boost the enrolment considerably, rescuing many of these Institutes from the clutches of their economic ills. In this way, the whole scenario of distance education of the country would undergo a radical change.

Another ugly spot of the system is the unhappy relationship between the Institutes and Open Universities. Though belonging to the same stream and pursuing the same goals, they look upon each other with suspicious eyes. The Institutes consider the Open Universities as having been super-imposed upon them, while the Open Universities look down upon the Institutes as the bastards of the system, totally incapable of pursuing the goals of distance education. One commentator very aptly describes the situation as, 'Not to speak of their working hand in hand with each other, their relationship is infact strained with mutual suspicion and acrimony. The Directorates in particular nurse the grievance that the creation of the Open Universities has pushed them into a secondary position..... new institutions (open universities)... not only perpetuated their existing problems but also created many more for them" (Editorial, *Indian Journal of Distance Education,* Vol.IV) This is indeed too sad a development. Unless both of these institutions work in close co-operation with each other, distance education system would continue to be fraught with a serious danger.

## REFERENCES

Aggarwala, S.K. and Ansari, M.M. (Eds). *Directory of Distance Education Institutes, Part-I (India).* New Delhi, Association of Indian Universities.

Bakshish Singh, Saroj Mullick and Neelam Chaudhry.*Correspondence/Distance Education in India, An Indepth Study Covering the Year 1989-90 (Research Report).* B.N.Koul (Ed.) New Delhi, Indira Gandhi National Open University, 1994.

Datt, Ruddar, 'Growth of Distance Education In India.' *Indian Journal of Distance Education.* (Chandigarh). Vol. IV. (1991)

Gupta, S.K. 'Development of Distance Education In India Problems, Priorities and Policies. *ICDE Bulletin* No. 23.

*Indian Journal of Distance Education* (Chandigarh) Vol. IV

Information Folder, Indira Gandhi National Open University, Regional Director, IGNOU, Karnal 1994.

Letter of Dr. B. P.Gangurde, Additional Secretary, UGC to Vice-Chancellors, D. O. No. F-3-14/93 (NFE-II) December 1993.

Shrimali, K.L. Quoted by G.Ram Reddy. Koul, B.N., Bakshish Singh and Ansari, M.M.(Eds) *Studies in Distance Education.* New Delhi: Association of Indian Universities and Indira Gandhi National Open University 1988.

CHAPTER III

# STUDENTS' PROFILES

THE absence of any age bar on entry to it raises certain interesting questions, such as, what type of people enrol themselves with the Institutes of Distance Education. Why do they come forward to have education through this mode ? What is their performance and so on and so forth? The answer to these questions provides a meaningful insight into the nature and role of this nascent system. This chapter is therefore devoted to the study of the student's profiles in the Institutes of Distance Education in India.

## II

To begin with, we study the type of students who enrol themselves with the Institutes of Distance Education. Going by the philosophical norms, distance education is actually meant for the grown-up persons who fail, for one reason or another, to receive education at the appropriate stage of their life. It provides to them an opportunity to make up that serious deficiency and thereby fulfil their life's ambition for education. Besides them, there are people who are educated, and in certain cases well-educated even, who too want more of education, maybe for the reason that they want to improve their station/status in life, to keep themselves occupied during their free time, or maybe they want to learn more of such things which they may not have studied at all earlier or studied but marginally. This system opens its portals for them as well. This is the reason why distance education is described as a second chance education.

However, the exigencies of the development process have also inducted into this system the freshers as well. 'The revolution of rising expectations', currently sweeping across the developing countries of the world, has infused into every mind, especially those who are newly enfranchised, to equip themselves with education. Too greatly inflated demand for education, coupled with an insurmountable constraint of resources on the part of the state, has led many a nation to divert a part of their school/college going youngsters to the Institutes of Distance Education, especially to those Institutes which are run by the conventional universities for the added reason that, being the extension wings of their parent universities, they provide the same study programmes through the distance mode as through the conventional mode. Thus, these Institutes contain a sizeable strength of the youngsters.

As for the distribution of the students between these two broad categories (the old and the young) the position in India has been fluid. At the earlier stages of the inception of this system, the older age group (those who were 25 years of age and above) out-numbered the youngsters and the freshers. In 1970's , nearly 2/3rd of the total enrolment in the Chandigarh Institute, for instance, comprised those persons who were above 25 years of their age. Almost everyone of them was employed and most of them were married and well-settled in life. One and a half decades that followed, marked a drastic change in this composition. Today, the picture stands upside down. A Study of the Chandigarh Institute 1987 reveals that 59.2 per cent students were below 22 years of their age and another 21.4 per cent were between 22-25 years. In other words, four-fifths of them fell in the category of the youngsters. (*Indian Journal of Distance Education.* Vol. I)

To compare the position obtaining presently in India with that of the developed countries, the two mark a serious contrast with each other. While the youngsters outnumber the older persons in India, it is the latter who dominate the scene elsewhere in the world. To quote a few studies. At the Athabasca University (Canada), 70 per cent of the students in 1989 were in the age group of 25-44 years. (*Research In Distance Education*). The Japanese University of the Air had in 1985-86 only 15.1 per cent youngsters. Conversely, 84.1 per cent of the students were above 25 years of age. Similarly, in the Indonesian Open University of Tarbuca, 80 per cent were the employed persons. (G.Ram Reddy, 1988 pp.154-56).

If in the 1960's and 1970's persons in the older age group (and, incidentally, the employed and the married) numerically dominated the scene of distance education in India, the reasons were two-fold in nature. On the one hand, there were a number of persons in the ranks of the employed whose promotional avenues had been blocked on account of lesser educational qualifications on their part. Besides them, there existed many such persons who nursed for long an ambition to pursue higher education, not necessarily with the object of improving their career prospects, but for various other reasons. These two categories of persons were frantically looking forward for any type of opening that may come on their way. As mentioned earlier, the introduction of distance education in the country was a God-sent opportunity for them. They brook no delay and caught it by its forelock.

On the other hand, the number of the youngsters, seeking higher education was not so large as to overflow from the colleges and universities (a phenomenon to be witnessed in later years). This was perhaps for the reason that most of our development plans (as for example rural reconstruction, community uplift, educational spread, agricultural improvement, employment generation and the like) had not made much of an impact upon our rural populace in general and the deprived section of society in particular. As a result, educational awareness had not as yet dawned upon the educational have-nots. Moreover, the pace of population growth was not so swift. Cumulatively, the number of education seekers was as much as could be absorbed easily by the existing conventional institutions, putting but little strain on the Institutes of Distance Education. Therein lay the secret of the dominance of the older and the employed persons.

That the youngsters constitute a sizeable section of our distance students provides evidence to the fact that we have been unable to cope with the growing rush of the education seekers through the instrumentality of the conventional system. Conversely, had distance system not come to our rescue, our ambitious goal of 'education for all' would not have been possible at all to achieve. In that eventuality, our democracy would have been badly put to jeopardy. For, millions of youngmen and youngwomen who would have gone without education (and also without jobs to their liking and aspiration), would have contributed to social unrest of the worst kind. Thus, distance education has been rendering yeoman service to the nation. Realising the paucity of resources for conventional type of education, on the one hand, and the immense potential of distance education, on the other, our planners have proposed that out of the additional inflow of one million of students in higher education in the course of the Eighth Five Year Plan period (1992-97), half of this number would be diverted to this stream (Para 11.7, 2.3 ) and that no more conventional type of colleges and universities would be set up.

An analysis of the profiles of the youngsters reveals that a large majority of them hail from comparatively poorer homes, who can afford neither to defray the heavier cost of the conventional education nor to tie themselves with conventional colleges on a whole-time basis lest they should be compelled to forego studies after they have succeeded in getting a job which is of a greater value to them than perhaps higher studies. Without courting a risk of this type, they prefer the Institute of Distance Education, the dominant consideration being that they can still pursue their studies after having been engaged in some employment. Distance Education thus holds out special appeal to this section of the people.

Another significant development of the past two decades is the marked change in the gender ratio of students in distance education. In 1970's the number of the women pursuing higher education through this mode was too little. In the Chandigarh Institute, it was 6.00 per cent in 1971-72 (Bhatnagar and Sehjpal, 1992, an unpublished study). Today, their strength has appreciated quite considerably. The MIIRD study (1980-81) puts the strength of the women at 22 per cent whereas Bakshish Singh, *et al.* study (1989-90) found that it has gone upto 39.6 per cent. The latter further reports that "the women percentage in both the Schools of Continuing Education, Delhi and Madurai Kamraj University is 45 per cent, followed by CCI's of Madras University 44 per cent, CIEFL 41 per cent, Sri Venkateshwara University 40 per cent, Panjab University, Chandigarh 38 per cent...." (Bakshish Singh, 1994, p.57)

It is further gathered that the strength of the women in the post graduate study programmes is greater than in the under-graduate study programmes. Mahajan conducted an in-depth study of the gender ratio in three M.A. courses, namely Punjabi, Hindi and English as offered by the Directorate of Correspondence Courses, Panjab University, Chandigarh and discovered that in 1989-90 the ratio of the women to the total number of students was, respectively, 49 per cent, 62 per cent and 55 per cent (1991). Making an identical disclosure, Ross and Powell report that at the Athabasca University, the female ratio surpasses their male counterparts in respect of their numbers (1990).

That women should come forward to receive higher education in an increasing number is a very happy development for an educationally under-developed society as that of ours. The induction of more and more of women in higher education would not only make them politically more articulate but would also enable them to foster their homes and families in a more enlightened manner. This is quite essential at this critical juncture of history.

It would not be an exaggeration to say that distance education as compared to the conventional system, is a better institutional mechanism to promote education among the women in particular. Besides involving comparatively lesser social as well as individual cost, it induces even the conservative parents to send their daughters for higher studies. That their daughters would pursue higher studies under their benign care without either being uprooted from their homes or exposed to the 'immoral ways' of the modern urban life is both a consolation and incentive for them. This is exactly what is being witnessed today. The newly affluent rural peasantry in Punjab and Haryana is also now bewitched of the desire to send their daughters for higher education so that not only do they enhance their social status but their daughters also get educated and are married to the affluent boys. They cast their preference for distance education partly because of the limited number of seats in colleges and university departments and partly because of the conservative nature of their elderly womenfolk in particular. This is precisely the reason why the rural-based women predominate the scene. Let us hope that our women should also attain that level of education as men, may be through the instrumentality of the distance system.

Another goal of distance education (in the context of our country) was to help eradicate the social imbalance of the rural and the other deprived sections of society vis-a-vis their well off urban brethren. It was hoped that once these sections acquired education, (preferably higher education) they would themselves make their way on the ascending curve of the social hierarchy. How far has distance education been able to achieve that goal is very difficult to assess in view of the lack of the requisite data. However, there are two general indicators which do affirm that this goal too has been achieved, by and large.

The first indicator could be the rural-urban ratio of the students. Bakshish Singh, study 1994 reveals that the position varies from Institute to Institute. In 1989-90 the highest percentage of rural students was in Utkal University 73 per cent, followed by Kurukshetra University 52 per cent, Gujarat Vidyapeeth 51 per cent, Tilak Maharashtra Vidyapeeth 50 per cent and Punjabi University 48 per cent (p. 57). In the Chandigarh Institute, we do not find much change in the ratio since the 1970's. Broadly, the proportion of the ruralities to the urbanites remains, more or less intact. However, the strength of rural boys and girls in the post-graduate section, particularly in Punjabi and Hindi disciplines, has, of late, marked an upward trend. As said earlier, the newly-dawned affluence in the rural areas of this part of the country (consequent upon the Green Revolution) has made the rich peasantry highly conscious of education. Their sons and daughters do their graduation in rural colleges and come to the nearby cities for higher education. Finding themselves ill-equipped to compete against the more advanced and well-groomed urban-based students, partly because of the poor academic standards of the rural colleges and partly because of their receiving education in their first generation, they get refuge only in the Institute of Distance Education. The girls prefer this mode for the added reason of the conservative attitude of their parents as explained earlier.

It may further be added that their comparatively poorer proficiency in English (again due to the rugged nature of the rural environments in which the schools and colleges where they receive their education, operate) handicaps them from pursuing higher studies in English or any other social science wherein too English constitutes the medium of instruction. They are thus left with no option but to go in for Punjabi and Hindi. Their better proficiency in these languages further reinforces their choice. Hence there is a comparatively greater rush of these ruralites in M.A. in Hindi and Punjabi.

The second indicator of our having drawn somewhat closer to the goal of equality is the tremendous increase of the younger students in such Institutes as are situated in big cities like Delhi and Chandigarh. A close look at their profiles reveals that almost all of them are the fresh school leavers and, further, they belong mostly to the socially and economically deprived sections of society (sons and close relatives of the peons, the factory workers, the daily wage earners and such other categories of the slum-dwellers and the like). As pointed out earlier, these youngsters, hailing from the poorer homes, are in a great need of some employment hence they opt for the distance system quite deliberately.

To look at the case of the Chandigarh Institute from a closer angle, what we find is that the share of the Chandigarhians in the total enrolment of students in the Institute was hardly one-fourth in the mid-seventies. It has gone upto 60-65 per cent by the end of the 1980's (Bakshish Singh, *et al*. put the figure of the urbanites at 85 per cent as per 1989-90 enrolment.) This tremendous increase of the local students in the Institute is predominantly due to the reason that Chandigarh is mainly a city of the '*babus*' who are invariably more conscious of education than perhaps any other segment of society. It is also partly due to the reason that the bulk of the population of this city (unlike that of any other city/town) is an *emigre* from the villages and towns of not only the neighbouring states of Punjab, Haryana and Himachal Pradesh but also of as far away States as Bihar and Madhya Pradesh. More significantly, these people still maintain their roots in their original home towns and villages. As a result, whenever anyone's relative's or friend's son finishes his schooling, he is sent to this city where he lives with his 'uncle'. The latter admits him to the Institute and also gets his name registered with a nearby employment exchange. In this way, the young lad both pursues studies and looks out for a job.

The case of Delhi is no different. This city too is resided by people who hail from almost all over the country and quite a few of them still maintain a live contact with their original homes. They also bring their relatives with them both for 'earning and learning'. Besides, the vast employment avenues that this city provides make hundreds and thousands of people come to this city on their own and combine job-hunting with distance education. This explains why the Delhi Institute is almost cent per cent an urban Institute (Bakshish Singh *et al.*, put their figure at 93 per cent) These two cases amply substantiate our hypothesis that distance education is discharging its responsibility of educating the socially-handicapped sections quite admirably.

As regards the employment profiles of the older age group of students, they fall in three broad categories, the working, the superannuated and the non-working. The former two categories comprise the present and the former civil servants, military personnel, bank officials, employees of the private and the public enterprises, accounts people and so on. The more noteworthy feature is that unlike the past years when only the lower and the middle level government and private management employees alone availed of the facility of distance instruction, now high officials also come forward to enrol themselves with these Institutes. This is probably for the reason that the nature of the study programmes given by these Institutes has undergone a radical change. Earlier when these Institutes offered the graduate and the post-graduate study programmes only, it was but natural that the lower and the middle level functionaries who did not possess that much qualification alone would get themselves enrolled with them. Now these Institutes and the Open Universities also provide for such professionally more useful additional study programmes as Master in Public Administration, Economics, Personnel Administration, Commerce, Business Administration, Electronics, Information Management, Diploma courses in Advanced Management, Accountancy, Distance Education, Creative Writing, Journalism, Mass Communication and the like. Naturally, the level and the quality of students would undergo a change correspondingly. As a result, these Institutes have on their rolls a number of officers of such superior civil services as the Indian Administrative Service, the Indian Economic Service, the Indian

Banking Service, the Indian Police Service, etc. etc. In the same manner, the officers of the armed services of such ranks as Majors, Colonels and even Brigadiers join these courses, largely with the objective of finding some meaningful occupation for themselves after their superannuation.

Equally significant is that distance education has now begun to catch the imagination of the superannuated and the non-working people as well. Earlier both these categories of persons would not do anything except reading the newspapers, dabbling in local politics or medling in the affairs of the others and would thus while away their time. Boredom, early ageing and premature death formed the characteristic features of their life. But of late they too have begun to avail of the facilities offered by the distance learning systems. To cite two typical cases.

First, we had on our rolls in the Chandigarh Institute a former officer of the Indian Police Service. For fourteen long years after having retired as an Assistant Inspector General of Police, he ran a private detective agency. When he found himself physically too feeble to manage that job, he joined M.A.Political Science. He says that he found these studies so much interesting that after having completed that two-year course, he went ahead with the study, first, of Economics and then English, again of the post- graduate level.

Second, one day this author saw an old lady in her mid-seventies taking swift strides to his office with her bent back and a long staff in her hand. On inquiry, he was wonderstruck to discover that she was an M.A.(English Part II) student.

These are just two illustrative cases. There are innumerable men and women who find in distance studies an ideal pasture during the closing years of their life. Besides keeping themselves meaningfully occupied, they also get the satisfaction of learning new things. There are persons who find superannuation an ideal time to fulfil their long pending ambition for they feel that they are now completely free from all their responsibilities of the office as well as the home. To cite the case of a student who had failed to successfully complete his M.A. course through this mode due to his persistent ill-health, was once asked by his friends as to why he was taking the trouble of studies, zealously replied. "Earlier Prakash (a fictitious name) was B.A. Pass. Now he is at least M.A. Fail". This simple innocuous statement was an expression of his long pant up ambition to have a post-graduate degree. In this way, we find that there are indefinite types of persons in this world who find in distance education a new message of hope and fulfilment.

Yet another happy sign is that the distance learning system has also of late attracted the attention of the housewives. Earlier the women who joined this system hailed from the ranks of either the young girls or the working women. But now even the housewives find some utility in this system. A study of the Dr.Ambedkar Open University discloses that the strength of the housewives among the women students of the University was 68 per cent in 1983-84, 87 per cent in 1986-87, and 85.3 per cent in 1991-92. The remaining students hailed from the ranks of the teachers and other categories of employees and unemployed unmarried girls. (Quoted by B.K.Kamala in Bakshish Singh. 1995, p.136).

The emergence of the nuclear families, the two-children norm and, above all, the simplification of the domestic chores have all contributed to the steep reduction in the drudgery of their domestic life. Abundant free time that the housewives now have at their disposal makes them think, among other things, of distance education. Some of them undertake distance studies to complete the study programmes which was once disrupted by an early marriage, a child birth or any other reason. Others take up a course simply to while away their time in a more constructive manner. They find such courses useful and interesting as Creative Writing, Accounts Keeping, Computer Application, Population Education, Gandhian Philosophy, Women Studies and the like. Thus, the housewives constitute a newly discovered area of clientele by distance education.

In sum, distance education and more especially the wide sweep of its course and the flexibility of its instructional mode, hold out a strong appeal to all sections of the people, young and old, men and women, the employed, the unemployed and the superannuated. Hopefully, it would usher in our society as well an educational revolution, pulling down the vestiges of illiteracy and conservatism.

## III

The next important issue that needs to be examined is, what motivates a person to take up a distance education course. The first great attraction that such courses hold out to the people is that of career building/career improvement. As we know there are a number of persons who are held up in their present position in the official hierarchy mainly because of the poor educational qualifications on their part. Some of them might not have been actually held up but they anticipate that they would not be able to go beyond a certain level because they do not have the requisite qualifications for the same. Such persons find in the distance learning system a convenient method to make up their deficienty. At the earlier stages of the inception of this system, such persons had out-numbered all other categories of the distance learners. Today, their number has shrunk, but they still constitute quite a sizeable group. These persons are mostly found inflating the ranks of the traditional B.A./B.Com. and M.A. courses. For, a university degree is still considered to be an essential qualification for a number of middle and higher level office and administrative jobs.

The second category of the career seekers comprise those lowly placed office, commercial and industrial workers who no longer derive much pleasure from the nature of their present employment. They are captivated by the desire to shift to a better station in life. An office clerk, for instance, wants to compete for the State/Central level administrative service, school teacher wants to be a college/university professor, a diploma-holder junior engineer nurses the ambition of becoming an executive engineer one day and so on. This desire of upward mobility motivates such persons to distance education. They seek in it the fulfilment of their ambition. The ready availability of such technically oriented study programmes as Bachelor or Master in Engineering, Computer Science, Journalism and Mass Communication, or advance diploma course in Management, Business Administration, Accountancy and the like, besides, of course, the traditional M.A. courses in such disciplines as Public Administration, Economics, Commerce, Political Science, etc. provide a strong inducement for such persons to attain their goal.

In this way, we find that distance education helps a variety of the employed, partially employed or even the unemployed to attain their ambition to make a respectable living in society. Career building thus constitutes a major cause of motivation for distance studies. A number of learned studies attest to this fact. Quoting a study *(Americans in Transition: Life Changes as Reasons for Adult Learning* by Aslanian and Bricknell) Iquacy Warriewicz says, "...while for the overwhelming majority, learning is utilitarian; people want some reward other than pleasure derived from learning. Career changes were named by 46 per cent as their reason for deciding to learn. . ." These data are very close to our findings in Ontario where the purpose of learning was job-related for 44 per cent." (1982).

While it is true that for a majority of the students career-building is important, there are people who are motivated to distance education not with any monetary or job consideration in mind but only for the sake of learning. Instead of whiling away their time in idle gossip or in such other unproductive pursuits, they think that it is better to learn something new or to enhance their knowledge of something of which they know but little. Such persons belong more often than not to the ranks of the superannuated officials and the house-wives. For, it is these two categories of people who have plenty of leisure at their disposal. The others are generally too busy with their other more productive pursuits. It is, therefore, but obvious that the number of such persons is not to be very large. Iquacy Warriewicz (1982) puts their number in his Ontario (Canada) study at 18 per cent as a whole. Though no such learned study has been conducted in this country, we do know on our experience that there is a sizeable strength of such students in almost every Institution. But it is certain that their number, compared to the developed countries, is not that large.

While discussing the issue of the motivation, one cannot help mentioning that there is a very large section of students in our Institutes which is inducted into the system without any proper motivation but by the sheer force of circumstances. As mentioned earlier, there are innumerable students, who being fresh from their schools and colleges, are keen to get admission in college/university departments. But being unable to face a stiff competition against the others they fail to be absorbed by the conventional institutions. When left with no chance, they make their way to the Institutes of Distance Education. Thus, they are here less by design and more by chance.

With a view to measuring the motivation level of the distance students, Mahajan (1991) conducted a study of the students of the Chandigarh Institute with respect to the timings of their admission. His hypothesis was that those who were fully motivated by distance education take admission as soon as it is opened or by the last date of the normal admission time whereas the undecided lot comes only towards the end of the extended period of admissions after having exhausted all other avenues. He discovered that only two-fifths (35 to 40 per cent) of the student fall in the category of the fully motivated ones for they take admission right in the beginning of the session. In other words, 3/5th of them constitutes that phalanx of students who opt for this system less by design and more by the force of circumstances. Incidentally, this percentage corresponds to the overall strength of the unemployed and the freshers in the Institute. This fact further establishes our hypothesis that the ranks of the unmotivated students are mostly filled by the freshers.

## IV

How do the distance students perform in their studies? This question assumes significance in view of the reason that distance students unlike their conventional counterparts, combine studies with their occupational responsibilities, thus there is an implicit danger that their occupational responsibilities might affect their studies or vice versa. It is also a fact that those who prosecute distance studies are generally advanced in age and as such do not possess a very sharp memory so as to help them perform well in the examination.

The yard-stick to measure the performance of students—distance as well as conventional—usually, is two-fold. Quantatively it is the rates of completion and of the dropout. In other words, how many students enter into a given course; how many of them drop out of it in between the admission and its conclusion; and , finally, how many of the remainder are successful in the terminal examination. Qualitatively how many of the successful candidates are placed in the merit list, how many obtain first class and so on.

The validity of this yard-stick even in respect of the conventional system has been questioned by a number of educationists. In so far as the distance learning system is concerned, it stands outrightly rejected for the following two reasons. In the first place, it is very relevantly pointed out that the terminal stage of a distance study programme is too difficult to be determined, the reason being the flexible nature of the distance education system. To dilate upon, a distance student unlike his conventional counterpart enjoys the freedom to enter and re-enter into a given study programme at will and similarly to bow out of it at any time and that too temporarily or even for good. To hypothetically illustrate, a student takes up a certain course and after having successfully completed, say, three out of eight credits, he discontinues his studies. In that case, he need not inform his Institute. After a couple of years, he again thinks of resuming his studies. He takes up the admission again for the fourth credit onward (he had already completed the first three, for which he gets due consideration and weight ) and proceeds further. Now in a fluid situation of this type it is pretty difficult to determine at any given point of time how many students had entered into a particular course, how many of them have completed it and so on. For, at every step, students continue getting in and getting out of it.

Secondly, a person takes up a distance course not necessarily to complete it. Unlike his counterpart in the conventional system, he is not wholly committed to it. Instead, this course is more of a supplementary nature to him. His primary commitment is toward his profession (or in case of ahousewifes toward her family) which provides bread and butter to him and to the other members of his family. It is not obligatory on his part that he must complete it. If he does it, well and good, and if he doesn't, he is not going to lose much. Moreover, being employed and perhaps married and having children, he is likely to face various types of problems (e.g. mid session transfer or employment, illness of someone in the family, unscheduled marriage, unplanned childbirth and so on) which may render it difficult for him to complete or carry on with his studies. The latter being peripheral in importance, can be conveniently given up, unlike a regular school or college student. Granville Rumble (1992) aptly remarks, " Many distance students choose to follow a course without necessarily planning to submit all the assignments or take the examination . . . many students never start actively studying the course and remain from the institutions point of view non-starters." (p. 87) Shale found that half of the students enrolled in the Athabasca University in 1978 and 1979 fell into this category. We also come across innumerable such cases in which the students do not remit the second instalment of fees or discontinue their contact with the Institute only to be found out later on that their interest in the studies had worn out.

As for the quality of performance in terms of the number of the merit positions or the first classes among the pass-holders of the university, this criterion too is misplaced. The nature of the composition of distance students (promotion-seekers, career builders, housewives, super-annuated officials, etc. etc.) provides us ample evidence that none of these categories of persons are interested in university merit positions. Instead, their only object is to have a degree. Some of them may not be interested even in degrees/certificates. To them reading and writing is the be-end and be-all of their life. To expect of them that they would burn mid-night oil and establish record in the university examination would be nothing short of betraying our common sense.

Thus, the yardstick originally devised to measure the performance of conventional type of students or to determine thereon the reputation of an Institute is totally irrelevant in so far as the distance system is concerned. The worth of distance education or the reputation of an Institute of Distance Education should be judged not by the examination results of its students but by the nature of the study programmes that the system offers. Are these study programmes commensurate with the needs of the society? Does this system help the nation in providing to its citizens the facilities of re-deployment? Does it also help it to effectively absorb the overflow of students from the conventional institutions, thereby helping the cause of educational spread? Does it provide enough avenues to meet the citizens' ambition for upward social mobility? and so on.

However, these traditional criteria have so much clouded our vision that we cannot think of any other criterion and go on measuring the performance of distance students by them even though they are too irrelevant. Anyway, even if we go by this yardstick, we find that the dropout rate which in the case of the Institutes of Distance Education is supposed to outstrip that of the conventional institutions, does not actually do so. The study of Bakshish Singh (1994) discloses that the dropout rate in the Annamalai, Panjab and Kurukshetra Institutes was respectively, 3 per cent (in 1990), 15 per cent (1989) and 21 per cent (in 1988) whereas in the case of the conventional students of their respective parent universities was 68 per cent in Annamalai and 47 per cent in Panjab (pp.49-50). The study of Jose Chander, (1984) of the Trivandrum Institute puts the dropout rate at 18.5 per cent (1983-85). Thus the performance of distance student as measured in terms of their dropout rate is quite good, even while the provocations for them to discontinue their studies are far too many.

To judge the effectiveness of this system on the basis of the performance of the students in the terminal examination, Bakshish Singh, (1994) observe that their study of the 29 Institutes "shows that their pass percentage ranges from 30 per cent to 97 per cent." (p.50) They had also taken up a sample of three Institutes and compared the performance of their students with conventional students of their parent universities and discovered that while in Annamalai the pass percentage of distance students was 97 (in 1990) whereas that of conventional students was 89 per cent. In Panjab, it was, respectively, 44 per cent and 53 per cent, while in Kurukshetra, it was 54 per cent and 64 per cent (pp.49-50). Sheath (1969) reports from Australia that while the internal students in the faculty of arts of the New England University showed in 1955-68 a pass percentages of 77.5 that of the external students during the same period in the same course was 78.2. As to the quality of their performance, we find that distance students too bag positions in the university. In our Institute (Chandigarh), we find that our M.A. Public Administration students in particular give as good a performance as the students of the university department and often bag a large number of merit positions. At the earlier stages of the inception of our Institute, there was hardly a year when a few merit positions might not have been won by our B.A. and B.Com. students. Jevons (1982) who conducted a study of Deakin University (Australia) also reports that " off-campus students fare no worse than on-campus students. Indeed, they do slightly better, though the differences are marginal". (Daniel, S, *et al.* p.126).

While judging the performance of distance students we must not lose sight of the manifold handicaps that they suffer from. They do not for example enjoy the facility of face-to-face interaction with their teachers. Their age as well as their occupational hazards go against them, and so on. However, the loss on this account is amply compensated by such other factors as their experience and wisdom, and, above all, by the high level of motivation on their part. Given these conditions, it is no wonder that they do as well in their studies as their counterparts in colleges and universities. Handicapped they may be, but they are certainly no worse than the latter.

## V

Finally, we come to the question how far do distance students attain their objective? As stated above, a great majority of them take up distance studies with a view to improving their status in life which fetches to them both enhanced social prestige and better standards of living. A number of studies in India and abroad reveal that most of these students do succeed in attaining their objective. In 1988, a survey was conducted in Fern Universitat (Germany) regarding the study motivation of distance students. Most of the students are reported to have said that they had fulfilled their ambition. (Christine von Prumme, 1990) Madurai Kamraj University also conducted in the mid-eighties an empirical survey into this very issue. Its findings reveal, "Those who have successfully completed the course through correspondence have benefited most in gaining social prestige and for those students the impact has been more social and educational than economic." (Enrolment Pattern, Research Note, *Indian Journal of Distance Education*, Vol. I).

We too have seen from time to time a number of students coming to the Institute or visiting their teachers in their homes (sometimes even carrying packets of sweet meat) to tell them that the degree/diploma that they had done through the Institute had been immensely helpful to them in securing promotion in their rank or to the next higher cadre of their official hierarchy. Some of them have even been successful in shifting over to the profession of their choice.

Once an ex-student related a very interesting experience of his life. He said that until recently he was only a matriculate, though a superintendent in his office. But compared to him, his three sons, two daughters, three daughters-in-law and his brother-in-law—all had much better educational qualifications to their credit (some of them were even M.A. or B.A.,LL.B's). Whenever there was a family get-together everyone of them affectionately jeared at him. In his heart of hearts, he felt too small. But because of the lack of facilities, he was helpless. To his good luck, one day he came across a news flash that the Panjab University would institute Correspondence Courses. He was overjoyed to see in it a ray of hope for him. The day admissions started, he found himself at the fee counter of the university. He was perhaps the first student to join the new Institute. In the years to follow, he did his graduation as well as a law course. These degrees not only elevated him in the estimations of his family members and friends but fetched to him the Under-Secretaryship in his office (a highly coveted position in the official hierarchy). After superannuation he set up his law practice. While relating this experience, his face was glowing with immense pleasure of self-pride and achievement.

## REFERENCES

Aslanian and Bricknell, "Americans in Transition, Life Changes, As Reasons for Adult Learning", quoted by Iquaey Warriewicz. in Daniel, John S, Martha A and Themposon, John (Eds). *Learning at a Distance, A World Perspective of Distance Education*. Athabasca University, 1982.

Bakshish Singh, Saroj Mullick and Neelam Chaudhary, *Correspondence/Distance Education In India, An Indepth Study Covering the Year 1989-90*. Koul, B.N. (Ed..) New Delhi, Indira Gandhi National Open University. 1994.

Bhatnagar, S. and Sehijpal, A.K., *Department of Correspondence Studies, Panjab University, A Status Paper*, 1992. An Unpublished Study.

Chander, Jose N., Kevin, S. and Sudhakaran, P., *Drop-outs in the System of Distance Education (A Project Report)*, Trivandrum, Institute of Correspondence Courses, University of Kerala, 1984.

*Eighth Five Year Plan* (1992-97) Vol. I. Government of India, Planning Commission, New Delhi.

Jeavons. in Deniel, John S., Martha, A. and Thomson, John (Eds.) *Op.Cit.*

Mahajan, Ravi K., 'Language Courses in Distance Education And Regular Set-up, A Study of Examination Results'. *Indian Journal of Distance Education* (Chandigarh), Vol. IV (1991).

Pummer Christins Von, 'Study Motivations of Distance Students', *Research In Distance Education,* Vol. 2, No. 2 (April, 1990).

Reddy, G. Ram, *Open Universities, Ivory Towers Thrown Open*. Delhi, Sterling. 1988.

Research Notes I, *Indian Journal of Distance Education,* Vol. I.

Ross, L. and Powell R. 'Woman And Distance Education', *Research In Distance Education*, Vol.2, No.2 (April, 1990).

Rumble, Granville, *The Management of Distance Learning Systems*. Paris, UNESCO Institute of Educational Planning And Research, 1992.

Sheath, Haward C., 'External Studies at University Level, Some Recent Developments, in Erdos, Renee (Ed.) *Proceedings of the Eighth International Conference of the International Council for Correspondence Education*. Paris, UNESCO House, 1969.

Warriewicz, Iquacy. *Op.cit.*

CHAPTER IV

# STUDY MATERIAL
## The Written Lesson

LESSON constitutes the key-stone of the educational edifice. It is an instrument by means of which a teacher imparts instruction to his students. In the class-room-based system of education, lesson is given generally orally, though teachers do make use of the black board and of such modern electronic aids as films, slides, overhead projectors and the like, in order to make their teaching both interesting and effective. In the non-contiguous environments of distance education verbal communication is well-nigh impossible. To overcome the constraints of spatial separation, the distance teacher must reduce his lesson to black and white, multiplicate it into copies and then mail one copy to each of his students. On their part, the students would study these lessons at their own time and convenience in their respective homes and would then send their reaction, response and performance rolls by mail to their institute. The invention of modern electronic-based educational technologies (such as radio, television, audio and video cassettes, telephone, computer, etc. etc.) has further facilitated the task of distance educators in inducting into their instructional process an element of directness, thereby making their teaching more forceful and effective. Fast growing use of these technologies notwithstanding, printed lesson continues to be the mainstay of distance education the world over. This is true not only of conventional correspondence courses but also of highly sophisticated multi-media presentations like the courses of open universities.* (Pathak )

Lesson, which thus forms the main instrument of distance instructions needs to be guarded against two major pitfalls—sub-standard quality and

*To empirically test this hypothesis, Kurt Timmons conducted a field survey in Australia on the effectiveness of the various teaching media such as the written lesson, telephone tutorials and computer based instruction and found out that ". . . students generally perceive the traditional learning guide and text-books to be more important than any other adjuncts. Interestingly, the learning guide produced by the teacher is more highly valued than the commercially produced text-books".

delayed delivery to its users. Unfortunately, most of our Institutes of Distance Education in India have miserably failed on both these accounts and, as a result, they have brought a bad name to themselves as well as to the system at large. It is, therefore, highly imperative that utmost care should be taken to ensure that the study material that we provide to our students is qualitatively, as good (if not better) as the instruction that class-room-based students of a first-rate-college get at the hands of their reputed teachers. It hardly needs to be emphasised that quality of the study material is the touch-stone of the success and failure of an Institute of Distance Education. All those Institutes which have established their reputation in the field have shown their extra-ordinary concern for quality. Equally important is that the administrative machinery of the Institute is so geared that its study material is delivered to the students at well-planned intervals of time so that their studies go on quite uninterruptedly. Timely delivery is as crucial for the well-being of the Institute as the quality of its study material.

Being a relative concept, quality is the product of a number of variables. Its major determining factor is the nature of the target group of students for whom the lesson is to be produced. Quality of the script needs be adjusted to the level of their ability as also to their aspirations, expectations and requirements. As for the type of students that we get in our Institutes, they are an assorted lot of the matures and the urchins, the knowledge/skill seekers and the college drop-outs, the experienced and the freshers. The lesson must, therefore, cater to the needs of those who want just a pass in the examination and the degree/diploma as also of those who are in quest of knowledge or seek to enhance their competitive capability, or to keep themselves occupied during their leisurely hours. The assorted nature of the learners and their varied expectations notwithstanding, we must bear in mind that a majority of the learners are adults who are definitely more demanding than the youth. Moreover, they are here for knowledge. Therefore, it becomes all the more imperative for us that our study material meets their expectations more than that of any other section.(Moore, 1987).

Keeping in view such a mixed group of students, the lesson should have the qualities, first, of comprehensiveness. The writer must dwell (preferably extensively) upon each and every aspect of the subject under treatment so that the distance learner (who, more often than not, is devoid of any other academic assistance does not fail to comprehend the lesson or a part thereof, simply because of poor explanation of the subject or the lack of adequate background knowledge of any aspect of the topic concerned. While the author of a book can afford to assume that its readers may look beyond it if they need certain help to understand the book's contents, the author of a lesson cannot make any such assumption. If in the process of developing a lesson, he feels that the explanation of certain aspects needs to be repeated, he should not hesitate to do so. For, repetitive explanation (of course, to a reasonable extent) would help facilitate the assimilation task of the distance learner. Besides, he should also make every effort to anticipate all possible questions and difficulties and to provide such assistance that might be needed within the context of the programme itself (Moore, 1987). Highlighting the qualities of a lesson, Erdos (1967) says, " It must guide the student's studies, aid him in the assimilation of knowledge and skill, give him practice in the use of this knowledge and skill and test his understanding and attainment to find out where he needs additional help." (p.14)

Although the dominant concern of the script-writer all through the development of the lesson would (should) be to bring home to his students the subject as effectively as he can, he should also relevantly quote the opinions of the other learned authorities on the subject, especially whenever he puts forward his own viewpoint, either by way of an explanation or in support/opposition of a certain proposition. By doing so, he would not only acquaint his students with a wide spectrum of viewpoints but would envelop his script with a halo of authority. He would also absolve himself of the charge (sometimes levelled against script writers) of unduly rubbing on the minds of the students one viewpoint only, thereby making an attempt to indoctrinate them. Above all, these quotations would help the students to earn a distinction in the terminal examination, particularly at the hands of the Indian examiners who have a weakness for quotations. However, the script-writer must also at the same time ward himself against his over-temptation of giving too many quotations, lest this jungle of quotations should eclipse the explanation of the subject. Many college teachers are in the habit of cluttering their texts with too many quotations. This style, while robbing the reader of the charm of smooth reading of the book, tends to dub the text as sub-standard.

The learned viewpoints, the excerpts of books/journals, the various types of statistical information and the like that may be incorporated in the lesson-script must be properly acknowledged in a scientific manner. Some script writers do not however care to do so. There is of course no doubt that a lesson is not a research paper by any means, yet the author should not let anything go unacknowledged. Such a method would not only save the author of the charge of plagiarisation, but would also go a long way in helping the students develops a proper context of the situations. Those who would like to consult the literature further would find this additional information all the more useful.

To reflect upon the lesson-scripts of our Institutes. In most of the cases they are weak both qualitatively and quantitatively. Apart from being deficient in subject matter, they are sketchy and short and also poor in explanation. Bakshish Singh, (1994) analysed the quality of the study material of (a sample of ) 24 Institutes with the help of the evaluators' feedback. Their findings are; (a) content adequacy is satisfactory in 50 per cent and poor in 42 per cent; (b) relevance of content is satisfactory in 50 per cent, poor in 33 per cent and good only in 17 per cent; (c) content density is poor in 58 per cent, satisfactory in 30 per cent and good only 12 per cent; and (d) the use of illustrations, examples, etc is poor in 83 per cent good in 20 per cent and satisfactory in 17 per cent.".

Projecting distance student's point of view, Rathore (1994) (who elicited the opinion of 200 students, hailing from 14 Institutes of the country) observe, "It is seen that only 52.66 per cent students are on the whole satisfied with the reading materials, whereas 42.33 per cent students are not satisfied. Thus, the observation that majority of reading material are not upto the mark, seems to be correct." (p.71). However, it would not be fair to sweep the entire lot of lesson-scripts with one broom. There are undoubtedly good many such lessons which can be described by any standard as by far the best. But unfortunately their number is not very large.

It may be underlined that most of the lessons which were found to be substandard were the handiwork of those teachers who work in the conventional system. They are too ill-qualified to do this job. For, as Repley Sims (1982) rightly observes, "Nevertheless, whatever the legitimate extentuating circumstance in a given case, the basic principle does not change, i.e. contiguous and non-contiguous teaching-learning environments require different approaches and techniques . . . A good classroom teacher may not be as effective in a non-contiguous teaching-learning situation, any more than text book material prepared for the classroom would be suitable for the learner at a physical distance from the classroom"( p.64).

Having been bred and brought up in the environment of the conventional system, the conventional teachers little appreciate the needs and requirements of distance learners and the unfavourable situations in which most of them are placed. As a result, they tend to write lessons in the same old stereo-typed way in which they teach their classroom students. This practice of getting lessons written by classroom-based teachers who have no idea of the correspondence method and no contact with distance students constitutes a serious anomaly.(Bakshish Singh in Inayat Khan, 1989).

Even though we are conscious of the fact that conventional teachers however learned and experienced they may be, are generally ill-suited for the job, ironically the academic activity of most of these Institutes is highly dominated by them. Those Institutes which do not provide for a whole-time faculty of their own (incidentally their number is far larger than those which make a provision for the same) put their exclusive reliance on the outside teachers for the preparation of their study material and for many other things too. Even the other category of Institutes, get their lessons written from the outsiders for one reason or another.

This too unduly big role that has been conceded to the conventionalists has made them overlook the difference between the conventional and the distance students. They consider the latter as good as the former and thus handle the writing of lesson for distance learners in the same manner as teaching a class. Little do they realise that unlike their own students, the distance learners are cut off from them by hundreds of miles. They, therefore, need to provide in their written texts additional pedagogic aids in order to overcome this barrier of separation, besides of course, other normal teaching techniques (Erdos, 1967, p.36). Lessons written by them thus tend to be sub-standard. Reflecting upon his Chinese experiences, Chan Dong Kim also feels that study material produced by external authors tends to be "insufficiently geared to the needs of distance learners. . ."(Ram Reddy, 1988, p.171). Corroborating this fact, S.P. Anand (1979) remarks that "lessons written by teachers enjoying immense reputation as first-rate professors were found to be either too 'soft' even for correspondence students or went beyond the syllabus to the extent of becoming irrelevant to the immediate task before the illumini" (p.81).

That lessons written by conventional teachers generally do not eminently serve the needs of distance learners does not imply that these Institutes should discard their services all together and, instead, drive their lonely furrow. By no means do we make any such suggestion. For, any hint to this effect even made obliquely, would negate the vary thesis that the conventional and the distance systems are mutually complementary and they must, therefore, closely draw upon each other. Moreover, such a touch-me-not policy would deprive these Institutes of the benefit of the vast reservoir of academic scholarship that the conventional system has built over the ages. That would be too big a loss for them to be easily sustained. The best way by which the services of these teachers can be availed of without compromising with the quality of the study material is to adopt the team approach in the development of the study materials. Open Universities and the other well-reputed Institutes of Distance Education the world over have already adopted it with a remarkable degree of success. We will dwell upon this approach a little later in this chapter.

Next to comprehensiveness comes the style of the presentation of the subject matter, another important variable impinging upon the quality of the lesson-script. The assumption with which a script-writer should proceed with his task is that the students for whom he is writing constitutes a lot of the socially and economically handicapped persons. Many of them may be living in villages where there may not be available any type of academic assistance or guidance. Some of them may be too deficient in their background knowledge to make out even the basic concepts. Some of them may be too old to keep themselves in touch with whatever little they had studied in their younger years. Thus, the lesson should be written in a style that none in this assorted lot faces any difficulty in comprehending its subject matter. In other words, the style should be easy and lucid; the language in which it is couched is not difficult (lest the student should have to consult the dictionary at every step) and the quotations that are given are not too long. The writer should make use of glossaries, tables, charts, diagrams and the like, thereby explaining the subject in various different ways.

Another consideration that the script writer should always keep in mind is that the person who is to study that lesson would seldom have a chance of face-to-face interaction with him. Therefore, it becomes incumbent upon him that he should so shape his script as to make his presence regularly felt by his students. He can do that by writing his script in an informal conversational style, as if he is talking straight in the face of his students. Holmberg (1989) describes this style as 'didactic conversation' which encourages a student to think aloud. (Granwille Rumble, 1992, p.29)

However, it has been observed that the lesson-scripts of these Institutes are invariably written in a typical text-book style. Mukhopadhyay (1989) rightly complains that "in a very large majority of institutions, the correspondence lessons resemble the conventional text books — very often unstructured, poorly laid out and produced. . . violating all principles of psychology of reading. What self-learning distance education material should serve, remains largely unfulfilled".

The script-writers in general and those hailing from the ranks of the conventional college/university teachers in particular do not prefer the conversational style. Maybe, they are not much familiar with it, or maybe they do not like it, perhaps for the reason that the various types of conversational adjuncts that are embedded into the script are obstructive in nature, interrupting the smooth flow of its reading. Their disliking for this style may be illustrated by one typical case. Once a lesson-script written by this author was referred for review to an eminently-placed university teacher. The only changes/modifications that the learned reviewer suggested were those relating to this style. He struck off all the conversational adjuncts that the author had put in here and there. At the end of his report, he remarked that these conversational adjuncts should be avoided as far as possible. That reviewer was not the only one of his kind. Many others had also to suggest likewise. Such a perception of the conversational style further reinforces our conclusion that those teachers whom these Institutes commission for writing their lessons are, by and large, little conversant or appreciative of the spatially-scattered nature of distance learners.

In order to get a constant feedback from his students as to how students receive his lesson, the classroom teacher keeps an eye on them. To make up this deficiency in a non-contiguous situation, the writer should better insert at places a few in-built exercises so that the students should pause at those places and answer the questions himself. These small exercises would enable distance learners to have self-assessment of their grasp of the instruction and would thus make their participation in their teaching-learning process both active and effective. (Sansanwal (1988) and Mani, (1988) . But, again, the lessons of most of our Institutes are lacking in this respect. Bakshish Singh, *et al.*, (1994) report, "So far as the use of conversational language and style is concerned 100 per cent of CCI course material is found to be poor. . . ."(p.91).

Finally, a lesson must be properly embedded into the totality of the framework of the syllabus. In other words, every lesson should be suitably correlated with the subjects/topics that precede it, so that the reader when embarks upon its study is well-acquainted with what has been dealt with immediately before it and what correlation that bears with the one in hand. Similarly, before he finishes its study, he must also have an idea as to what would follow it and what link the latter would have with it. Such a treatment would enable the student to understand how one topic dovetails into the other and continuity is maintained in the entire course. This approach will ultimately help the student to have an integral view of the course, facilitating his thorough understanding and comprehension of the subject.

The ideal method of presentation of a subject/topic is to develop it step by step in a proper pedagogic manner. The script writer must, first, state in brief the objectives of the lesson and then delimit its scope. After having done so, he should develop its details. It is not necessary that he should follow the essay-type approach. Instead, he may choose any method, ranging from visual effects to exhaustive verbal explanation. The idea behind this exercise is how best to make the script a self-learning lesson as to enable the distance student to understand and assimilate the subject matter in as easy a manner as possible. This is the approach which is generally adopted in situations where the teacher and the taught do not have any face-to-face interaction with each other.

Its merits notwithstanding, this approach does not appear to be acceptable to either the teachers or the students of these Institutes. The identical nature of the syllabi of the courses of study of these Institutes as also of the mode of performance-evaluation of their students with their counterparts studying in class-room based college and university departments constitutes a major stumbling block for the application of this approach. This commonness of courses and the syllabi thereof makes the students of these Institutes expect their teachers to furnish to them long essay-type lessons so that they may be able to suitably tailor them to their examination needs. The prefacing of these lessons with such introducing headings and sub-headings as objectives, scope and the like, and, further, embedding them with various other explanatory aids and illustrations may cause some confusion to them. Some studies have attested to this fact. It has even been observed that when lessons were written in accordance with this approach, many a student discarded them and, instead, sought the help of cheap bazar notes. This is the reason why the script writers adopt invariably the conventional text-book approach.

It is further desirable that the script-writer should give at the end of his lesson an exhaustive list of further readings on the topic concerned. The fact cannot be denied that however exhaustive a lesson-script may be, it is not possible to encapsule in it the entire information or material, available on a subject. Although the writer tries to put into his script as much of it as is relevant for the needs of the rank and file of his students. Yet there may be some students who may like to go beyond the lesson and seek more of information and knowledge. This list would be found highly useful by this category of students. This type of informatry guide is all the more essential for such lessons as are written for higher classes, as for instance the post-graduate classes. At this level the students are expected to do extensive reading in order to acquaint themselves with as wide a spectrum of knowledge as possible. This ready-made list of further readings will facilitate their task of looking for greater and wider information and knowledge.

To further cater to the needs of the latter category of the students, the teacher-in-charge of a course should try to continuously feed his students with excerpts of relevant text-books and encyclopedias, copies of the learned articles and such other worthwhile literature that he may find useful for them. However, none of these Institutes not even the well-reputed universities, like the IGNOU, adopt this practice. The teachers think that once they have despatched the lessons, their duty towards the students is over. If anyone of them requires any additional help, he may manage it on his own. Thus, the only type of study material that they provide consists of written lessons, nothing more, nor less than that.

As alluded above, one of the most crucial factors that goes a long way in determining the quality of the lesson is who writes the lesson and in what manner is it written. A lesson may be the product of either an individual subject specialist or a team of experts. The individual author approach requires an individual subject expert (who may belong to the Institute's faculty or may be hired from outside on a short term basis) to handle the entire task of writing the script, right from the development of its outlines to its final editing and the preparation of its press copy. (Since the Institutes do not generally make a provision for the services of such experts as designers and editors, these tasks are also got to be done by the author himself). He alone decides as to what are the requirements of the students and in what manner are these to be met. It is upto him whether he may seek the consultation or assistance of anyone else or may choose to depend upon and exploit his own expertise and experience. What is required of him is that he should produce a first-rate lesson-script, which may serve the needs of the students in an ideal way.

In the team or corporate approach, the task of preparing the study material is entrusted to the care of a team of experts rather than to an individual subject specialist. In view of the scope of the task being larger, the team includes, besides a number of subject specialists, a host of such experts as language masters, designers, editors, computer scientists, audio and video technical script-writers and the like. The lesson script that finally emerges, is the product of the collective efforts of all of these experts.

To explain the *modus operandi* of the team approach. To begin with, the subject experts discuss and decide in the course of a number of their sittings the parameters of the topic in hand, and then develop the broad outlines of the subject matter and the lay-out of the script. They also indicate the sources of information, which task though seemingly simple, may turn out, in certain cases, quite formidable. Having finalised these details, the subject specialists would then entrust the task of writing out the full-length script to some one amongst themselves. The latter would take some time to produce the draft. As soon as the draft is ready, it is circulated among the various members of the team. After these persons have studied the draft, a plenary session of the entire team is convened wherein each member expresses his opinion. Since the master script of the lesson is yet to be finalised, the subject specialists are conceded the privilege of monopolising the deliberations of the session. They examine the draft from the various standpoints and try to finalise it. If they find it necessary, they may send the draft back to its author for reconsideration, recasting and even for radical modification. After they have fully satisfied themselves about each and every aspect of the script, it is finally ready and their job is over.

Now commences the work of the other experts. The language masters would vet and polish its language; the designers would prepare the diagrams, tables, charts, pictures and the like; the editors will edit it; the computer experts will feed the subject matter into the computer and thereby initiate the process of printing. In case audio and video scripts are also to be prepared, their respective experts will also get down to work. Since one expert following the other works on the draft as soon as it reaches his table, the whole exercise can be compared to that of an assembling workshop of a factory where the various types of the technical personnel are busy assembling the components of a machine. This nature of the task makes Granville Rumble (1992) to call this approach an Assembly Line Approach (pp.55-56).

To compare the team approach with the individual author approach, the former has an edge over the latter. Under the former, the chances of mistakes (both omission and commission) are completely ruled out. For, when a certain subject is examined again and again by a number of experts and that too over a number of sittings which are interspersed by a few intervals of time, it is bound to be certain that no aspect of it is left out of consideration or is stated/interpreted wrongly. The script would always be wholesome, balanced and exhaustive. On the contrary, when one individual works on it single-handedly, without being academically accountable for his product to anyone else, there are an endless number of chances of his script getting deficient in various different ways. Nôt only is he likely to overlook certain aspects of the subject (deliberately, inadvertently or out of his shallow knowledge of the subject), but also of presenting the subject matter in a manner that may ill-serve the needs of the students. His interpretations of certain propositions or factual data may be biased or even wrong. In other words, his unbridled whims and caprices may cost the students very dearly. Eulogising the corporate method of lesson writing Lord Perry, the first Vice-Chancellor of the British Open University had once remarked, "There seems to me no doubt that a course produced by this method will inevitably tend to be superior in quality to any produced by an individual". (Quoted by Andrew Blowers,1989).

As for the actual practice in India, the lessons-scripts of almost all the Institutes of Distance Education with the exception of one or two Open Universities, are the product of the individual teacher's efforts. The team approach is practically unknown, the reason being its time as well as money consuming nature. Obviously when a script is to be handled by a number of experts and that too in as detailed and leisurely a manner as highlighted above, its preparation is bound to consume a lot of time. If such an approach is to be adopted, it is necessary that not only should the syllabus of the course and the split-up into lessons/units is finalised a year ahead of the launching of the study programme, but the lesson preparation work through the team of experts is commissioned in time so that the lessons in their printed, audio and video forms are ready for despatch well in time. The hasty and hotch potch manner in which we work rules out completely the feasibility of perspective planning on these lines and action thereon.

Our nature of rushing the things through at the nick of time apart, there are certain in-built constraints in the system which inhabit us from adopting a leisurely approach. One such constraint pertains to syllabus formation. In every university, open or conventional, this function falls in the purview of its Academic Council. While in the case of an Open University the Academic Council consists of distance teachers and perhaps none else, that of a conventional university is primarily a show of the class-room-based teachers. Those who hail from the Institutes of Distance Education get but marginal representation on it. Thus, they do not have any say on its decision-making with the result that the interests of these Institutes fail to get due attention, much less protection at the hands of the Council.

The upshot of this attitude of indifference comes in the form of the delayed finalisation of the syllabi of the various courses of study. Though the rules stipulate April-end as the outermost limit for this task, the process invariably drags on till the middle or the end of June, sometimes even later than that. Delay is not the only feature of its functioning, more significant than this is its tendency to change the syllabi, wholly or partially, every now and then. Repeated changes and that too when decided quite late land these Institutes in situations of great inconvenience and awkwardness.

Unlike class-room-based teaching where teachers take but little time to deliver their goods, distance teaching is done primarily through the medium of written lesson-scripts whose preparation is a long-drawn process. Obviously the question arises, when the syllabus is finalised as late as June-end, when would the lessons be commissioned for writing, when would the script writers complete their assignments, when would those hand-written scripts be printed and despatched to the students. The time left for the entire process to go through smoothly and efficiently is quite short. In order to meet the time schedule, the whole process is to be rushed through post-haste. In a situation of this type, it is the individual author approach that alone can save the Institute from awkward situations. Even by adopting this approach, lesson-preparation and their despatch often get delayed, badly upsetting the delivery schedule and thereby creating unknown difficulties to the students. On the contrary, Open Universities do not face any such problem. Distance teaching being their exclusive concern, they so schedule their entire time-frame that the question of delay does not arise at all. Precisely, this is the secret of their being eminently placed to adopt the team approach. In sum, if these Institutes fail to derive the benefit of the team approach, the entire responsibility for this loss rests with such 'foreign' decision-making bodies as the Academic Council, which are but little considerate to their interests.

Yet another aspect of the functioning of the Academic Council which too impinges upon the lesson preparation work of the Institute is that even though it is the highest academic body of the university, its deliberations are sometimes tinged with acrimonious debates of a highly non-academic nature. It is observed that its members sometimes bitterly clash with one another in order to get their books officially prescribed by it. This is more so in the language courses than in either the social or the physical sciences. One component of the syllabi of the under-graduate courses of English, Hindi and Punjabi consists of the compulsory study of some standard text-books. These text-books are the anthologies of the poems/prose of certain well-known writers on the subject. These are compiled by the college/university teachers. The compulsory nature of their study and the lucerative market, resulting therefore, make the various members of the Boards of Study and the Academic Council to press their claims for the selection and approval of their anthologies. The ensuing clash of interests not only delays decisions but also leads to frequent changes in the syllabi. Another dimension of this clash of interests is that the claimants are not sure till the end whether or not the die would be cast in their favour. Once a person comes to know that his anthology has been finally selected and prescribed, he would sit down to compile it. This process too takes its own toll of time, thereby creating further delay. It has been observed that the prescribed text-books generally do not reach the market till half of the academic session is over. Surprisingly, once it so happened that the person concerned failed to compile his text in time, thereby creating a highly ticklish situation both for the teachers and the students. At long last, the Board of Studies had to decide that the text-book, prescribed for the preceding year, would continue for that session as well. In such situations, the plight of the distance teachers can be better imagined than described.

That conventional universities do not pay heed to the difficulties and problems of their own Institutes of Distance Education, particularly those arising out of the delayed finalisation of the syllabi of the courses of study and their frequent tempering with them was discussed time and again at a number of fora including the University Grants Commission but with little fruit. The latter even tried to impress upon the universities concerned through the guidelines that it issued to them at various times, regarding the functioning of these Institutes, to so schedule their syllabus formation calendar that it leaves sufficient time to their Institutes to prepare their study material in time. (Guidelines Para 5.02) It even suggested that syllabi should not be revised earlier than three years and whenever a revision is affected, it should be decided at least one year ahead of the commencement of the academic session when it is to be implemented. Some of the universities have even taken decisions to implement these directions But when things come down to actual implementation, little respect is shown either to the U.G.C. guidelines or to their own decisions. These directions/decisions are implemented more in their breach than in their observance. The net result is that the Institutes continue to suffer and their image distorted badly.

As alluded above, the team approach is also cost prohibitive in so far as these Institutes are concerned.. The individual author approach requires them to pay to one individual teacher only, one who authors the lesson and to none else. (Since his duty spans over the writing of the script as well as over its editing and the preparation of the press copy, noneelse is associated with him for the latter jobs.) On the other hand, the team approach involves a large number of experts, belonging to such diverse fields as language vetting, designing, editing and computer science (even if we exclude electronic media experts), besides, of course, the subject specialists. Not only is the team large in size but its deliberations must spread over a number of days and months. The Institute would, therefore, be required to pay remuneration for the work of each one of them in keeping with their expertise as well as the time devoted by them to this task. Thus, the cost involved in the preparation of the lesson-script in accordance with this approach is far too exorbitant as compared to the individual author system. To cite one case, the Chandigarh Institute spends only Rs.500 on the writing/preparation of a lesson script for post-graduate classes. But for this amount, which constitutes the remuneration of the individual author of the script, there is no other expense involved in this work. On the contrary, the IGNOU engages a number of subject specialists (who alone in the whole team are hired on contract basis from outside the University) and pays Rs.1,000 to each one of them, in addition to their travelling and daily allowances for attending the sessions of the team. The indirect cost of the salary and other perquisites of the various other associate experts who belong to the IGNOU itself, is in addition to all this. Keeping in view these hard realities, one inside expert frankly confesses, that the underlying reason for the Institutes not adopting the team approach is that "this method is expensive and, at the same time, slow." (B.K.Sinha, 1989, p.107; also refer to Murthi and Krishna, (1992) p.160)

Taking an overall view of the lesson preparation work, we find that neither the teachers nor the Institutes take this work seriously. Obviously, quality is the first casuality of this deplorable state of indifference. As far as the Institutes go, they are more concerned with the timely despatch of lessons (lest their image is not tarnished) than about their quality. That is why they prefer individual author approach to the team approach. Their apathy toward quality further manifests itself in their tendency to avoid having their own whole-time faculty, and instead, get this work done from the outside teachers on contractual basis. Furtheron, the remuneration that they pay to script writers is ridiculously too low. Some of them pay as little as Rs.75 per lesson. What quality would this pittance fetch for the

Institute can be better imagined them described.

Yet another faulty aspect of their policy is that they entrust this highly difficult task of writing lessons to every. Tom, Dick and Harry on their faculty. This is due mainly to the reason that the persons at the helm of affairs of these Institutes, being themselves the product of the conventional system, do not appreciate that writing, compared to lecturing to a class, is a very difficult task. It is all the more so with respect to the lessons for distance students. In fact, lesson-writing is an art which one acquires by training and research as well as with experience and practice. It is the domain of the experienced and the seasoned teachers. Conversely the inexperienced and raw hands cannot do justice to this work. But unfortunately the men at the top of the hierarchy do not appreciate this fact and consequently associate every member of the faculty with this work, without consideration to one's standing or experience as a teacher, much less as a distance educator.

This policy is doubty counterproductive. While the quality of their lessons suffers at the hands of the freshly recruited and inexperienced teachers, the energies of their senior and seasoned teachers are frittered away on such pedestrian tasks as marking of the students' home assignments or lecturing in the personal contact programmes. If this policy of equal distribution of work among all faculty members is revised and the senior faculty is vested with the exclusive responsibility of writing lessons, there is no reason why the quality of the study material does not improve considerably. It may be added that this type of division of work and responsibility is a recognised policy pattern of all the reputed Institutes of Distance Education the world over. The Indian Institutes need to draw a leaf from their book.

As far as teachers are concerned, they too do not appear to take much interest in the preparation of the study material. Those who work in these Institutes on a whole-time basis have, by and large failed to identify themselves with this nascent system of distance education. Most of them constitute a desgruntled lot, despite their having been put at par with their counterparts working in other departments of the university. They feel dissatisfied with the nature of their work and always clamour for their transfer to the conventional wings of their university. With such a given low morale, how can we expect them to produce qualitatively high study material?

Then on the top of it comes the lack of accountability on the part of the teachers. Following the individual author approach these teachers tend to become the judge of their own work. The lesson-scripts, produced by them, are not subject to any type of review, internal or external. Though rules stipulate that an individual author must first discuss the outlines of his lesson with his departmental colleagues and when the script is ready, he should submit it for their perusal and review. Whatever suggestions they offer at both the stages shall be given due weightage by him. But all these stipulations remain enshrined in the rule-book of the Institute, to be seldom invoked and put into practice. Over the years, these teachers have come to be so much overwhelmed by a deep sense of apathy and alienation that they would not like to spare even a minute to listen to what anyone of their colleagues has written for his students. They may lend an ear to their colleague's research paper but not to his lesson-script. This is the degree of their involvement in such a crucially significant aspect of the system.

However, this deficiency can be overcome by means of a sound system of external review. The ideal system is that as soon as a lesson-script is received from its author it should be sent to an outside subject specialist for review. Simultaneously, it should be administered to a select group of students in order to ascertain whether or not it meets their requirements; whether it is too soft or too hard for them. The results of this pre-test as also the comments of the learned reviewer should be communicated back to the author concerned. The final script that would thus emerge would ideally meet the requirements of both the discipline and the students. As for these Institutes, they do not provide for any such system. Some of them did care to have it at the initial stages of their inception but have discontinued it long since. Besides the apathy of the authorities and the loathsomeness of the teachers, heavy expenditure involved in this system accounts for its discontinuance. The obvious result is the degeneration of quality of their study material. Both the U.G.C. and the NCDE have repeatedly tried to impress upon these Institutes the vital importance of this system of review in the overall scheme of distance education, but in vain. (Refer to the letter of Additional Secretary, U.G.C. to the Vice-Chancellors, December, 93 and also to the Report of the Directors' Conference, New Delhi, 1974). Individual authors continue to rule the roost with all their academic strengths and weaknesses.

It may be mentioned that the teachers working in these Institutes on a whole-time basis are somewhat over-worked (Murthi and Krishna, 1992). This fact too impinges upon the quality of their written texts. A study conducted by this author (1994) reveals that in the Chandigarh Institute "the eight member faculty of Political Science Department handles 160 lessons of post-graduate classes and 270 lessons of under-graduate classes (90 lessons of each medium, English, Hindi and Punjabi). In the same manner, the two teachers of the Department of Philosophy handle 270 lessons of B.A. classes." Dispelling the impression that this work is not so taxing, the author of the paper observes, "It is true that all the lessons are not written every year . . . However, every lesson needs to be vetted, reviewed and revised every year, so that it is duly updated and corrected from various other angles. Further, it is also true that in so far as the under-graduate classes are concerned, the lesson are prepared only in one medium, generally English. The other two versions are got ready from the outside expert translators on contract basis. Nevertheless, the fact remains that the faculty must handle them thoroughly. This handling implies that the teachers must read each and every lesson between the lines so as to ensure that no mistake of any type—spelling, syntax or printing is left. They must also update them by inducting into them the latest information that has poured in since the lesson was revised last. Sometimes the plethora of new information is so large that a better part of the lesson is got to be redone altogether. In this context one may not lose sight of the fact that teachers also need time for the collection of the requisite information and also for updating their knowledge of the subject. Thus, we find that the work of lesson-vetting, though seemingly a simple exercise, is no less time-consuming."

"As regards the Hindi and the Punjabi versions," the author adds, "these are also vetted by the teachers themselves. To pass them on to the translators every year for this purpose is neither feasible nor academically sound. They must also be handled by the internal teachers in the same careful manner as those in the English medium, for those who are serviced by them are as good students of the Department as these who opt for the English version." (p.4)

In passing, the issue of reducing the workload of the teachers and thereby improve the quality of the study material may also be considered. To this end, the Institute needs to adopt a two-pronged policy. First, it must bifurcate the responsibility of the teachers into two halves. The first half should comprise only writing, vetting and up-dating of the lesson-scripts, while the other half should consist of the marking of the students' home assignments and lecturing in the personal contact programmes. As suggested above, the former chunk of responsibility be entrusted to the exclusive care of the senior faculty, and the latter half to the junior faculty. The second aspect of the new policy should relate to the regional networking of the various Institutes. As we discuss at length in one of the chapters to follow, the various Institutes, located in close geographical vicinity of one another, should develop a network among themselves, with a view to forging mutual collaboration, *inter alia*, for the development of the study material in all its different manifestations. Such a networking would further help cut down the workload of the teachers, making them concentrate increasingly on the preparation of the study material. Its quality would then improve automatically.

In the end, it may be observed that all-out efforts may be made by everyone concerned—the Institutes and University authorities, the teachers and the U.G.C.— to ensure that the study materials that these Institutes provide to their distance learners is by far the best so that no one should be able to raise his little finger against its quality. It must also be emphasised that if timely steps are not taken in this behalf, our Institutes would miserably fail to achieve their lofty goal of human resource development even though they may continue attracting students towards them. By their sheer indifference they would thus betray a great national cause.

## II

After a lesson is written by the subject specialists and the various other experts have worked on it, it is now ready for servicing to the students. But before that task is taken in hand, another massive operation is to be gone through. It is to be printed into thousands of copies. This 'industrial aspect' of distance education demands that the 'goods' are produced efficiently and are supplied to their users as per their demand.

It may relevantly be underlined that distance education is an 'industry' of its own kind in the sense that its production and marketing operations are closely conditioned by a tight time- schedule. These operations are to be gone through within a course of 8 to 9 months, i.e. between May and the following January. This work cannot be taken in hand earlier than May because by then the Academic Council hardly completes its work of finalisation of the syllabi of the various courses of study. On the other side of the continuum, the delivery schedule can also not be stretched beyond the January-end in view of the consideration that the students should be given reasonably sufficient time for preparing themselves for the examination which commences in April. This constraint of time makes this 'industrial operation' all the more difficult.

Its time-bound nature apart, the operation itself is monstrous in size. A study of the Chandigarh Institute reveals that the Institute printed during the academic session, 1992-93, as many as 1,038 units of lessons in three different mediums (English, Hindi and Punjabi). They ran into a length of 62,380 pages (Bhatnagar and Sehjpal). More revealing than these statistics are the tedious details of the production operation which not only consume a good deal of time and money but also keep the authorities continuously on their tenter-hooks.

Surprisingly, these Institutes which seek to provide instruction through the medium of the written/printed lesson-scripts still employ the age-old letter press technology for printing their scripts, which technology has long since been discarded the world over. Even when these Institutes know that it is on account of this slow and sluggish technology that they have to face a good deal of embarrassment at the hands of their clients, they do not propose to go in for a newer and more efficient technology. New technologies, a plenty of which are available in the market, are not only fast but far more cost-efficient than the one they use at the moment. It is high time that they go in for this long over-due change.

To briefly explain the details of the production process. Lesson scripts, as received from the script-writers, are generally hand-written. In order to make them easily readable, they are put on manually-operated machines (another anachronism) and typed. After these are typed and corrected, they are transmitted to the printing presses, where they are manually composed, letter by letter, by the semi-literate composers who are prone to commit more of mistakes. To rectify these mistakes, the proof-pages are read and reread, first in the press itself ( generally twice) and then by the professional proof-readers of the Institute, again, at least twice, depending upon the efficiency of the press concerned. Finally, the composed script is presented to the author for the print order. He too would give a reading in order to satisfy himself that the subject matter has been composed correctly and as per his directions. After a script has passed through these tedious stages, it is put on treadles and the required number of copies are printed.

The whole of this process consumes nearly two months provided that all those persons who are associated with this work at its various stages attend to their duties conscientiously which, more often than not, they seldom do so. The time-span is thus bound to stretch far beyond the prescribed limit, putting the whole delivery schedule in jeopardy. The above-quoted study discloses that there have been cases where a lesson has taken as long as six months to arrive at the delivery counter. These details drive one to the conclusion that it is the composing part that consumes the maximum time whereas its printing aspect is far simple an affair.

Another drawback of this technology is that once the printing work is over and the required number of copies are obtained, the plate containing the composed matter is destroyed in order to release the lead for some other work, waiting to be executed. If thereafter the need arises for a few more copies, the whole process is to be gone through *de novo*. This means that there is no in-built mechanism whereby more copies may be obtained without repeating the whole process.

Compared to this tedious and time-consuming process, the Desk Top Publishing (DTP) technology is far simple and also time as well as cost efficient. Primarily based on computer technology, the DTP completely eliminates manual operations. The hand-written manuscripts are fed straightaway into the computer. The subject matter going into its memory recesses, is stored there permanently. In order to ensure the correctness of the composition, a copy of it is taken out and presented to the author for his satisfaction. In case he finds mistakes in it, these would be corrected computerically which is far easier than the manual process. Once the corrections are made and the composition work is over, the floppy is ready to multiplicate the script into as many copies as are needed. The multiplication is done by the printer attached with the computer or in case the number copies required is very large, then through the off-set printing process.

In the subsequent years when lessons are vetted and up-dated, the existing subject matter is retrieved from the memory recesses of the computer, necessary changes are made by the author and then these changes are incorporated into the body of the lesson, again computerically. Thereafter, the same process of multiplication through the printer is repeated. Thus, the superiority of this process lies in the complete elimination of all those tedious stages that are associated with the composition of the entire subject matter afresh every year, as is the current practice today.

To compare the two technologies, the letter press technology is far more defective. Being slow and tedious, it takes unduly long time for the finished product to reach the delivery counter. As a result, it is widely observed that these Institutes are seldom in a position to adhere to their delivery schedule. Delayed despatch of lessons is an established pattern of their functioning. Sometimes these despatches get as much delayed as March-end. It is but obvious that the students at the other end must feel exasperated and agitated, rushing enquiry after inquiry to the headquarters. The reputation of the Institute would naturally suffer a serious setback.

Secondly, the letter-press technology, based as it is on manual operations, leaves a wide scope for printing errors. The casual manner in which many composers and proof-readers function heightens the incidence of error further. It is an open secret that lesson-scripts of these Institutes abound in printing errors. The printers' devil plays such a havoc that sentences after sentences are either left out or mingled badly with one another, putting the readers to a quandary how to make a sense out of them. On the contrary, if the author is a bit vigilant at the time of feeding the subject matter into the computer (which he would naturally be in the interest of his own reputation), the problem of committing printing errors is thus overcome. For, the subject matter once fed into the computer, is not to be tampered with. In other words, DTP ensures errorless printing.

Another disadvantage of the letter-press technology is that it involves a heavy printing cost. It is the composition part which eats away a lion's share of the cost, whereas printing *per se* accounts for an insignificant part of it. The irony of the situation is that composition work is alone repeated every year. If the repetition of this work is eliminated somehow (say by preserving the plate) leaving behind only the printing part, even this technology could have been cost-effective. This advantage is available with the DTP system wherein the subject matter, once composed, computerically, can be retrieved whenever need be by just pressing a button and then as many copies of it can be obtained as needed. Therein lies the secret of the cost-effectiveness of this technology. Bhatnagar and Sahjpal's study (1994) further reveals that the printing cost is cut down to one-third. The Chandigarh Institute which spends Rs.16 lacs per annum on printing can reduce this cost to Rs.3.15 lacs if it switches over to DTP system..

The exorbitant nature of the cost as involved in the letter-press technology led many an Institute to print their lessons in bulk so as to suffice the needs of a couple of years, generally three years. This experiment did not however, help them much, for, in the first place, they could not correctly estimate their requirement over the next three years in view of the fluctuating nature of their student enrolment. As a result, the stocks would sometimes fall short of their requirements or sometimes go surplus. The wide prevalent manace of pilferage of the lessons (due to their being in great demand by the conventional students and the others) further accentuated their difficulties.

The second danger against which this technology could not provide these Institutes an effective bulwark was the inhospitable attitude of the Academic Council to suitably protect their interests by not changing the syllabi every year. Even if there was a little change, the Institute had to prepare the addendum to their already printed scripts.

Above all, locking the capital to print a huge stock of lessons for three years as also the warehousing facilities neutralized the gains (if any) occurring from the advanced printing. Thus, this experiment created more of difficulties than it actually solved them.

Yet another disadvantage of the letter-press technology is that its application makes the Institute employ a number of copy holders and proof-readers to cope with the massive task of proof-reading. The DTP system, on the other hand, is free from any such personnel encumbrances, as this technology completely eliminates the need to read the proof pages time and again. Whatever little of proof-reading is involved in it, it is done by the author himself. By offsetting the need to employ this personnel, the new technology further brings down the cost of the printing operation.

Doubts are often cast about the heavy capital investment needed to instal the DTP system as also to employ the highly qualified technical personnel to make the system work. All these doubts are ill-founded. The only sophisticated gadgetry that this system requires consists of a couple of Personal Computers (PC's) and a laser printer, the former to store the subject matter and the latter to bring out the copies. The number of the PC's would depend upon the number of the lessons and the mediums in which to publish them. The requirements of an Institute of 10,000 students can be conveniently met by half a dozen of PC's. It may be underlined that once the floppies of all the lesson-scripts are ready (which work may either be got done from outside agencies on payment basis or may be undertaken in phases by the Institute internally on its own machines) the current work would not be heavy so as to require a very large number of PC's. Since the subject matter is already in the computer, it is retrieved and the necessary changes/modifications as pointed out by lesson-vetters are to be incorporated into the body of the script (which work, as pointed out earlier is not very difficult), 2 to 3 PC's can cope with this work. Thus, the gadgetry required is neither very elaborate nor technically very complex.

As for the technical personnel, we need only a couple of data feeders/processors. This job is not very difficult or technical in nature. A few departmental clerks can operate the PC's after a little of training. In fact what needs to be done is that the clerks of the various subject departments who are charged, *inter alia*, with the duty of typing out the lesson manuscripts of the departmental teachers, should be trained for this purpose. Without affecting the basic nature of their job (they would now be typing these manuscripts computerically rather than manually), the quality of work would improve and that too without incurring any extra expenditure. Besides doing this work more scientifically, they would be made to gradually computarise the other administrative operations of their departments.

So far as the cost component of the new technology is concerned, it too is not very large. A few hundred thousands of rupees (less than five) is sufficient to meet the capital cost of the DTP system. This amount is so small that every Institute can easily manage to squeeze it out of its own funds. If somehow it cannot do so, the U.G.C. may be asked to assist it in this respect.

There is yet another advantage of the DTP system. The convenience and speed with which it takes care of the various production operations helps the Institute to bring about modifications in the lesson-scripts that last-minute changes in the syllabi necessitate. Today, the Institutes clamour, though in vain, that changes in the syllabi should be introduced at least one year in advance so as to give to them time to incorporate the changes into their lessons. The new technology is so efficient that it can take care of these changes even if they are announced late. The Institutes should no longer plead mercy at the door of the Academic Council and instead, assert their independent entity.

To sum up, the introduction of this technology would put these Institutes on the track of modern scientific management of their multi-facetted administrative operations. As alluded above, this technology would not only modernise the production system, but would also help them computerise their various other administrative services particularly those relating to students' record maintenance, establishment and library. It would induct efficiency in the overall functioning of the Institute which, in turn, would furnish its image considerably in the eyes of its clients and the general public at large. It is in keeping with the immense benefits of this technology that the Commonwealth of Learning has provided DTP systems to a number of African Institutes of Distance Education in order to assist them in the production of distance learning material" (*Comlearn*, Vol.4 No.1.) Thus, this technology deserves to be given a trial. Moreover, when the entire publishing industry of the country can successfully reap the fruits of this technology, why should these Institutes which are in no way less concerned with printing and publishing, form islands of anachronistic technology!

## III

Finally comes the delivery aspect of the study material. The success and reputation of distance education is cardinally hinged with its delivery system, as much as on the quality of its lessons. However academically sound and nicely brought out the lessons may be, if they do not reach the students well in time, of what use would they be for them. It is, therefore, virtually essential that lessons should be delivered to their users in some well-planned rhythmic order.

To compare oneself with one's counterparts is a natural propensity on the part of every human being. The students of an Institute of Distance Education, particularly those belonging to conventional universities, tend to compare the facilities that they get from it with those of their counterparts in sister colleges and university departments. In case the supply of lesson to them fails to synchronise with the start of the class-room work in other institutions, they feel highly let down. In the same manner, their disappointment and indignation know no bounds if the final packet of lessons does not reach them before their counterparts break for the holidays, preparatory to the terminal examination. But the irony is that while it is essential to be vigilant on the delivery front, it is here that a majority of the Institutes cut an utterly sorry figure. As alluded above, they often fail to maintain a regular and timely supply of the study material. There is no denying the fact that every Institute does draw out an ambitious time schedule for the delivery of its lessons and that it also strives hard to adhere to it meticulously. But it is either the script-writer or the printer, or even both of them who miserably fail it by not discharging their part of the responsibility conscientiously. The distruption of the schedule that they cause fatches a bad name for the Institute.

Though the script-writer and the printer are the notorious villains of the peace, sometimes the Institutes themselves create situations of suspense and uncertainty for the students. Since most of the Institutes do not have control either on the writers (as most of them do not maintain a whole-time faculty of their own and hence depend upon the goodwill of outside teachers) or on the printers (as they, with hardly any exception, get their lessons printed in the market on contractual basis), they are not sure when would their lessons be ready for despatch. As and when a few of of them are received from the printer, these are immediately passed on to the students. This situation of administrative uncertainly does not allow these Institutes to draw out in advance any delivery schedule, much less communicate it to the students. Such a situation leaves the students in a state of suspense as to when would they get their lessons and in how many instalments. Obviously, they would not be able to plan out their studies and will have to work in an hap-hazard manner.

The students' difficulties apart, even the Institute has to pay for this situation of uncertainty and confusion, a heavy price in administrative and financial terms. In the absence of any preplanned delivery schedule, the Institute is not in a position to decide the number and date of the despatches in advance. Despatches are made subject to the availability of the lessons. In the initial stages, they are sizeable in volume and contain a reasonably large number of lessons. But towards the end of the academic session, their size shrinks and the number begins to increase. The reason is that by then many lessons remain undespatched, forcing the student to make persistent demands to expedite their despatch. The panic that is thus let loose, makes the Institute despatch lessons with top speed, unmindful of the consideration whether or not a despatch is wholesome. The number of despatches would thus go up, making the delivery cost escalate.

The question that assumes importance is, in how many despatches should the study material be made available to the students? There are two schools of thought. First, the students should be given lessons at an easy pace, irrespective of the number of despatches. It is argued that in the class-rooms, students are taught as much in the course of a day/week as they may assimilate it thoroughly. Distance students, it is argued, are no different from them; they too should be given instruction in gradual doses. A proper feedback in the form of their home assignments should be taken at the end of each exercise. Disapproving this approach, the other school contends that distance students are not urchins so as to be taught in this halting and faltering manner. Being a lot of the responsible and mature people, they should be left to themselves so that they may plan and prosecute their studies at their own convenience and choice. It is, therefore, argued that the wise course would be to send the study material of the entire course in one single despatch. Let the students work out their own strategy of study for themselves.

To us the latter approach does not sound much logical. By sending the entire lot of lessons in one instalment, we would be off-loading the burden of our responsibility towards our students rather than helping them. The very purpose of instruction is defeated. We sincerely feel that one who is charged with the duty of teaching even by the distance mode, is supposed to give instruction in small doses and at the same time keep a constant eye on his students so as to ensure that whatever he teaches is properly digested by them. Therefore, the former approach appears to be correct.

It may further be underlined that of late the complexion of the students, joining these Institutes, has undergone a radical change. The proportion of the older age group who are generally looked upon as mature and responsible people, has considerably shrunk, yielding place to the younger element who are either the freshers or the drop-outs of the conventional system. This lot needs to be as carefully nurtured as we nuture the class-room based students. To send to them lessons in one single lot is to play with their career rather than doing some tangible help to them. To sum up, the former approach of sending lessons in easy instalments is more logical than the latter approach. That is the reason why most of the Institutes adopt this practice.

Another allied question that needs to be suitably answered now is, what is the ideal number of instalments which an Institute should send? There are no hard and fast rule which may determine this number. Every Institute has developed its own norms. Bakshish Singh, (1994) study discloses that 16 out of the 20 Institutes despatch their lessons in 2 to 4 instalments, 2 Institutes in 5 to 8 instalments and another 2 in 10 to 12 instalments. (p.88)

The Chandigarh Institute fixes this number at 4. It binds all the lessons of a paper/subject into four small booklets of a more or less even size. As soon as a student takes admission to the Institute, a packet containing the first booklet of each paper/subject is mailed to him. The second despatch follows in about six weeks. All-out efforts are made to ensure that before he comes to attend the first series of the Personal Contact Programme which commences in early October, he must have received half of the total number of lessons. The other two instalment are sent in the months of November and January, again with the target that before he attends the second series, he receives the entire lot of lessons. This is how planning is done and the students are provided with this mailing schedule much in advance. However, a good deal of deviation does take place every year because of the non-cooperation of the printers as also that of the teachers. This deviation would continue to occur so long as printing process is not streamlined by installing the DTP system. Once it is done, the delay caused by the sluggish working of the teachers would also be effectively curbed and consequently the delivery schedule would cease to be disturbed for all times to come.

As regards the mode of despatch, the registered mail remains perhaps unsurpassed by any other mode. To quote the case of the Chandigarh Institute again, it experimented with all methods. At the initial stages, it used to send these despatches by ordinary mail. That method, though saved the Institute from the heavy expenditure on the registry, often resulted into the loss of the packet during the transit. Those students who failed to receive their packets were provided with another, thus making the Institute face both embarrassment and monetary loss. To overcome that problem a proposal was made to replace that system by registered post. That proposal was opposed by the authorities on the ground that it would strain the finances of the Institute quite unduly. The teachers and the others would also disapprove of the suggestion on socialistic grounds that it would tax the students unnecessarily. At long last, it was decided to give an option to all out-station students to get their lessons either by an ordinary mail or by registered mail. Those opting for the latter mode would pay Rs.50.00 as mailing charges. The response of the students was remarkable. More than 70 per cent of them opted for the registered mail in the first year. Encouraged by that response, the Institute made the registered mail compulsory from the following year onward. The local students were however given the option of collecting their packets at the public counter of the Institute, if they so liked. Since then the system has been working quite satisfactorily.

## REFERENCES


Anand, S.P., *University Without Walls*. New Delhi, Vikas. 1979.

Bakshish Singh, 'Lesson-writing in Distance Education', in Inayat Khan (Ed.) *Teaching at a Distance*. Delhi, Amar Prakashan. 1989.

Bakshish Singh, Saroj Mullick and Neelam Chaudhary. *Correspondence/Distance Education in India. An Indepth Study Covering the Year*, 1989-90. A Research Report Koul, B.N. (Ed.). New Delhi, Indira Gandhi National Open University, 1994.

Bhatnagar, S., 'Networking for Qualitative Improvement of Study Material, An Action Plan.' Paper presented to the National Seminar on Distance Education and the Challenges of the Twenty — First Century, Chandigarh, May, 1994.

Bhatnagar, S. and Sahjpal, A.K., 'Lesson-Production, A Comparative Study of the Letter-Press and Desk-Top Publishing Technologies, An unpublished paper. 1994.

Blowers, Andrew, 'The Open University of the U.K. ideals under challenge'. (1994) *I.C.D.E. Bulletin No.20*. (May, 1989)

*Comlearn* (News Letter of the Common Wealth of Learning). Vol.4. No.1.

Erdos, Renee F., *Teaching by Correspondence. UNESCO Source Book*. London, Longman. 1967.

Kim Chan Dong, G. Ram Reddy (Ed.) *Open Universities, The Invory Towers Thrown Open*. Delhi, Sterling 1988.

Letter of Dr. B.P. Gangurde, Additional Secretary, U.G.C. to Vice-Chancellors, D.O.No.F.3-14/93 (NFE-II) December, 1993.

Mani, Ganathi, in B.N.Koul, Bakshish Singh and M.M.Ansari (Eds.) *Studies In Distance Education*. New Delhi, Association of Indian Universities and Indira Gandhi National Open University, 1988

Moore, Michael G., 'Learners and Learning at a Distance', *ICDE Bulletin No.14*. (May, 1987)

Murthi, N. Linga and Radha Krishna S., 'Some Reflections on Social Sciences Teaching in Distance Education', *Kaktiya Journal of Distance Education*, ( Warangal) (Andhra Pradesh). Vol.1 No.1 (January, 1992)

Mukhopadhyay, M., 'Networking in Distance Education', *Indian Journal of Distance Education.* Chandigarh Vol. III (1989)

Pathak, Anil, in B.N. Koul, *et.al. Op.cit.*

Ramanujam, P. Ranga, 'Distance Learning Materials of the Developing Countries : How About Their Quality ?' *Indian Journal of Open Learning* (New Delhi) Vol.2, No.2.

Rumble, Granville, *The Management of Distance Learning Systems.* Paris. UNESCO International Institute of Educational Planning. 1992.

Sansanwal, D.N. in Koul, B.N. *et.al. Op.Cit.*

Sims, Ripley, *An Inquiry into Correspondence Educating Process* (Concise Version). International Council for Correspondence Education. (1982).

Sinha, B.K., 'The Lesson Objective and Content', Inayat Khan (Ed) *Teaching at a Distance.* Delhi. Amar Prakashan, 1982.

Timmins, Kurt, 'Educational Effectiveness of Various Adjuncts to Printed Study Materials in Distance Education'. *Research in Distance Education*, Vol.I, No.3 (October) 1989.

CHAPTER V

# STUDY MATERIAL
## The Audio-Visual Lesson

MODERN electronic technology has placed at the disposal of man a variety of new modes of communication. While telephone, computer, e-mail and fax make him communicate with his fellow-beings, both quickly and directly, however distantly located they may be, television enables him to see with his own eyes as to what is happening across the globe. No longer has he to wait endlessly for the postman to bring a message of welfare of his friend or relative and that too a week or ten-day old. Now he talks face to face with others, irrespective of their situation. Thus, these inventions have spanned distance and shrunk the wide world into a global village.

To distance teachers and students, these newer technologies have come as a great boon. These have considerably facilitated their task, enabling the former to teach the latter both by the word of their mouth and by the expression of their face and gestures of their hand. Now they explain the things with the help of diagrams, pictures, tables, charts and the like, creating as profound an impact on the learners' mind as traditional teachers used to do with the help of the chalk and the blackboard. Distance has ceased to be a handicap with them and communication has become direct as well as fast. In fact, the instructional process has become more "exciting, effective and inexpensive". (Kiran Karnik in Bakshish Singh, 1995. p.62). The printed word which, until recently, was the only medium of distance teaching, has now been relegated to the position of a complementary aid to it. A revolution has thus swept across the realm of distance education.

Neither among themselves nor in relation to the printed word, these electronic technologies are mutually exclusive. In fact, each one of them makes a contribution of its own, quite distinct from the others. If radio/ audio cassettes enable the distance teacher to talk straight into the ears of his students, television/video cassettes make his presence virtually felt by them, thus endowing the instructional process with a closer personal touch. In the same manner, if the written script provides to the student a comprehensive account of the subject in black and white which they can read again and again to digest it thoroughly, tele-conferencing affords them with an opportunity to ask questions and seek clarifications directly at the hands of their teachers. In this way, we find that none of these technologies can be a substitute for the others, different media serving different educational functions. (Anthony Bates as quoted by Avtar Singh 1991). Therefore, the ideal way to derive the maximum benefit from them is to integrate all the available instructional technologies (both electronic and print) in a suitable manner and goad each one of them to that particular task for which it is best suited. (Pathak in Koul, 1988). Peters describes this as the Industrial Model of distance education.(1992). This model was first introduced by the British Open University and has since been functioning very well, suitably meeting its needs.

The range of gadgetry that modern electronic technologies have furnished to the distance teaching mode is vast indeed. We have radio, audio cassettes, television, video cassettes, video tape, video disc, telephone, computer, fax, e-mail, optical fibres, and perhaps a few more. However, all of them cannot be employed for distance education, partly because some of them may not be very relevant to this system and partly because they may not be available in the country or if available, they may be cost prohibitive for the system or the Institute concerned. That is the reason why only a few select technologies are widely made use of by distance education everywhere in the world. Most highly developed nations of the West may perhaps be the exception which might be using all of them together.

In India, most of the Institutes still bank upon the print medium alone. The newer instructional technologies are, by and large, still foreign to them. However in those parts of the country where the regional stations of the All-India Radio extend the hospitality of their broad-casting services, the Institutes avail of this facility. So far, the IGNOU and a few other Institutes and Open Universities enjoy the privilege of having access to this highly sophisticated gadgetry. Of late, the UGC has sponsored with the munificence of the Doordarshan (National television) a television programme of higher education called 'Country-wide Classroom' wherein educational programmes developed by a chain of Educational Media Research Centres (EMRC's) are telecast for the common use of distance learners from all over the country. But this programme could not catch the imagination of these Institutions as well as the learners thereof for various reasons. (We will highlight these reasons at length a little later in this chapter.) Resultantly, these newer technologies remain by and large, beyond the reach of these Institutes.

However, a realisation is fast dawning upon these Institutes as well that these technologies would alone help them carry their courses to the door step of their students. (Tackwale,1995). Unless they adopt them soon, they would lose their appeal among the prospective learners. Already they are being dubbed, though erroneously, as the Institutes of (only) Correspondence Education as contra-distinguished from the Institutes/ Universities of Distance Education simply because they do not employ these newer technologies. In its Chandigarh (1994) Meet, the NCDE deliberated on this issue at length and then resolved that "the conventional universities-run Institutes of Distance Education should increasingly employ modern electronic technologies (more specifically audio, video and computer) in order to enhance the quality and effectiveness of their study material. Keeping in view the high cost of the hardware and technical components of these technologies, the U.G.C. be urged upon to give specially earmarked grants to the universities for the creation of these facilities." (Proceedings of the Sixth National Seminar on Distance Education and Challenges of the Twenty -first Century'. Chandigarh, May, 1994).

Earlier, the high-level Power Group, constituted by the U.G.C. to look into the problems of these Institutes and suggest remedial measures had also made recommendations on these very lines. Accepting its recommendations, the U.G.C. had commended these technologies to the universities concerned. It suggested that, to begin with, they may use the existing audio and video cassettes of the IGNOU and the others. "In the long-run, the EMRC's in the States should help in the development of video/audio cassettes for the distance education institutes" (Letter of the Additional Secretary to Vice-Chancellors). Thus, it appears that the day is not far off when these Institutes would also fall in line with their counterparts the world over by harnessing these technologies for their use.

We may now switch over to the detailed study of these technologies, one by one, and analyse their uses and limitations thereon. We begin with the Radio Broadcasting Service.

## Radio Broadcasting Service

The only universally available and easily accessible electronic technology is the radio. Unlike most of the other technologies, this technology does not require the Institute either to procure or install any type of hardware equipment. The high capital cost of gadgetry and (more significantly) the vast populace that it seeks to serve, demand that the network of its broadcasting service should be developed and maintained by as elaborate and extensive an organization as the government. The Institute, being one of its users, may also, among others, avail of this facility by preparing and broadcasting its specially designed lessons. Thus, this technology while putting the minimum of financial and technical burden on the Institute helps it to broadcast its instruction straight into the ear of its learners, thereby supplementing the written lesson with the vocal word of its teacher. Thus far, the main point of criticism against distance education was that it sought to teach the students through the medium of the cold print; the warmth of the teacher's word was missing. Radio has filled up that badly felt void.

From the students' point of view also, radio is handy as well as cost beneficial. All that one requires to catch the voice and the word of one's teacher is just one transistor set. It is so moderately priced that everyone, even of the humbler means, can buy it. In so far as the teachers of the Institute are concerned, they too are not taxed. Instead, they are paid by the broadcasting service a handsome remuneration for the time and energy that they spend on the preparation of the radio lesson script.

In India 4 Institutes (namely Chandigarh, Patiala, Delhi and Madurai Kamraj) and all the 4 Open Universities (Bakshish Singh, *et al.*, Research Report, 1994) enjoy the hospitality of the All-India Radio which broadcast special programmes for distance learners of their respective regions. The Chandigarh and the Patiala Institutes, for instance, are served by the Jalandhar station of the AIR. Synchronising (what it describes) its University Broadcasting session with the academic session of the universities concerned (July to May), the AIR (Jalandhar) broadcasts every day from 5.45 p.m. to 6.00 p.m. a specially prepared talk for distance learners in particular and for the others in general. Before the commencement of the Broadcasting session, a tripartite meeting comprising the Directors of AIR and the two Institutes concerned, is held. In that meeting the Institutes faculties decide the topics as well as the calendar of the talks. All those disciplines in which distance instruction are imparted by the Institutes concerned are covered by these talks. The talks are written by the teachers keeping in view the requirements of their students. Then the AIR studios record and broadcast them.

Despite the immense usefulness of this technology to distance learners, the AIR does not make its services available to them in as lavish a manner as it ought to do. This is evident from the fact that out of a large network of its stations only 4/5 extend the benefit of this service to the Institutes of Distance Education. This niggardly attitude of the AIR needs to be revised urgently.

The attitude of the AIR notwithstanding, the fault of not making full use of this technology also lies with distance learners. The surveys conducted by the AIR, Jalandhar, as well as by the Chandigarh Institute reveal that a very small percentage of the students of these beneficiary Institutes listen to these talks. Even though each one of these Institutes furnishes to the students a detailed calendar of this programme in advance of the commencement of the broadcasting session, besides its repeated reference in the prospectus and other informatory documents that it sends to them from time to time, a number of students confessed ignorance of this programme. Those of them who listened did not find them much useful. Tony Bates who was commissioned in 1980 by the International Institute of Educational Planning (Paris) to conduct a survey of the use of the Audio-Visual Media in 12 distance learning systems of the world, reports that there is "a clear movement away from using broadcasting in distance learning system." (John S. Daniel ,1982 p.8).

A number of reasons account for the unpopularity of the radio broadcasting service. In the first place may be listed the unsuitability of the timings of the broadcast. As mentioned above, the AIR schedules its University Broadcast generally in the evening hours, which time is quite odd. This is the time when the office-goers, who constitute a sizeable percentage of distance learners, return home after a heavy day of work and strain. This is the time when youngster—another sizeable section of the Institutes' students, go out for either walk or play. This is the time when Doordarshan telecasts either feature films or some equally captivating programmes of general entertainment. This is the time when the housewives are busy cooking food in the kitchen and the lowly paid workers struggle for their living at their respective work places. Thus, nobody is either free or willing to spare his/her time and listen to these talks.

It may be underlined that these talks, not being casual, require their listeners to mentally prepare themselves suitably if they are keen to assimilate them properly. It is therefore advisable that before they sit down to listen to them, they should recaptulate the lesson, and afterwards do post-talk review. The whole of this process consumes a minimum of one hour. This is too long a time to be easily spared at this too busy a juncture of the day. Thus these talks generally go unlistened.

The odd nature of the timings of this broadcast was repeatedly brought to the notice of the AIR. But they, on their part, express their inability to spare any other time, especially during their peak hours. The limitation of the AIR is twofold: first that a number of other programmes, perhaps of a greater importance, vie with one another for accommodation in this slot, and secondly the audience of this programmes is so small and specialised that the interests of the general public cannot be sidetracked.

The second major cause of the ineffectiveness of this programme is the poor quality of these talks. They are generally ill drafted, poor in content and, above all, unimpressively delivered, with the result that they fail to evince the listeners' interest. It appears that those teachers who write the script of these talks fail to do justice to them mainly because of the lack of the requisite training. After all, writing a radio script is not an easy job. It is infact an art, pretty different from the writing of a lesson for print. The former in particular require training and practice. Unless suitable arrangements for training are made, the quality of talks cannot improve.

Equally important aspect is the delivery of the talk. Every Tom, Dick and Harry does not possess radio worthy voice. But in our case the tragedy is that audio testing is not done by the AIR and as a result, all teachers, irrespective of the quality of their speaking talent, are drafted for this work, little realising that ill-suited persons would spell doom on the programme as a whole.

Lack of training apart, there is another reason why radio talks are qualitatively deficient.The AIR avowedly maintains that it is a free forum, anyone can speak anything, subject, however, to public decency, law and order and such other universally recognised constraints. But it has been experienced that its officials who record and broadcast the various programmes, are obsessively cautious lest some word uttered by a speaker may not mitigate against the policies of the government. (*The Tribune*) This attitude of 'more loyal than the king' causes a good deal of irritation to the teachers of the social sciences in particular. For, there are an endless number of subjects in Political Science, Public Administration, Economics, Sociology and the Laws where teacher cannot do justice either to the subject concerned or to those whom he is acquainting it with, unless he highlights both the points of view, for and against it. Obviously, the radio talks would remain qualitatively weak and unbalanced if only one view point is presented. Once it so happened that a teacher of Political Science was to record a talk on Fundamental Rights, as enshrined in the Indian Constitution. When he tried to criticise the Preventive Detention Act as an encroachment on citizens' rights, the official on recording duty objected to his saying so. The wordy duel that ensued between the two made the teacher concerned to permanently boycott that Radio Talks programme altogether. In short, those script-writers/ broadcasters who succumb to these pressure tactics, compromise with the quality of their talk. This is one reason why audio cassettes are being increasingly preferred by the teachers of repute.

There is yet another reason why radio talks programme has failed to make much of an impact on the students. With the given limitations of this technology, radio talks are delivered but once (unless the AIR authorities choose to broadcast them again) and that too at a particularly given point of time. If a person misses a talk, he misses it for all times to come. There can be several reasons for the talk being missed. One may have more highly pressing engagement at that fixed hour. One's radio set may not be functional, either due to some mechanical defect in it or due to the energy breakdown. In this connection, it may not be out of place to mention here that the States of Punjab and Haryana where there is a perpetual shortage of power, often apply power cuts of longer durations almost every day. These cuts not only descent hundreds and thousands of homes to darkness but also make their inmates miss many an interesting radio and television programme. Thus, one may not be able to listen to these talks for one reason or another. However some one may like to rebut this argument by referring to the alternative technology of tape-recording the radio programmes. But the question is, how many people possess that machine. All said and done, radio talks are prone to be missed and herein lies the biggest weakness of this technology.

## Audio Cassette

Another technology that closely resembles the radio is audio cassette technology. In this case, audio programmes are recorded on small cassetted tapes with the help of a small machine, called a tape recorder. These can be listened to by playing them, again on a small machine, the record player. These days both the tape recorder and the tape player are generally clubbed together in one compact apparatus, nick-named as two-in-one.

For purposes of distance teaching, audio cassette has far outstripped the radio both in utility and popularity. Reporting from the British Open University as early as 1983, A.W. Bates says that most of the programmes of the U.K.O.U. are now being recorded and relayed on audio cassettes instead of being broadcast on the radio network. It is learnt on authority that when the Chandigarh Institute initiated in 1988 the programme of providing to the students cassetted audio talks on no-profit-no-loss basis, as many as 550 students procured these cassettes by mail in the very first year besides hundreds of those who listened to them in person in the Institute's studios. On the other hand, the survey conducted by the AIR Jalandhar in that very year reported the number of serious listeners of their university broadcasts as very poor. A further proof of the growing popularity of this technology is manifest in the growing number of the Institutes going in for audio cassettes.

What is the secret of the increasing patronage of this technology by the Institutes of Distance Education? In the first place, we find that this technology is so simple and cost beneficent that every Institute can easily go in for it. As said above, it does not need heavy capital investment. Secondly, it saves the Institute from the awkward dependence on another organization. Thirdly, the authoritarian attitude of the radio authorities, particularly in the allocation of the timings for the Institute's programmes and in obstructing the objectivity of their contents, is too bitter a pill to be easily swallowed by any self-respecting person. Once the audio cassette recording studio is set up, it may prepare its own cassettes on any topic it likes and its teachers may treat a subject in as objective a manner as they wish to. As for the listeners, they too would no longer be trammelled by the constraints of the timings. They may listen to these cassettes whenever and wherever they may like.Tony Bates (1982) rightly remarks that students like these cassettes because of "their convenience (they can use cassettes whenever they wish to study), the control students have over them (they can play parts of the cassette as many or as few times as they need) and their informality. Students frequently comment that cassettes are like having a personal tutorial with the course author in their own room, a quality that appears to be lacking in radio programmes. . . . ." To sum up, audio-cassette commends itself to distance education is every respect.

No wonder then that within a very short period of its invention, audio cassette has become an indispensable hardware component of distance education. Today, all Institutes, particularly of the developed nations, make a very lavish use of this technology. Their printed lessons are invariably accompanied by their audio supplements. The latter are provided as indiscriminately to all the students as the former. As mentioned in the preceding chapter, all types of lesson are collectively prepared by a large team of experts which team includes, besides subject specialists and the others, audio experts as well. When subject specialists are busy finalising their text, the audio experts also keep track of the need as to which aspect of the text should be transformed into its audio version. After the subject specialists have finished their job, the audio experts exchange their notes with them and then all of them collectively decide the content and form of the audio (as also the video) versions of the lesson. Thus, we find that the written, the audio and the video scripts/cassettes are almost simultaneously prepared and mailed to the students.

As far as our Institutes are concerned, we cannot think of working on these lines for at least one decade. For, we are yet to release ourselves from the limbo of one-dimensional approach to distance teaching, namely the printed scripts. Even if we convince ourselves about the acute need and desirability of inducting audio technology into our instructional mode, it would take a very long time to prepare the audio version of all the lessons of the various study programmes. The task is not easy, particularly in view of the specialized nature of the art/technique of developing the audio version of the written text. Every Institute shall have either to obtain the services of audio experts or to impart training to the entire faculty. Those Institutes which maintain whole time faculties may not find it difficult to achieve this goal. Already providing for an elaborate organisational set-up, they may not hesitate to spend a little more money on the training of their staff or even on the recruitment of a couple of audio experts. But the problem would arise with regard to those Institutes whom the profit motive has coerced to the extent of getting their lessons written from outside on contractual basis. In case they decide to go in for this technology, they will have first to go in for the recruitment of a few audio experts (for, in the absence of the whole-time faculty, this is the only alternative left for them) and then to make their script-writers sit with the audio experts and help them develop the audio version of their lessons. All this would entail huge expenditure on a recurring basis. Would they be prepared to spare funds for this purpose at the cost of their earnings, particularly in view of the fact that this work is only of a supplementary (rather than of primary) nature ?

Even if the requisite will to employ this technology is mustered up, the cost factor would always continue to haunt the Institutes. At best they could be pressurised to meet the capital cost of the studio and other allied facilities and also of its staff component. But they would certainly not agree to provide for the recurring expenditure on the cost of the blank cassettes (thousands of which would be required to meet the students' demand). For, to begin with, only a few randomly-selected lessons would be transformed into their audio version and these would then be sent to the students, maybe to all those who are on its rolls or only to those who ask for them. Even in the case of the latter option, the expenditure would be quite sizeable and it would go on inflating as the number of audio lessons increase and also as this technology catches the increasing imagination of the students. The only safe course is to ask the students who want to be served by this additional facility to bear the cost of the blank cassettes. They may either send to the Institute their own blank cassette or may ask it to procure the same for them on no-profit-no-loss basis. As for its mailing charges, let the Institute bear them. This experiment has been working very successfully in Chandigarh Institute.

Another riddle that needs to be sorted out pertains to the incentive to the teachers who write audio scripts of these texts. It would be quite difficult to expect the teachers to do this job in addition to their already well-defined nature of their duties. Today, those of them who are commissioned by the AIR to write and broadcast radio talks (even for their own students) are paid a handsome remuneration, would they do this job on gratis for the Institute? Some sort of monetary incentive shall have to be given to them and that would constitute yet another financial strain on the Institute concerned.

**Television (T.V.)**

By depicting the instruction in a picture form, television creates a profound impact on one's memory, perhaps more profound than does the radio or the audio cassettes. The nature of the human brain is such that the images received visually, if properly decoded, are better understood and retained for a longer time. In other words, human brain understands the iconic language better. (Pelach and Ribot, 1994 ).

Powerful nature of this technology has made television an important instrument of distance education, the world over. A number of countries like China, Thailand, Russia, etc. etc. make television their main medium of distance instruction, relegating other educational technologies to the background. In India, however, this medium remains largely under-utilised, perhaps for the reason that it has made its nation-wide debut (even as a source of information and recreation) only too recently. With the passage of time, it might make its services increasingly available to distance education. But this cannot be vouched with certainty, partly because of the inherent weaknesses of this technology and partly because of the vastness of this land and multi-cultural character of its population.

Television, like radio, being centrally controlled and operated through a country-wide network of its relaying stations, suffers the same constraints of timings, lack of objectivity in presentation, incapability of repeating the programmes at the will of the listeners, complications arising from the energy breakdown and the like, as in the case of the radio broadcasting service. These shortcomings have earned for this technology as well an element of unacceptability as a suitable mode of instruction at the hands of distance students and teachers.

The other problem with this technology, particularly in the context of India, is that the country is so vast in size and is inhabited by a people with so varied a range of cultural and social backgrounds that one centrally controlled television network cannot satisfy the aspirations of all ethno-cultural groupings. In the field of education, the problem becomes all the more complicated, because there are a bewildering number of universities and institutes, each providing for a syllabus different from the rest. How can one television programme (and for that matter, even a couple of programmes) meet the requirements of such a diverse range of university students. This is one reason why the Country-wide Classroom (a television programme for higher education telecast by the Doordarshan) has not been able to catch the attention of the students from all over the country. It is often complained that disjointed and stray programmes on subjects, not selected systematically but in a most hap-hazardly manner (any programme that comes in its way is telecast, provided it meets the technical standards of the Doordarshan) ill-serves the aspirations and requirements of the students. Mahajan (1994), a keen student of distance education, carefully observed this programme for thirty consecutive days and then discovered that "the level of discourse is highly inconsistent, one programme presents a simple introductory talk suitable for a novice; the next presents case studies meant for specialists". An educational programme meant for teaching can be successful only if it is built around some theme or the syllabus of some university. This is, of course, not possible in a large and culturally diverse nation as that of ours. No doubt we have a chain of regional television stations, besides the central station, but all of them suffer from one constraint or another, hence incapable of serving the needs of distance students.

However, at the root of the problem lies the lack of both the will and the appreciation of the role of television in education on the part of those who control this media. Had they wished, one channel could have been conveniently spared exclusively for educational telecast. An arrangement of this kind would have provided such a wide range of programmes as to cover a large chunk of students from the various regions and universities of the country.

Yet another problem is the paucity of suitable programmes. Our resources are too limited to meet the requirements of even one programme, the Country-wide Classroom. The U.G.C. has set up a chain of 10 Educational Media Research Centres (EMRC's ) to make programmes for higher education. The Doordarshan is also engaged in this task. But the combined effort of all of them hardly meets the present requirements. This is one reason why Doordarshan is not in a position so far to allow its regional stations to undertake the venture of telecasting educational programmes for the university students of their respective regions. To produce a television programme is too difficult a task to be easily accomplished by people with ordinary qualifications. It needs large cadres of trained technical personnel of various different types of trade, besides. an elaborate hardware of a highly sophisticated technology. All this cannot be procured overnight. By and by, we are turning the corner even on this front.

### Video Cassette

A viable alternative to television (like the radio) is the video cassette. Being easy to handle and capable of operation at will, it is free from all those encumbrances as checkmate the popularity of television in the realm of distance education. Video cassette has become an essential component of instructional technology of this system. Again, to quote Tony Bates (1988). He says, "The value of video cassette lies not just in its ability to allow students to view the programmes at more convenient times. It also enables learning from television to be much more effective. Indeed, the video cassette is to the broadcast what the book is to the lecture." p.34)

In India, this medium has not so far been fully explored. As mentioned earlier, it is only the IGNOU which has the access to this technology. As far as the other Institutes are concerned, if they do not make use of this technology, it is not so much for the reason that either they are unaware of the utility of this technology or do not want to employ it, as due to their incapability to afford its exorbitant cost. The handy nature of this technology as also the independent identity of each Institute (in the sense that the courses of study and the syllabi thereof are pretty distinct from one another) demand that everyone of them should have its separate arrangement for the production of video programmes, so that they may prepare them as per their own requirements. Only then will this technology be useful to them. This suggestion may sound too bold and radical, but in fact it is not so. For, whichever University/Institute has harnessed this technology for its own purpose, has made its own separate arrangements for both the hard and the soft wares. Conversely, if an Institute is to depend upon the goodwill of another Institute or a production centre, its enthusiasm and initiative may sap after some time.

The merits of this suggestion notwithstanding, there are a number of hurdles in the way of its implementation. In the first place, there is the problem of finance. This technology is so costly that no Institute on its own can afford it. To build a modest studio with a bare minimum of the essential hardware would involve millions of rupees. On the top of it, this technology is changing so fast that what is the latest today would become obsclete tomorrow. This change further escalates its cost. From where would the funds come? Already the budgets of most of the Institutes are in the red. They survive on the financial support of their respective universities. As for the latter, they are obsessed with the disgust that these Institutes are an unwanted drain on their growingly tender finances. To expect these universities to divert millions of rupees toward the creation of the video production facilities would be putting the premium too high. Thus in the long run the onus of making these facilities available to these Institutes lies on the U.G.C. Already pressure has begun to be mounted on it.

The technical personnel needed to operate the hardware and to commence the production of the cassettes is again a costly proposition, in no way less costly than the hardware component. Moreover, these personnel is a rare commodity not easily available in as great a number as they are required. Equally scarce are the script-writers for the video technology. In the absence of suitable training facilities, we do not have experts, especially among distance teachers, who may be able to write good scripts for video lessons.

Given these conditions of scarcity, even if we succeed somehow in creating an enough number of production centres, from where shall we find the suitable personnel to run them? Further assuming that we find the staff for these centres, shall we be able to create enough work to keep them fully busy? Shall our teachers, even if they are fully trained, be in a position to produce enough number of video worthy lesson scripts? All these issues are critically important for the successful spread of this technology in all Institutes of our country.

Keeping in view the twin consideration of the exorbitant cost of the hardware as well as the software of this technology and our teachers' inability to furnish video scripts in adequate number, particularly at the initial stages of the proliferation of this programme (when the training facilities are in the process of their creation) it would be prudent to create these facilities at the regional level, rather than at the level of each individual Institute. Let the Government/the U.G.C. rapidly expand the number of the EMRC's on a scale so as to have one such centre in each region of the country. The regional centre should then make its services available to all the Institutes and to all other departments of the conventional universities of the region concerned. Centrally created and efficiently managed as these regional centres would be, they would meaningfully assist these Institutes in harnessing the video technology in a worthwhile manner. At the same time, the nation would be able to conserve its highly scarce financial and technical resources.

**Telephone and Computer**

Telephone and Computer are two such electronic gadgets which have gone a long way in revolutionising both the theory and practice of distance education. Until recently telephone was occasionally used by individual distance learners to call on their teachers and seek clarifications from them on certain aspects of their lessons which posed to them problems of comprehension. In the same manner, computer assisted the teachers in storing, processing and interpreting information and data that they need from time to time. They also used it to prepare tables, charts and other illustrative aids which they insert into their lesson-scripts or display them on overhead projector or black board in order to enhance the learning effect of their teaching. This type of assistance, these two gadgets still render to distance learners and teachers perhaps in a bigger and bolder way. But the more significant development is that telephone and computer have combined together to pave the way for an altogether new mode of distance instruction. Together they have introduced, what is called Computer Mediated Communication (EMC) or what Pelton ( 1992) describes as 'tele-education'.

CMC generally takes two forms in so far as distance education is concerned. The first is Tele-Conferencing. This is a method by means of which a teacher speaks simultaneously to a number of his distance students, all of whom are situated at different places, quite cut off from one another, and discuss with them a certain subject and may even deliver a full length lesson to them. The recipient students who listen to him as also the others who attend that 'lecture session', can raise questions from their respective places and seek clarification from him and also from their peers. The fast developing electronic technology has now added a new dimension to tele-conferencing. Now the participants (teachers as well as students) not only listen to one another's voice but also see their live picture, with all their movements and gestures. This is the new method of Video-Tele-Conferencing.

In this way, we find that tele-conferencing (audio as well as video) helps create the environments of a classroom, extended over the length and breadth of the country, thereby enabling the students to enjoy the same facilities of direct face-to-face interaction with their teachers and also with their peers, as are characteristic of the conventional system. Besides helping them enhance the cognitive effect of instruction, conferencing breaks down the isolation of the students from their peers thereby eradicating the most serious disadvantages of independent learning. (Hurlbut Roberts, 1988)

What about the future prospects of these techniques. The *Comlearn* reports, " The application of voice-based tele-conferencing technology has gained increasing prominence in modern distance education, especially a complement to traditional print and postal-based method.". As for Video tele-conferencing, it says, "With technological advances, the emergence of international standards, and rapidly declining transmission cost, video-tele conferencing will become a major vehicle for communications in the 1990's.... the use of video tele-conferencing for instructional purposes has begun to grow."

The second form of CMC is e-mail (electronic mail). As the letters that we write to our friends and relatives are carried to their destination by the postman and deposited in the addressees' mail boxes from where the latter collect them at their convenience, in the same manner, "the messages are sent down the telephone line and stored in `electronic mail boxes' on a mainframe host computer for accessing by the addressee at his or her convenience. The communication is personalised, asynchronous and definitely faster than regular postal services."(Some Naidu, 1989).

In this way, we find that computer/tele-conferencing has revolutionised the mode and method of message transmission in general, facilitating the task, among others, of distance educators. Space and time, which hampered their task earlier and weakened the thrust of their instruction has been remarkably overcome by this new electronic device. It may be interesting to know that the Off-Campus Academic Programme (OCAP) of the University of Sains Malaysia (USM) has completely dispensed away with face-to-face teaching as was done earlier in the form of PCP and have since been providing distance instruction through tele-conferencing. The experiment has been working quite satisfactorily.(Nordin, 1992).

To us in India, all this sounds like a fairy-tale at least for the present. Today, we are to wait for years to get a telephone connection and those who have got one, often complain of faulty service as well as of unduly heavy bills, partly because of the high tariff and partly because of the bungling of the tele-communication officials. With these given conditions, how can a distance learner of ordinary means ever think of calling on his teachers telephonically and seek academic help from him? Even if someone is kind enough to extend that courtesy to him, who knows whether or not the teacher concerned has a telephone at his residence or office? There is no guarantee of the latter possibility, for the teachers generally do not belong to that elite group which have an easy access to such a luxury as telephone. Further, assuming that the teacher has the facility of a telephone and his students too enjoys someone's hospitality, would he able to meet the expenses of a telephonic call which when relating to the clarification of a certain academic issue, is bound to be of a longer duration and hence very costly.

To cite a case of the utilization of telephone facility by the students. In 1976, the Chandigarh Institute installed a network of telephones providing one connection to each subject departments. The students were informed about that facility and were advised to speak to their respective tutors whenever they faced any problem. But what was observed over the years was that no student ever sought telephonically any assistance from the teachers. Occasionally, they might make an enquiry relating to some administrative difficulty. Information gathered informally revealed that many students did not have a telephone at their place. Some of them frankly confessed that they would not like to have some one's obligation for this purpose. They would further underline their incapacity to bear the exorbitant cost of a telephonic call. Instead of making use of the telephone, they would prefer to write a letter to their teacher or even to call on them in person.

To conclude, so long as telephone does not cease to be a luxury and its network does not extend to every hamlet of the country, it would remain out of bounds for distance students. Let us hope that tele-communication revolution which has, of late, begun to make its impact felt even by us in this country, may sweep, sooner than later, at the door of distance education and make the rapidly multiplying uses of tele-education available to our distance learners as well.

As far as tele-conferencing is concerned, it is not that difficult to employ even by our distance learning system, in view of the fact that tele-conferencing does not involve either an elaborate or very costly hardware. Comprising as it does only three gadgets (a computer, modem and telephone), it can be easily managed by each invididual Institute both at its head-quarters and the regional centres. However, the difficult part of this system is the non-existence or inadequacy of the study centres. To make tele-conferencing a success we need a chain of well-established study centres where the students can assemble and the teacher-in-charge of those centres may co-ordinate the tele-conference. Once we have set up a chain of composite study centres (we will spell out this concept in one of the chapter to follow), tele-conferencing would then become possible.

As for the computer, its academic uses apart, it is an invaluable administrative aid. There are an endless number of administrative operations in an Institute of Distance Education which computer can take care far more efficiently than the manner we perform them today. To identify a few such areas, every Institute has on its rolls thousands of students whose fees are collected and reckoned under various different heads, and whose admission forms carry varied types of information which too needs to be properly classified for further use. Further, each one of these students submits every year a couple of response sheets whose proper record is to be carefully maintained. Those of them who come to attend personal contact programmes and reside in hostels are to be catered to in various different ways. Above all, there is the most elaborate and intricate process of preparing lesson packets and mailing them to the students. All these student services can be maintained at a level of greater accuracy and efficiency if computer is pressed into service. Besides student services, there are many other things on the establishment, accountancy, purchase and sales side which again can be manipulated better by the computer. How immensely helpful can a computer be in the field of printing and production of the study material has already been exhaustively dealt with in the previous chapter. Yet another area where computer can render great service is the library. The Yashwantrao Chavan Open University has identified the following areas for computerisation. They are, (a) Study Text Production, (b) Office Automation, (c) Multimedia learning materials development (d) Development of evaluation technology, and (e) Multi-media learning centres. (Tackwale, 1995) Thus, computer's range of utility to an Institute of Distance Education is as unlimited as in any other sector of the daily life of man.

But the pity is that our Institutes ( as also hundreds and thousands of our government offices) have not so far fully appreciated the vital role that computer can play in their day-to-day functioning. The office routine is still being manipulated manually in the same old stereo-typed fashion as it was done, say, a hundred years ago. Even when it is widely known and experienced that by streamlining their operations a computer can help them cast off the stigma of inefficiency and public criticism, our administrators do not bother to pay any heed to this technological revolution. But happily, things have, of late, begun to turn a corner. Let us hope that computer overtakes our offices (including our Institutes) in a bold manner, sooner than later, making better days dawn over their client.

**Other Electronic Technologies**

As mentioned at the outset, there are a number of electronic technologies which have been helping distance education in developed countries for quite some time. A few more new technologies may be in the pipeline of our laboratories. But most of them are beyond the reach of an under-developed country like India. Even if they are available indigenously, they may not be harnessed by our Institutes mainly because of poor financial standing on their part. Moreover, these technologies are so sophisticated that they require a well-developed infrastructure of certain other technologies. As for instance, electronic mail or computer-conferencing require for their operationalisation a well-developed network of telephone and computer. Keeping in view these limitations, it is, therefore advisable that these Institutes should concentrate for the time being, on such tried technologies as audio cassettes, video cassettes and the computer. They may also harness the new mode of tele-conferencing which too is not difficult to be put into operation. Once the functioning of these technologies is efficiently geared up by their intensive use, these Institutes may go in for other more sophisticated technologies. It may be emphasised that the Institutes of the developed nations, even if they have procured all types of latest technologies, put their main reliance on the printed scripts, audio and video cassettes, the computer and the telephone.

**Integrated Approach**

The question that needs to be suitably answered is how to make use of these technologies. As mentioned at the outset, these technologies are not mutually interchangeable in the sense that one may be a substitute for another. It is not that a lesson is first written in a prose form and then its versions are prepared verbatim in the audio and video forms. By doing so, an Institute may take legitimate pride of having harnessed all the necessary technologies and also of putting them into their proper and regular use. The students may also have the satisfaction of getting their study material not in one but in three forms. The Institute may also then be listed among the highly developed ones. This is a typical case of a multi-media approach, wherein we juxtapose the various technologies without suitably blending them with one another. In doing so, we are led by a highly erroneous impression that one technology may be substituted for another.

This approach does not serve the purpose of our distance learners. For, whatever is given in the printed form is available in the audio and the video forms as well. In what way then would these verbatim versions be useful to the students in overcoming their comprehension problems. Our labour would thus go waste. Avtar Singh (1991) makes a right and timely warning . He says, "Every effort should be made to ensure that the programmes complement rather than duplicate the printed material, otherwise the viewers, who tend to be more conscious of time, will not watch more than one or two programmes before abandoning them for text books that cover the same ground".

The best way is to properly integrate these technologies with one another and make use of them at those places where they are most highly suited. The subject specialists themselves know as to which area/aspect of a certain topic is difficult and needs a pun. Their experience of the day-to-day teaching and their mutual discussion with one another, especially while developing the outlines of the lesson-script, further sharpen their sense of distinguishing between the more difficult aspects and the comparatively easier ones. Later on, when they interact with the audio and the video experts, they are in a position to tell the latter as to which aspect needs to be given an audio treatment and which video treatment. After these areas have been identified the media men would produce the audio and the video tapes. This is the only way to put these technologies to their best use.

Identifying the areas where audio-cassette technology is ideally suited, Tony Bates (1,982) says that it can be used for "mastery learning, for commenting on diagrams, charts, tables, texts.... (p. 11). In the same manner, Laverne Miller (1994) tells us that a film/video cassette " can explain graphically an idea and thus enhance or reinforce the basic purpose of a lesson. In this sense, it is cognitive in effect. It can provide an effective experience about which the students may be expected to describe their reaction and their emotions in discussion or in some form of composition or writing." Endorsing it, Otto Peters (1982) says, "When video is used instead of printed material, higher test-scores cannot be expected. But the amount of time needed to understand the given concept may be shorter.... Good learning results in a shorter time could also be achieved by showing a supplementary video cassette before the course material is studied... using it as an advanced organiser." (pp.86-87).

Following this integrated approach, the audio and the video components of the study material would not be the verbatim copies of the written text. Nor is it necessary that these versions should contain the entire subject matter of the latter. Instead, they would pertain to those aspects only which need to be explained by means of these electronic media respectively. In fact, these technologies being complementary to the basic text, help the latter to be understood and comprehended in a more effective manner. A student might, therefore, be required to switch over repeatedly from the text to the video and back to the text and then from it to the audio and so on and so forth. If after having gone into this exercise for a couple of times, he still feels the necessity of further clarification of a certain point or aspect of the lesson, he may contact the teacher whether on telephone (if that technology is within his reach) or in person. This is the right and the latest method of distance teaching and learning.

## Teacher, the Crucial Factor

Actualisation of the wish of the Institutes to supplement the written text of their study material with audio and video cassettes depends mainly upon two factors, namely, finance and teachers. Though finance is scarce, efforts are being made seriously to bring round the U.G.C. to concede to these Institutes sizeable grants, (if not proportional to their actual share as calculated on the basis of the proportion of the students that they cater to). Hopes have also dawned that the U.G.C. would accept this proposal. Once funds are available, this aspect of distance education would be taken care, for finance would then cease to be an obstruction in their way.

It is, however, the teachers who would be very difficult to be persuaded to undertake this task. Like the written script, the preparation of the audio-video programme too is dependent upon their active involvement and co-operation. As alluded above, it is the teacher who is the best judge as to which aspect of his lesson needs to be presented in the audio form and which in the video form. Again, it would be he who is to indicate where to lay emphasis and in what form. Though the conversion of the written text into the audio and video forms would ultimately be done by the audio and the video experts, they need to be guided and even directed by the teacher concerned because of his being the master of the subject as also having the onerous duty of providing to his students rich, wholesome and easy-to-comprehend study material. Thus, the teacher would act as the central arch around whom everyone would revolve. The cruciality of his role demands that he must be psychologically prepared to undertake this task not only actively but also enthusiastically. He should then be imparted the training to write the audio and the video scripts. Once he himself develops these scripts, then quality is bound to improve, for they would then be the product of the combination of his mastery of the subject and his art of audio and video script writing.

But to persuade the teachers to lend their willing co-operation to this programme is not an easy task. It is not that they oppose it but they give cold shoulder it by not coming forward to undertake this responsibility. To illustrate, the Chandigarh Institute set up a small audio-video production unit in 1989. In the course of the last six years, it could produce only six video programmes and about 300 audio talks. If the number of the latter appears to be somewhat impressive (though in fact it is not, in view of the large size of the faculty, 73), the secret is that all those who are commissioned by the AIR to deliver talks, are requested to get them recorded in the Institute's studio as well. Even in doing so, most of them show a good deal of hesitation and they have to be persuaded a lot to do so. Another parallel case is that of the neighbouring university of Patiala where the U.G.C. set up in 1988 an Audio Visual Research Centre. Till the middle of the year 1994 they had not produced even a single programme. Among the various reasons advanced for the Centre not getting functional, the most important was the non-availability of programmes. In other words, teachers do not come forward with the proposals and if at all they do, they do so in a half-hearted manner.

That teachers are luke warm to the idea of undertaking teaching also through the medium of audio-visual aids is not peculiar to India alone. It is a world-wide feature. While delivering his presidential address to the International Council of Educational Media in 1993, Asgeir Gudumundsson said, " From the media world we often get the message that teachers are reactionaries, that they are the barriers that prohibit the use of new technology in schools." Carnegie Commission (U.S.A.) had discovered in 1972 "that instructional technology is not uniformly welcomed by the academic community and that faculty members interested in developing new materials for instructional technologies are not properly rewarded for their effort." Among the five factors identified by D.W. Spuck (1988) that hinder the successful implementation of these technologies in U.S.A. the most important was "the resistance of the present university faculty."

There are a number of reasons that account for this attitude of the teachers. In the first place, we find that our teachers, by and large, are not given either to flexibility or innovation. Though speaking in a slightly different context, Bakshish Singh (1994) rightly points out, "The main reason is that conventional universities do not allow the requisite flexibility and innovations which are a must for distance education system. Unfortunately, this problem is faced by most of the distance education institutes and even by open universities because most of their teachers are also drawn from the conventional system. The academics in the conventional universities are generally averse to changes and innovations. Most of them are obsessed with the idea that there can be no teaching without face-to-face contact."

This conservative attitude of resistance to change and innovation manifests itself nowhere so glaringly as in their non-acceptance of the new electronic technologies. This is a problem which is too deep-rooted to be easily overcome.

Traditional ties of the Institute's teachers with their counterparts working in other departments of their parent university make them compare their lot with the latter at every step of their functioning. When they find that the others continue teaching their students through the same old uni-dimensional medium while they are required not only to write lessons (which in itself is quite a difficult and taxing job) but also to prepare the audio and the video scripts, their sense of false discrimination and inferiority complex (vis-a-vis their colleagues) gets accentuated, which in turn, further reinforces their opposition to these innovative technologies (Otto Peters, 1988)

The third important reason is the absence of any recognised system of reward and punishment. Those who do not do their work or do it shabbily not only go unpunished but keep on getting their seniority-based dues (no higher authority can dare to deny these benefits to them because they are not productivity linked), whereas those who work diligently with a sense of commitment and devotion and try to innovate new paths and practices do not get any reward in tangible terms except perhaps a boss's pat of 'shabash' on their shoulder. This is a nation-wide feature of our administrative structure and the Institutes are no islands of it. In our system, a distance teacher's work is measured in terms of the number of lessons he writes, the response sheets he marks and the lectures he delivers in the personal contact programme. If anyone of them spends some of his time in assisting the administration, in developing an audio/ video lesson or doing any other worthwhile thing for the system, he would not be shown any leniency towards his daily/weekly quota of work. In such a rigid rule-bound system why should one waste his time and energy on some innovative task? Carnegies Commission (1972) also complains that "faculty members interested in developing new materials for instructional technologies are not properly rewarded for their efforts."

The problem thus appears to be quite formidable both on the psychological and systemic levels. It is very difficult to change the approach of the teachers or the system at large. The only viable alternative is to bifurcate the faculty into two halves. As suggested in the previous chapter, the senior faculty comprising the readers and the professors should alone be entrusted with the task of preparing the study material while the marking of the response sheets and lecturing in the personal contact programme should be the responsibility of the junior faculty of the lecturers. Once the senior faculty is given the exclusive duty of preparing the study material, they would not mind either the writing of the texts or producing the audio and the video versions of the former. For, this work would constitute an explicit term of their contract or the duty chart. Such an arrangement would alone force them to accept these newer technologies. Once a beginning is made, adaptation would acquire speed and the process of their assimilation by the system would be accomplished in no time. Our Institutes would then successfully stake their claims for being included in the privileged category of distance education.

## REFERENCES

Avtar Singh, 'Use of Audio-Visual Media in the teaching of Shakespear's Hamlet' in Distance Education System'. *Indian Journal of Distance Education*. Vol. IV (1991)

Bakshish Singh, 'Distance Education Problems and Challenges', *Indian Journal Distance Education*. Vol. IV. (1994)

Bates, A.W. Quoted by Faus Jaspers, 'Speech and voice in instructional programmes', *Educational Media International*. Vol. 31, No. 2. (June, 1994)

Bates, Tony, in Daniel, John S., Stoud, Martha, A. and Thompson John (Eds.), *Learning at a Distance: A World Perspective*. Edmonton Athabasca University, 1982.

Bates, Tony, 'Television, Learning and Distance Education', *ICDE Bulletin* No. 16 (January, 1988)

Carnegie Commission (U.S.A.) (1972) Quoted by Spolls, Thomas H. and Bowman, Mary Annu, 'Increasing Faculty Use of Instructional Technology, Barriers and Incentives', *Educational Media International.* Vol. 30, No. 4. (December, 1993)

Comlearn (News Publication of the Commonwealth of Learning), Vol.5, No.1 (November, 1994).

Gudumundsson, Asgeir, Presidential Address to Barcelona Conference (1993). *Educational Media International.* (London) Vol. 31, No. 1. 1994).

Karnik, Kiran. 'TV for Education: The Way Ahead', in Bakshish Singh (Ed.) *New Horizons in Distance Education*, New Delhi, Uppal.1995.

Letter of Dr. R. P. Gangurde, Additional Secretary, U.G.C., D.O.No.F-3-14/93 (NFE-11), December, 1993.

Mahajan, Ravi K., 'Knowledge from a box'. *Chandigarh Newsline*, 5 September, 1994.

Miller, Laverne, Education Media Literacy With Films and Video', *Education Media International.* Vol. 30, No. 1 (March, 1994)

Naidu, Som, 'Computer Conferencing in Distance Education'. *ICDE Bulletin* No. 21. (September, 1989)

Nordin, M.R. 'Costs and Benefits of Using Teleconferencing in the Off-Campus programme, University Sans Malaysia'. *ICDE Bulletin* No.30. (September, 1992)

National Seminar on Distance Education and the Challenges of the Twenty—First Century', Chandigarh (May, 1994) *A Report.*

Pathak, Anil Koul, B.N., Bakshish Singh and Ansari, M.M. (Eds) *Studies in Distance Education.* New Delhi, Association of Indian Universities and Indira Gandhi National Open University, 1988.

Pelach, Joaquin and Ribot, Maria Dolors de. 'New Technologies and Educational Instruction'. *Educational Media International.* Vol. 30, No. 3 (Setember, 1994)

Pelton, J. Quoted by A. W. Bates, 'Third Generation Distance Education, The Challenge of New Technology'. *Kaktiya Journal of Distance Education,* Vol.1, No.1. (1992).

Peters, Qtto, Quoted by A. W. Bates, *Ibid.*

Peters, Qtto, in Reddy, G. Ram. *Open Universities, The Ivory Towers Thrown Open.* Delhi, Sterling, 1988.

Roberts, L.H., 'Computer Conferencing: A Classroom for Distance Learning'. *ICDE Bulletin* No.18. (September, 1988).

Spuck, D.W Quoted by Robert, 1.H. *Op. Cit.*

Tackwale, Ram G., 'Application of New Technologies in Distance Education', in Bakshish Singh (Ed.). *New Horizons in Distance Education*, New Delhi, Uppal, 1995.

*The Tribune*, (Chandigarh), 11 December, 1994.

CHAPTER VI

# COUNSELLING AND PERSONAL CONTACT PROGRAMME

NEXT to the study material, counselling/personal contact programme constitutes another principal mode of distance instruction. This instrument enables the distance learners to get their lesson — comprehension problems sorted out at the hands of their teachers by means of their direct face-to-face interaction with them. However, the role of counselling/personal contact programme is being increasingly questioned of late. In fact, there are two schools of thought, one which pleads for making counselling compulsory for all types of distance education programmes and the other which wants it to be completely dispensed away. (Holmberg, 1985). The former feel that "beyond the package of materials, there is a need for individualised advice, support, interpretation and mediation capable of meeting the diverse needs of the students. The success of a distance education system rests upon the correct balance between the teaching package and the mediating function." (David Sewart, 1982) Those who stand for the abolition of counselling hold the view that distance education, unlike its conventional counterpart, is an independent self-study. The students enjoy full freedom not only to pace their studies according to their own time and convenience, but also to decide what, when and where to study. This freedom apart, those who opt for this system are generally grown-up adults, responsible and mature to take their own decisions independently. Obviously, these students want to be left exclusively on their own, instead of being fettered by such pre-determined obligatory conditions such as the PCP and compulsory attendance thereof. Obligations of this type constitute an unwanted intrusion in their freedom to pursue their studies. The philosophy of distance education (viz. none is to be debarred from education, nor anyone is to be forced for it; one may have as much of it as one likes) further rules out the desirability of hinging distance education study programmes with any obligatory pre-condition. Distance learners need to be freed from all such conventional controls and conditions as are characteristic of the other system.

However, in the Indian context, the philosophy of doing away with counselling and such other academic adjuncts does not cut much ice. Distance students as well as distance teachers, being the product of the conventional system, cannot feel at home psychologically unless the education system provides for direct face-to-face interaction between the teacher and the taught, may be for a limited period of time. This type of an interaction is a vital component of a learning process. Students are after all students whatever may be the level of their maturity and hence need the fostering care of their teachers. The rapidly swelling ranks of the distance learners by the growing number of the youngsters demands that counselling and such other additional pedagogic aids need be strengthened. These factors and forces drive us to the conclusion that counselling is going to stay on as a vital component in our system of distance education, may this system be managed through the open universities or the conventional university-run Institutes.

However, the fast developments in the realm of communication technologies and more specifically their revolutionary impact on our day-to-day verbal interaction with one another cannot be overlooked. It may not be a surprise if the format and the manner of conduct of the PCP undergo a radical change tomorrow. Already the University Sains Malaysia has, of late, dispensed away the traditional lesson scripts as well as counselling. Instead, they conduct their distance education study programmes through the new technology of tele-conferencing. No longer the teachers give counselling to the students within the four walls of the class room and answer their questions and queries in the traditional way. Now they conduct it electronically on a mammoth scale, addressing large groups of distance learners, who sitting at their respective study centres (spread over the length and breadth of the country) interact with their teachers as well as peers both through their live voice and visual gestures and movements. The whole process, as explained earlier, is mediated through such electronic gadgets as telephone, modem, computer, TV and the like. If today the University Sains Malayasia could harness this technology, it would not be a wonder if we also remodel our educational process on these very lines. In fact, the day does not seem to be far when the manifold difficulties and constraints that our system presently suffers from, may make us adopt this technology which, besides being cost-effective, is untrammelled by the whimsical conduct of the individual.

This debate, as also the growing impact of the newer communication technologies on distance education notwithstanding, counselling constitute an important, nay the most important (next only to the study materials) plans of both teaching and the feedback in our system of distance education. In this chapter, we discuss it in all its different manifestations.

## II

Counselling, though a simple term, meaning to give advice to those who seek it, has a significance of its own in so far as distance education is concerned. Containing both instructional and socio-psychological overtones, counselling is an important instrument in the hands of the teachers by means of which they help their students to iron out difficulties not only of comprehension of distance lessons but also of personal and para-academic nature. Though counselling can be sought and given by mail and even on telephone, the more prevalent and well-established mode is direct face-to-face interaction between the teacher and the taught. Every Institute organises from time to time short-duration camps, week-end sessions or summer schools wherein distance learners assemble from far and wide and get counselling. In order to derive the maximum benefit of this exercise, the students are supposed first to study their lessons, identify their difficulties and then come to these camps thoroughly prepared. When they meet their teacher face-to-face, they should pose their difficulties to them. The discussion that follows would help them get clarity. As for their personal problems, these may be discussed with their teachers in camera if they so choose. These camps apart, students can seek counselling by contacting their teachers/counsellors either at the headquarters of the Institute or at the study centres as per their mutual convenience.

In India, counselling is given in two slightly different forms. General counselling in the form of PCP and individualised tutoring. Personal Contact Programme, or PCP, as it is popularly called, is a short duration instructional camp where distance students from moffusil areas assemble to recapitulate and revise at the hands of their teacher the lessons which they received in the form of written or even in audio-video forms, and thereby get their problems solved. The real objective of an exercise of this type is to encourage the students to pose their difficulties to their teachers and peers so that they may get clarifications of the same in the course of the discussion that ensues. But in actual practice, PCP has been degenerated into a series of lecture sessions which teachers dominate while students listen to them passively. The system that has come to actually operate is that during these days, full-fledged classes are held, one after the other. The teachers are supposed to so adjust their teaching schedule that they encapsule in the prescribed number of their lectures the entire syllabus of the course. The one-hour or the three-quarters of an hour (the usual duration of one lecture) remains too packed by the teacher's lecture to allow a student to raise his little finger to seek clarification of a certain point or doubt. Those who have anything to ask or discuss, should meet the teacher afterwards.

This method of typical classroom teaching and scanning through the whole syllabus of the course in a series of few lectures, gives immense satisfaction to both the teachers and the students. (Rathore, 1983, p.131). While it simplifies the task of the teachers, it gives a good deal of consolation to the students and also helps them comprehend and digest their written lessons better. Sudhakaran (1984) aptly remarks, "Personal Contact Programme assumes significance when viewed from two angles, psychological and instructional. It is important psychologically as it tries to reduce the helplessness felt by students who, during their formative period, have become accustomed to the customary or traditional method of oral teaching and later on admitted into the system of distance education with a new orientation. The difference in the new system usually gives rise to some adjustment problems and it is personal contact programme that helps to a large extent to make the system more palatable. From the instructional angle, these programmes... help the students to understand the lessons better, familiarise them with the examination system and prepare them for better performance in the examination". (Jose Chander, 1984 p.87).

That the students are too keen to derive the maximum benefit of this exercise by learning as much as possible at the hands of their teachers is manifest in the common observation that those teachers who show a little of devotion and commitment towards them (and there is no dearth of such teachers) are virtually chased by the students after the classes. These teachers even organise extra-classes for them and also invite them to their rooms and spend hours with them. The popularity of the teachers as also the devotion of distance learners to their studies attain the highest water mark during the days when the examinations draw close at hand. At that time, the offices of most of the teachers remain crowded with the students.

Besides providing academic feast to them, PCP provides an opportunity to know and socialise with their peers. In a short period of a week or ten days, they draw quite close and even become friendly to one another. This is manifest in cultural functions and tea parties that they invariably organise at the conclusion of these programmes. A Personal

Contact Programme lasts usually for a week or ten days. In the case of certain higher classes (as for instance master in education or management), it is spread over two weeks or even longer. Though a week or (for that matter) even two weeks are too short to do full justice to the entire syllabus of the course, (students have often been heard requesting for an extension of the duration), a continuous stretch longer than a week or so is convenient neither to the students nor to the teachers. Those who are employed in the public and the private organisations find it difficult to obtain leave from their offices for a longer duration. Similar is the case of the house-wives who too cannot afford to be away from their homes for more than a week or ten days. On the other side, the teachers, if they are detailed for an out-station duty for a longer period, face difficulties to clear the backlog of their work which meanwhile accumulates on their desks in the department.

The Chandigarh Institute faces a different type of problem in providing longer duration Personal Contact Programmes. It administers to each class two spells of the Personal Contact Programme, of one week each. The first spell begins in early October and continues till the third week of December, while the second spell starts in January and lasts till the end of April. The number of days vis-a-vis the number of classes among which these are to be allocated, is so limited that it is practically impossible to give more than seven days to each class. Thus the accepted norm all over the country is a week or slightly more than this. Some Institutes make a provision for the Sunday classes, either in lieu of or in addition to the PCP. Following yet another practice the Delhi Institute organises for the unemployed students regular morning classes for a couple of months at a stretch. Thus, while the Personal Contact Programme is a well-established nation-wide practice, the Sunday classes and various other types of meets are special arrangements made by certain Institutes as per their own convenience and requirements.

The other form of counselling is Individualised Tutoring. Unlike the PCP, it is neither an institutionalised nor a formal exercise. In fact, it is (what we may describe) an informal way of seeking guidance from one's teachers. Since the latter are always present in their rooms, any student may walk in without any prior intimation or permission and may pose any problem to them. Committed to their welfare, as most of the teachers are, they warmly welcome the students and help them solve their problems. It is not necessary, that guidance may be sought on academic issues only (though lesson-centered issues invariably make the students knock at the door of their teachers),personal problems are also discussed, depending upon the equation one builds with one's teachers. Sometimes the students even bring their assignments (response sheets) and want their teachers to evaluate them in their presence so that they may know their deficiencies and shortcomings. The teachers do not hesitate to do that work even. Thus, they try to help their students in every possible way.

Though this type of individualised tutoring goes on round the whole year, it becomes more intensive as well as extensive during the couple of weeks preceding the examination. Individual students or even batches of them are found closetted with the teachers one after another for hours at a stretch. They get their academic difficulties solved and also seek guidance how to improve their performance in the examination. The Institute's building thus remains heavily thronged with students and the teachers also find themselves highly occupied but without a wrinkle on their face. Thus, counselling in the Indian context, is a much wider concept. The teachers teach the students, counsel them on issues ranging from lesson-learning to personal difficulties, and, above all, prepare them for the examination. The Delhi Institute organises for the unemployed students regular morning classes for a couple of months. Thus, while the Personal Contact Programme is a well-established nation-wide practice the Sunday classes and various other types of meets are the arrangements made by the Institutes as per their own convenience and requirements.

The philosophy of distance education enjoins upon every Institute that it should not only deliver the study material by post but should also organise counselling and PCP's as near to the homes of the students as possible. The rationale of this philosophy is that in order to facilitate distance learners to carry on their studies at their own pace and time, they should not be dislocated from their homes and that all types of study aids should be made available to them right at their door-step. This philosophy, therefore, demands that PCP should be organised not only at the headquarters but also at as many places as there is a sizeable concentration of students. Many an Institute follows this practice. In this respect, the example that the IGNOU has set is really commendable. Drawing students from all over the country, the IGNOU has set up more than 300 study centres, each one of which provides the venue for the PCP which it holds in the form of the Saturday and Sunday classes.

A number of Institutes have, however, discontinued the practice of holding Personal Contact Programmes at mofussil stations. Instead they concentrate all student activities at the headquarters. Rathore's study (1983) puts this number at 7, i.e.50 per cent of the sample. The main reason that accounts for this change is the growing regionalised character of these Institutes. Besides, the organisation of out-station PCP's poses a number of administrative problems, the most important of which is the inability of these Institutes to create on their own the necessary infrastructure in mofussil towns. In the absence of that infrastructure, these Institutes have to depend upon the goodwill of the local colleges and schools for sparing their buildings to them for the PCP's. Many local institutions are not in a position to do so because of their own limitations. Sometimes these institutions dictate too heavy terms, putting the guest Institute in a great quandary. When the Chandigarh Institute used to organise its PCP at Delhi (discontinued long since), it would find all the Delhi institutions busy in the evening hours on one account or another. The only place then available was the DAV College, Nehru Nagar. Though the host institute had commodious buildings and its authorities too were highly co-operative, it was located in one corner of the metropolis, making it difficult for the students to easily commute. Thus, to find out a suitable venue is too difficult a job.

The only solution of this problem is that the U.G.C. should set up a chain of composite study centres, one in each big city. These centres should have, besides other facilities (to be spelled out later in this chapter) a number of class-rooms where the various Institutes may be able to organise their PCP's. The creation of these centres would save these Institutes from the botheration of running from pillar to post in search of the accommodation. The heavy financial expenditure that the creation of these centres would entail is much beyond the capacity of these Institutes, both singly and collectively. The UGC alone can help them have this facility. Pressure is being mounted on it (Refer, among others, to the Report of the Round Table On Quality Assurance in Distance Education, June-July, 1994), let us hope that it concedes this demand sooner than later.

Another corollary of this problem is the temporary housing of the faculty and other administrative staff that is detailed on this duty. Though they are paid their daily allowance and are thus supposed to make their own lodging arrangements, the non-availability of suitable accommodation makes many of them decline this duty, further creating difficulties for the Institutes.

Yet another reason for not holding PCP at places away from the headquarters is the non-palatable nature of out-station duty by the faculty and the others. The non-availability of suitable lodging accommodation apart, they do not want to be dislocated from their homes at all. It has been experienced that out-station PCP duty creates a lot of bitterness and bad blood among the faculty members every year. The Institutes are often forced at the nick of time to make alternative arrangements. If the Institutes' faculty is not deputed for this work, the local college teachers who are asked to handle the PCP's, generally fail to do justice to this work, partly because of their non-familiarity with the task, especially with the technique of 'capsule teaching' and partly because of their non-identification with the cause. More often than not, they do the job of the filling up of the blanks only. The students too complain of the unsatisfactory performance of these teachers.

The entrustment of the PCP to the hired hands dilutes the Institute's control over this activity of crucial significance. Not only the hired faculty fails to do the job properly, but sincerely as well. Malpractices like truancy, fictitious roll calls of the students, financial bunglings and the like, also become rampant. Finally, the organisation of the PCP's at outstations is a costly proposition. Apart from the different types of payments that are made to the host institution, remuneration is paid to those persons (teachers and the others) who are locally engaged for various duties. If headquarters staff is deputed for this work (as is the general practice), they are to be paid for their travelling and lodging. Quite often this expenditure far exceeds the benefits that accrue from this exercise, as reckoned in terms of the number of the participating students.

These problems notwithstanding, the trend over the past few years is that the number of participants at the mofussil stations has marked a decline whereas that of the headquarters has been on the increase. Only those who belong to the town concerned alone care to attend it while those who hail from the nearby areas prefer to go to the headquarters. Their argument is that in case they are to go out of their homes bag and baggages why should not they attend the PCP at the headquarters which offer to them more than one attraction. They point out that the quality of teaching at the headquarters PCP is much better than that of the mofussil towns, perhaps for the reason that at the former place the PCP's are handled exclusively by the Institute's faculty. By interacting with the latter, many of their doubts and difficulties are solved. Then on the top of it, they can also get some of their long-pending administrative problems sorted out during their visit to the headquarters.

The administrative difficulties, further supported by the above-mentioned trend, led the Chandigarh Institute (to cite one illustrative case) to do away with the practice of holding its PCP's at a number of places, and, instead, concentrate this activity at its headquarters. As mentioned earlier, it devised a near fool-proof system of giving two PCP's of one week duration to all classes/courses. In order to further ensure that the attendance does not dwindle, it provides the additional facility for the lodging and boarding in the university hostels at subsidised rates to those of its students who care to attend these PCP's from far off places. The experiment has since been working successfully and to the satisfaction of everyone involved in it.

Besides the venue, another important variable that closely impinges upon the students' attendance in the PCP is its timings. To go by the suitability of the timings, distance students can be divided into three broad categories. They are: the employed, the unemployed and the women. While the employed students prefer the evening hours because of their being busy during the day, the women find it somewhat difficult to leave their homes at that time because of the compulsions of their domestic chores. As for the unemployed, though they are free at all hours of the day, they too prefer the day timings. Until recently, almost all the Institutes used to hold their PCP's in the late afternoon. They would begin their 'day' at 5 or 5.30 p.m. and carry on till 9 or 9.30 at night. They had fixed these timings in view of the consideration that the bulk of their students comprised the employed persons. But the change of the complexion of distance learners' community over the years, the unemployed and the women (far outstripping the number of the employed persons) made most of these Institutes to switch over to the day time. As mentioned earlier, the Delhi Institute holds regular classes in the day time for the unemployed and the women. The employed people whose number in that Institute is quite large avail of the facility of the Sunday classes, which too are held in the morning hours. Thus, the number of those Institutes which still adhere to the older hours has shrunk considerably.

The question that further arises is that while the theorists commend PCP as a great help to distance learners in alleviating their problems of study and the Institutes also take a good deal of pains to organise a series of PCP's both at the headquarters and at a number of mofussil stations, how many students avail of this facility? Is it a really worthwhile institution or a mere prestigious adjunct? A number of studies have been empirically made to find out both the percentage of those students who attend the PCP and the reasons that account for their participation/non-participation. Almost all these studies rate the percentage of attendance at around one-third of the total number on the rolls of the Institute. By way of an illustration, we cite two studies: the Kerala University Study (1982) (quoted by Jose Chandra. pp.91-93) and the Chandigarh Institute Study.

The Kerala University study, being quite exhaustive, has two very interesting facts to reveal. They are, briefly, as:

(a) "The attendance in 1980-81 was, the first round, 39.84 per cent; the second round, 32.76 per cent, and the third round, 31.34 per cent – a declining trend from the first round to the third round". It may be interesting to compare these findings with those of the Chandigarh study. The latter does not show any variation of attendance between the first and the second rounds, though many of the students who attend the first round keep at home during the second round while many who fail to make it earlier, come later, thus maintaining the balance, on the whole; and

(b) "The percentage of attendance of the pre-degree course is higher (45.82 to 35.22) than that of the degree students (37.32 to 30.22 per cent)".

Conversely, these studies reflect that two-thirds of the distance learners do not avail of this facility and further, some of those who come to attend the first-round do not turn up for the subsequent rounds.

Why do not such a large proportion of students attend the PCP? The various reasons of non-participation as reflected by these studies as also by our own interaction with a cross-section of students, year after year, may be reproduced, as under:

First, the most common reason adduced by the non-participants is the non-availability of time on their part for the PCP. Those who are in service complain that they do not get leave from their offices while the housewives point out that they are too engrossed in their family affairs to find time for the PCP. The latter further add that to keep themselves away from the home for such a long time as a week or ten days, brings about a lot of dislocation in the day-to-day routine of the family. This is especially so when the kids are small and the parents old. Kurt Timmon's study of Australia (1989) also corroborates that "attendance at a residential school is a very expensive and disruptive event. The student must take a week of leave from work and travel a considerable distance leaving behind family and home".

Second, whom to bother/exploit for their stay and hospitality for a week or so is another very common complaint. Since the Institutes do not undertake the responsibility of providing lodging facilities to the participants ( the Chandigarh Institute may perhaps be the only exception), the students find it difficult with whom to spend that long period of time.

In India, hotels are too expensive, while the institution of the 'sarais' (inns) which at one time was a highly popular place to spend a few days while on a trip away from the home, has fallen in disuse. Moreover, one feels it beneath one's dignity to stay there. As for one's relatives and friends, they too do not tend to welcome a guest these days partly because of the high cost of living and partly because of the individualised way of modern urban life.

Third, sometimes the dates do not suit those who are otherwise keen to attend the PCP. The Kerala study (1984) rates the number of such persons at one-third (35 per cent) of the whole. Bakshish Singh, *et.al* (1994) study discovered that a large chunk of students do not attend the PCP not because of the non-suitability of dates but because of the non-receipt of intimation of dates (p.122). This problem can be overcome to a great extent in case the Institutes chalk out in advance the dates for all the PCP's that are to be held at various places in the course of the whole academic session and announce the same right at its commencement. This is one of the many suggestions that students gave to Bakshish Singh, (1994) while discussing the issue how to strengthen PCP. (p.124). This advance information will facilitate the students in general and the working persons in particular to adjust their engagements or to obtain the leave from their work accordingly. The percentage of those persons whom dates do not suit would automatically come down. Our own experience of the Chandigarh Institute tells us that so long as we worked on an ad hoc basis (deciding the dates and venues for the various PCP's just a few days before their commencement and sending this information through press notes and individual letters), a very large number of students would complain that they were unable to attend the PCP as they had already fixed an unavoidable engagement during the days of the PCP or were refused the leave from their work because of the short notice. But ever since we have adopted the practice of taking an advance decision and incorporating the schedule of the dates of the various PCP's in the body of the prospectus, not only has the number of such complaints vertically gone down, but the attendance at the PCP has also marked an upward trend. Above all, the unnecessary expenditure that we used to incur on flashing out numerous press advertisements and letters to the individual students, has also been saved. Incidentally, the excuse about their ignorance of the PCP dates that a number of students used to make has also lost its validity.

Fourth, there is a sizeable section of students in every Institute who live in remote areas, as for instance, the armed forces personnel guarding the nation's frontiers on snowy mountains, high seas and on such like difficult terrains, or the residents of the remote hamlets. Though their number in absolute terms is not very large, they do help inflate the ranks of the non-participants.

Fifth, there is yet another category of those persons who do not find much utility in PCP and consider participation in it as a mere wastage of time. They are too sure of themselves that they can do better on their own than those who seek to walk on PCP crutches. The Kerala study puts their number at one-fifth (21 per cent) of the whole.

Sixth, another very crucial variable which determines both the rise and fall of the participants' number is the attitude and performance of the teachers. The distance learners, particularly the new entrants to the system, who know their teachers only as the author of their lessons and have had no opportunity of meeting them earlier, are generally very keen to see them. They hold them in high esteem and also have a lot of expectation from them. With this given degree of eagerness, respect and expectation, they come to attend the first series of the PCP. If the teachers give a healthy response, attend to their problems sympathetically and, above all, impress them with their lectures and academic guidance, the students' morale goes up. They feel happy and contented. Seldom would they then think of missing any further PCP. Instead, they would eagerly look forward to avail of all such opportunities of academic feast. They would also advise and persuade those who could not make it earlier, to attend it.

If, on the contrary, teachers cold shoulder them, keep them at bay, or do not impress them by their academic scholarship, they feel highly disillusioned and would never think of coming again. They would also discourage others from indulging in this game of the wastage of time. Corroborating this fact, the Kerala study underlines that "many of the first year students attend the first round as it is a new experience for them, perhaps they expect the teachers to show them an easy way to study the lessons. Once this belief is shattered, they lose their interest in attending any more of these programmes." (*op. cit.*, p.92)

Bakshish Singh, (1994) study shows that of the Open University students 53 per cent were either not satisfied or not much satisfied with the performance of teachers at the PCP, while in the case of Institute's students only 48 per cent were fully satisfied (p.123). Obviously, such a large percentage of the dissatisfied students would affect their attendance at the PCP.

Thus the teacher plays a cardinal role in the success and failure of the PCP. It has also been observed that the students' response varies from teacher to teacher. Those teachers who impress them are the highly sought-after persons both in and out of their classes. Most of the students like to attend their lectures. Whereas they do not bother the least for the others. They also build social ties of permanent nature with the former. The teachers therefore, need to be highly competent and devoted, particularly when they are required to attend to distance learners. The latter being the grown-up persons, having a more mature sense of judgment of both men and matters, are not easy to either impress or satisfy. But once a teacher impresses them, those students become their total devotees or '*bhagats*' while those teachers who fail to cut much ice with their students suffer from a deep sense of guilt and inferiority complex.

To sum up, there are a number of causes why students do not come to attend the PCP. It is the responsibility of the teachers and the Institutes' authorities to combinedly ensure its success. The former can do so by their quick-responsiveness to their students as well as by the competent display of their scholarship, while the latter by means of a sound policy and prompt attendance to the students' problems and difficulties. By and large, both these pillars of our Institutes are acquitting themselves very well on this account as is manifest in the rate of attendance of the PCP which favourably matches with the turn-out in other Institutes of the world.

What about the experience of those who come to participate in it? All studies are unanimous in their findings that "not even a single respondent has stated that the classes were not useful" (Kerala study, p.83). The reason for this wide range of satisfaction is two-fold. First, distance learners' level of motivation is comparatively very high. They attend the PCP with a desire more to learn and get benefited from it than to perceive it with a critical angle. Even if the attitude and response of a certain teacher is not satisfactory they would tolerate him and try to make the most of what he delivers rather than criticise or pick up a row with him. The second reason of this phenomenon of wide-spread satisfaction is the high degree of commitment on the part of our teachers. By and large, they treat distance learners very warm-heartedly and attend to their difficulties seriously and sympathetically. Very seldom a teacher would evade his responsibility on this account. Moreover, a couple of years of their experience in these Institutes has made them pick up the technique of 'capsuled teaching' and (thus) the knack of meeting their students' needs and expectations to their satisfaction.

It has been widely observed that once a student is convinced of the sincerity of the teachers and (hence) the utility of the PCP, he would not miss it at all, unless held up by certain unavoidable situations. Their keenness is manifest in their endeavour to conserve their leave (casual as well as earned) for the PCP and the examination and the advance steps they take to obtain it. Once it so happened that we scheduled the PCP for M.A. (Public Administration) students for the middle of March, a number of students working in the State Secretariat and the Legislative Chambers of Punjab and Haryana made a mass representation to us that those dates did not suit their convenience as they were then too busy in the annual exercise of budget-making for their respective States. Since they were not prepared to miss the PCP at any cost, we had to reschedule the dates.

It is very thrilling to see young women coming with their small kids or old persons with bent backs and staff in hand briskly walking to their classes. Some students who are (were) eminently placed in the civil and military services would even go to the extent of writing letters to the Director in appreciation of the dedication and diligence of their teachers. Bringing presents to the latter as a token of their love and regards for them is a commonplace occcurrence. All this provides an evidence how amply satisfied students go after the PCP. There is hardly a person who might have felt disillusioned with this exercise.

## III

### Study Centres

In its endeavour to further assist the distance learner by taking all essential educational facilities to the door-step of his house, an Institute sets up a chain of study centres in all such towns and cities as have a sizeable concentration of its students. Providing all essential services under one roof, a study centre serves the purpose of the Institute's headquarters in its miniscule form. It makes provision for the organisation of counselling, audio-video listening/viewing facilities, a small library containing books, journals, lesson-sets and the like, and, above all, a clerk's office to sort out students' academic and administrative problems. The objective behind the study centre is to save the students of the botheration of paying repeated visits to the headquarters in order to consult books or to seek the guidance of their teachers. "But for it", a commentator observes "many a distance learner would have been deprived of an opportunity of either peeping into the library or getting even a glimpse of their teachers and would have done their studies in their respective isolated homes, exclusively through the medium of the cold print." (Bhatnagar and Sehjpal,

1994) In this way, the study centre helps the Institute to translate the philosophy of distance education in its actual practice.

In India, the concept of the study centre could not get much popular somehow with the providers of distance education, particularly the Institutes. This is manifest from the fact that 14 out of 27 Institutes (that cared to furnish the requisite information on this account to Bakshish Singh, 1994) do not maintain any study centre at all. Of those which provide for them, 3 Institutes make a provision for only one study centre each (namely Shivaji, Kerala and Jammu), one (Shimla) has 2 study centres another one 3 (JNTU) has three study centres. There are only 2 Institutes which have a respectable number of study centres - Barktula (10) and Delhi (20). Rathore's study (1983) also discloses that only 35.71 per cent (i.e. 5 out of 14 respondent Institutes) provide study centres. (p.150) In comparison to the Institutes, the Open Universities make a much more elaborate provision for these study centres - IGNOU (202), Kota (29), B.R.Ambedkar (85) and Y.C. Maharashtra (78) (Bakshish Singh, 1994).

As for the facilities, the study centres as maintained by the Institutes, mainly cater to the library needs of the students. Even in this regard the services that they offer are generally too poor, for the libraries are both ill-equipped and ill-managed. In most of the cases, these libraries comprise a few book shelves which the Institute puts in some mofussil college/ school. To manage these study centres, the head of the host institution and its librarian are paid small honoraria. More often than not, this honorarium is too little to make these officials take interest, much less to motivate the distance learners to make use of the books. Reports often pour into the headquarters that these librarians not only cold shoulder the distance learners but also discourage them from the use of the centre. These centres are seldom inspected by the head of the Institute nor are their books replenished regularly. That is the reasons why these centres have failed to gain popularity with the students. Rathore tells us that hardly 32 per cent of the students make use of the library facilities (p.156). Similarly, Bakshish Singh, (1994) discloses that in the case of 75 per cent of these study centres, the average attendance is 50 per cent or less (p.115).

To make up that deficiency of the study centre on account of its poor library services, most of the Institutes try to maintain their central library services in high gear. Almost all of them have built up well-stocked central libraries, very well-equipped with reference and text books; they also subscribe to a number of learned journals and other periodicals. In addition to loaning facilities at the counter, some of them maintain postal services as well. All these factors combine together to make these libraries quite popular. Their reading rooms remain generally jam-packed with students. Invariably, they are open till late in the evening, especially during the few months preceding the examinations. Nonetheless, the fact remains that however effective and well organised the central library services may be, by no means do they provide a substitute for the study centres.

Besides library facilities, these centres are supposed to provide for audio-video listening/viewing facilities, information counters and PCP/ counselling. In so far as the study centres of these Institutes are concerned, most of them do not provide for these services. To quote Bakshish Singh, (1994) 20 Institutes out of 23 do not make a provision for audio-video facilities and, similarly, 6 out of 10 do not set up information counters at their study centres (p.116). Most of these Institutes also do not make use of their study centres for PCP. Invariably, they hold these exercises elsewhere, for the reason that these centres are both too small and too ill-organised to undertake as elaborate as exercise as that of a PCP. Thus, for all intents and purposes these study centres are non-existent; neither the students are aware of their existence nor are the Institutes' authorities keen to maintain them efficiently.

In comparison to these study centres, those that belong to the Open Universities are very well-equipped and also functionally very active. The study centres of the IGNOU, for instance match favourably with the international standards in every respect. To describe their structure and functions in some detail an IGNOU study centre is generally housed in a college or school which extends to it the facility of accommodation for such purposes as library and the reading room, class work, audio-video. listening/viewing, clerks office etc.etc. The head of the host institution or some one suggested by him is appointed its co-ordinator. The other staff required to manage the centre, such as assistant co-ordinators, office personnel, library attendants, technicians to operate the electronic gadgets, etc. etc. are also recruited from within the institution concerned or from the outside if need be. All of them are paid an honorarium which is quite handsome so that they work with a sense of commitment. In order to handle the counselling service, a large number of teachers of diverse disciplines are recruited from the host institution and elsewhere to act as counsellors. They work on contractual basis.

The Centre is very well equipped with all sorts of necessary instructional aids. It houses a small library which contains books, journals, lesson-sets and the like. The library loans books as well as provides the photo-copying services to its students. The Centre is further equipped with all types of electronic gadgets (such as television sets, tape recorders required for playing the audio and the video cassettes.

The Centre generally functions on Saturdays and Sundays. Its main activity is to organise counselling. The Co-ordinator draws out a comprehensive plan for the organisation of counselling for different courses and holds its numerous sessions accordingly. Besides, the Centre also makes arrangement for the evaluation of the student's home assignments which task is no less elaborate. Yet another activity of the Centre is to supply all types of information to the students as also to those who want to take up a course with the IGNOU. Every year, its office sells thousands of copies of the University prospectus and handles piles of other information and data. Thus humming with activity round the year, the study centre serves as an ideal agency of the IGNOU to provide all types of services to its students and the others.

It is an open secret that until the emergence of the IGNOU, the Institutes had not grasped fully the concept of a study centre. That is perhaps the reason that most of them did not then bother much whether or not they had any study centre, and if they had created a few, they would not care to properly manage them. But when the IGNOU began to set up these centres, one after the other, with a dazzling speed, these Institutes became increasingly conscious of this shortcoming on their part. Ultimately, this consciousness generated the demand for composite study centres.

One big reason why many Institutes did not create study centres or those which created some, did not staff them properly, was the lack of finances on their part. The creation and the day-to-day maintenance of a study centre (as elaborate as that of the IGNOU) requires huge piles of money. Even the very well-off Institutes cannot afford to have these 'white elephants'.

Keeping in view the immense utility of these centres, on the one hand, and the financial and administrative inability of these Institutes to create and maintain them, on the other, composite study centres (if created by the U.G.C. or any other such super agency) is the only viable solution. The demand for them, that is being made of late, is the outcome of a long, mature thinking on the part of those persons who have been in the system for a long time. They propose that the U.G.C. should setup, in phases, a chain of these centres. Each such centre should comprise a large building complex which should provide such accommodation as a few class rooms (large as well as small), two or three auditoria (for audio, video and television viewing), a conference hall, a library, a reading room, common rooms for the men and the women students and a few office rooms. In addition, it should also have a small guest house for the visiting faculty. This study centre should be fully equipped with all types of electronic gadgetry required by modern instructional technology, books (both reference and text), journals, lesson-sets of all the Institutes of the region (if not of the country as a whole), audio and video cassettes as produced by the various educational institutes of the country, and such other equipment as is needed to make the Centre efficiently functional. For its management a governing board, comprising the heads of all the Institutes of the region may be set up, while its day-to-day administration may be entrusted to the care of the local Institute. The annual maintenance grant will however be provided by the U.G.C.. This Centre should be made available for use to all the Institutes of the country as also to the students thereof. The former may hold their PCP's here, instead of depending upon the goodwill local colleges/schools. All the Institutes which make use of its class-rooms, electronic gadgetry, library and the guest house will pay for it.

Such composite centres alone will help these Institutes to realise the lofty objective of decentralising the facilities of distance education in various towns and cities. These centres will not only relieve them of their constant headache of finding suitable accommodation for their PCP's as well as for the boarding and lodging for their faculty when on PCP duty, but also immensely benefit their students who will then have access to books and journals and, above all, to the study material of all the Institutes of the region. These Institutes will then come at par with any first-rate Institute of Distance Education anywhere in the world. A big deficiency on their part will be made up.

## REFERENCES

Action Plan for Quality Assurance in ICC's/DED's, A Report of the Round Table Conference, organised by Commonwealth of Learning, University Grants Commission and the Distance Education Council in New Delhi. 30 June - 2 July, 1994. *Open Ideas* (An Official Organ of Indian Distance Education Association). Vol. 2, No.1 (February, 1995).

Bakshish Singh, Saroj Mullik and Neelam Chaudhary, *Correspondence' Distance Education In India, An Indepth Study Covering the year 1989-90.* Koul, B.N. (Ed.). New Delhi, Indira Gandhi National Open University.1994.

Bhatnagar, S. and Sahjpal, A.K., 'Role of Study Centre in Distance Education: A Case

Study of the Expanding Dimensions of the IGNOU Study Centre·Chandigarh'. *Indian Journal of Distance Education*. Vol. IV, (1994).

Chander, Jose N., Kevin, S. and Sudhakaran, P., *Drop-outs in the System of Distance Education (A Project Report)*, Trivandrum, Institute of Correspondence Courses, Kerala University, 1984

Holmberg, Borje, ***Status and Trends*** *of Distance Education*. Luna Lector Publishing, 1985.

Morrison, Terrence R. and Saraswat Deepak in Reddy, G. Ram (ed.). *Open Universities, the Ivory Towers Thrown Open*. Delhi, Sterling, 1988.

Rathore, H.C.S., *Management of Distance Education in India*. New Delhi, Ashish Publishing House, 1983.

Sewart, David, 'Individualising Support Services', in Daniel, John S.; Stoud, Martha, A; and Thompson, John (Eds.), *Learning at a Distance: A World Perspective*. Edmonton, Athabasca University, 1982.

Sudhakaran, R., 'Attendance at PCP's in Jose Chander and Kavin, S. (Eds.). *Distance Education: An Indian Perspective*. Trivandrum, Institute of Correspondence Courses, Kerala University, 1984.

Timmons, Kurt, 'Educational Effectiveness of Various Adjuncts to Printed Study Materials in Distance Education', ***Research in Distance Education***. Vol. I, No. 3. (October, 1989).

CHAPTER VII

# STUDENTS' RESPONSE SHEETS

TEACHING is a two-way process the effectiveness of which depends upon the quality of instruction that teachers impart as well as upon the nature of the students' response. In case the latter is not positive or encouraging (whatever may be the reasons), the whole process loses its utility and even becomes futile for those whom it is directed to. In that eventuality, the teacher concerned must either improve the content and (or) communication of his instruction or yield his place to some one else who can deliver the goods in a better way. In this client-oriented world, the teachers are the market managers who, though shape and determine the demand of their clientele, must measure their success by the satisfaction that it (clientele) derives.

In the class-room setting where teachers directly deliver instruction by the word of their mouth, occasionally though making use of the black-board and other modern electronic instructional gadgetry, students' response is judged by the nods of their head, the glow of their eyes, the expression of their faces and even by the murmur of their tongues. A vigilant teacher whose eyes are constantly fixed on their faces, adjusts the tone and the temper of his delivery and even modifies the contents of his lecture, in keeping with the changing moods of his audience. In distance teaching where the teacher and the taught are spatially separated from each other by hundreds of miles, this face-to-face interaction is not possible. The teacher must, therefore, devise new methods to judge the efficacy of his instruction. Though the telephone and video conferencing have, of late, considerably facilitated his task, students' home assignments or (what we describe in India) students' response sheets continue to form the main channel of the feedback of their response to the teachers' instruction.

A response sheet is a set of questions or such knowledge/information-eliciting exercises relating to a lesson or a couple of lessons which a student is supposed to answer in writing and then mail it to his teacher, in order to apprise the latter with the degree of his assimilation of the lesson. The teacher on his part will go through it thoroughly, pointing out the deficiencies in it. More importantly, he would give profuse comments by way of his guidance how to improve his performance. If rules require, he may grade it as well. Afterwards, these response-sheets are mailed back to the students so that they may not only preserve them for their future reference and reading but may also know their shortcomings and make improvements as desired and directed by the teacher. In this way, the response-sheet provides a highly meaningful channel which forges closer ties of understanding and friendship between the distance learner and his teacher. They may not be able to meet each other even once during their stay in the Institute for a couple of years, but they maintain their continuous dialogue with each other through the medium of the response sheets. It has often been observed that students when draw closer to their teacher through this medium, seek his guidance on many a personal problem as well, besides appending their answer to the various questions relating to the lesson. Thus we find that response sheet is "the single most important mechanism for prompting and for pacing the individuals' study and offers the only vehicle available to all students for feedback and dialogue with a tutor about their individual progress." (Mary Thorpe, quoted by P. Satyanarayana and C.Sesharatnam; 1992).

That a student is required to communicate to his teacher in writing as to how much grasp he has developed over the lesson provides to distance education an edge over the conventional classroom teaching where everything is conducted orally. It may be underlined tnat the writing that a distance student is required to do, is not a simple exercise of random writing. In fact, it is a guided exercise done, first, in response to his teachers' questions and then to meet the requirements of his comments. This repeatedly done exercise helps him to attain knowledge and pass the examination with a degree of distinction. The attainment of these objectives is further facilitated by the added advantage that every time he sends his response sheets to his teacher, he receives his individual attention, which a classroom student cannot look for conveniently. This is the big advantage of the distance system. (Erdos, 1967 ).

Designing of a response sheet is a difficult task in the sense that the teacher is supposed to frame such questions as may bring out the student's level of comprehension of the lesson as vividly as possible. This is all the more imperative in view of the response sheet being the only channel of the feedback. Its designing, therefore calls for much thought and creative imagination (Holmberg 1995) as well as a candid sense of distinction among the various aspects of the lesson which need to be tested and which to be left out. Keeping these broad parameters in mind the response sheet designers generally prepare three types of questions: objective, short answer and long essay type answers.

In every lesson, there are certain aspects which demand less of comprehension and more of the reckoning of information regarding the statistical data and the like. The objective type questions are ideal to test one's level of such information. In the same manner, there are certain other aspects which too are informatory in nature. But the information acquired thereon is not very precise so as to be answered in 'this or that' fashion. Instead, it requires to be explained, though briefly, but in a fewer words. Here we need short-answer type questions.

There is yet another aspect of the lesson where we need long essay-type questions. The mature nature of the graduate students demands that they should not only be equipped with bare information of the various aspects of our work-a-day world but should also develop the analytical and critical faculties of their mind. They would then acquire the capability of deciphering the subtle differences between right and wrong, good and bad, and also of putting across their viewpoint clearly, cogently and vehemently. To test this type of knowledge, we need question that require long essay-type answers wherein one may give coherent expression to one's thoughts and feelings, supporting his viewpoints with logic and sound argumentation. A response sheet will be complete only when it includes all these three types of questions.

Most of the response-sheet designers do not however tend to tax their mind so much mainly because they are guided by the consideration that their students should fare well in the examination. With that limited object in mind what they generally do is that they pick up few questions from the university question papers of the past few years and fit them into their response sheet. Since these papers have also, of late, started including all the three types of questions as mentioned above, the task of these designers has become somewhat easy. Some of them do however display their sense of innovation by formulating questions different from the beaten track.

Response sheets may be evaluated manually as well as mechanically. Those response sheets which carry objective type questions are generally mechanically evaluated with the help of a computer. They are described as CMA (Computer Marked Assignments). Those response sheets that carry short answer and essay type questions are evaluated manually by the teachers. They are described as TMA (Tutor Marked Assignments). Most of the Institutes make a provision for both types of response sheets.

The British Open University makes the submission of 8 TMA's and 8 CMA's an obligatory part of the continuous assessment for a full credit course. In the IGNOU, their number varies from course to course. While for the Management Course, the requirement is both TMA's and CMA's, the DDE Course requires only TMA's and not CMA's.

Response sheet constitutes an indispensable component of the system of distance education. Besides providing to the teachers a feedback channel to know how their lessons are being received by their students, it provides to the system at large a potent instrument of control over the students.

To this end, every Institute requires its students to submit a certain minimum number of response sheets in order to earn eligibility to appear in the terminal examination. The number and percentage of response sheets, however, varies from Institute to Institute and from course to. course even within an Institute. Bakshish Singh, (1994). tried to gather the requisite information on this account from the various Institutes and Open Universities by means of a questionnaire. Out of 29 Institutes, only 13 provided this information. As Table below shows, 4 Institutes require their students to submit 2 response sheets per subject, 3 requires 3-4 response sheets, 2 require 5-10 response sheets and only one requires 11 or more response sheets per subject. There are 2 Institutes which prescribe 5 to 10 response sheets per course. As regards Open Universities, 2 of them (IGNOU and Kota) require their students to submit 3 response sheet per course (In the IGNOU, 8 credits constitute a course). The Y.C.Maharashtra Open University requires one response sheets in 2-5 credit courses and 2 response sheets in 6-8 credit courses.

**TABLE 7.1: Showing the Minimum Number of Response Sheets Required to be Submitted and the Number of Institutes**

| *Requirement* | *No. of Institutes* |
|---|---|
| 2 per subject | 4 |
| 3-4 per subject | 3 |
| 5-10 per subject | 2 |
| 11 and above per subject | 1 |
| 5-10 per course | 2 |
| 11 and above per course | 1 |

*Source* : Bakshish Singh, *et al.*, Research Report.

Whether or not a student who does not submit the minimum number of response sheets is debarred from appearing in the terminal examination, Bakshish Singh (1994) discovered that of the 27 Institutes, 20 claimed that they insist on the fulfilment of that condition while 7 submitted that they did not do so. Further, of the 69 per cent of the Institutes which make response sheets compulsory, only 52 per cent counted their scores toward internal assessment. As for the Open Universities, 3 of them (75 per cent) make submission of response sheets compulsory as well as count their scores toward internal assessment, while one Open University (Dr.B. R. Ambedkar) did not insist on the submission of response sheets at all. There is yet another dimension of this situation, and, that is that there are a number of Institutes which while making the submission of response sheets compulsory, do not actually take cognizance of those students who do not comply with this condition. This laxity on their parts reduces this institution to a face. The Director of one leading Institute of the country confided in this author that response sheet has long ceased to be an instrument of communication between the teacher and the taught. Neither the Institutes insist upon the students to write the response sheets nor do the students care to submit any.

The factual position, as explained above, does not reflect a very healthy situation. Not to make the submission of response sheet compulsory or to claim that they do and then not to take notice of those who do not fulfil the prescribed condition and to allow everyone to take the examination is to make a mockery of the system. For, distance education has the unique distinction, among other things, of making the students maintain a lively two-way contact with the Institute through the instrumentality of response sheets. If this basic condition is not fulfilled, then how does this system distinguish itself from such academically unsound practices as 'private appearance'. The Institutes lose their control over their students. They do not know whether they pursue their studies properly and how is their study material being taken by them. Above all, this laxity on the part of the Institutes reinforces the impression of the conventionalists that this system too is academically unsound.

It is, therefore, of utmost importance that no Institute/Open University should allow anyone of its students to take the terminal examination without his having fulfilled the condition of the submission of the minimum number of response sheets. Further, it should also insist that the required number of response sheets should be submitted in a properly phased manner throughout the course of the academic year and not that all of them are sent in one or two lots toward the end of the year. Further on, if it is possible it should count their scores toward internal assessment. The

National Workshop On Academic Counselling in Distance Education, organised by Dr. B. R. Ambedkar Open University in 1992 had made such recommendations. It is high time that concerted efforts should be made to make the institution of response sheets effective.

However, the trouble with some of the Institutes is that having been lax with regard to the submission of response sheets in the initial stages of their inception (perhaps with a view to making their courses popular), they appear to have now been caught in a peculiar situation of indecisiveness. While, on the one hand, they are now keen to enforce this eligibility condition strictly in letter and spirit in order to establish their credentials in the world of academia, on the other, they are unable to do so. The long-hardened tradition of conniving at the recalcitrant element has inflated the number of the latter to such high proportions that if they were to enforce this eligibility condition now, they would debar a large majority of the students from taking the examination. That might perhaps be too harsh and unjust a decision on their part. Besides, it would seriously damage their 'reputation'. Cut-throat competition among the Institutes might spell doom on them in the sense that their enrollment might come down steeply in the following year. They have thus been caught between Cinderala and Charbidis.

These difficulties notwithstanding, these Institutes shall have to take steps sooner than later to enforce this conditionality upon which hinges the credentiality of the system at large. Already their social acceptability has suffered a good deal of erosion. Further delay would prove suicidal for them.

The only viable method to enforce this conditionality is that all Institutes of a region should take a collective decision not to allow those students, who do not submit the minimum required number of response sheets, to sit in the terminal examination. Once this decision is taken and enforced, Institutes would no longer have the apprehension that others would absorb their rejectee.

To come to the administrative handling of response sheets. It is undoubtedly an enormous task. Every Institute receives in the course of an academic year thousands of response sheets. Supposing an Institute has on its rolls 10,000 students and each one of them studies four subjects/papers and in order to qualify one-self for the terminal examination, one is required to submit a minimum of three response sheets, the Institute would receive 1,20,000 response sheets. This is the bare minimum. Their number may cross this limit, for there would always be on the rolls a sizeable number of such students who are quite serious about their studies and try to answer as many of response sheets (if not all) as they may conveniently do. These sheets are not received in one or a few lots. Instead, they continue pouring in tens or even in hundreds throughout the course of the year.

The tremendous number and their continuous inflow apart, the administrative, handling of response sheets is a multi-stage operation. To begin with, each individual packet is to be opened. Its contents generally comprising three to five response sheets and invariably relating to different subjects/papers are to be carefully sorted out and their receipt is to be recorded in the appropriate columns against the name/enrolment number of the student concerned. Then, subject and paper-wise packets are prepared for their transmission to their subject-wise Department. In his turn, the departmental clerk forwards them to the evaluators — the departmental teachers and (in case the number of response sheets exceeds the absorption capacity of the inside evaluators) the outside teachers who do this work on small contract basis. Again, a proper record of their despatch and receipt is to be maintained, especially with regard to those response sheets which are sent outside for evaluation. On their receipt after evaluation, the clerk would take necessary steps, to despatch them back to the students,on the the one hand, and to make the payment of remuneration to the outside evaluators, on the other.

Before they are despatched back to the students, the score of each and every response sheet is to be entered into the column where its receipt had been recorded. This aspect of the task is of crucial importance, for it would be on the basis of this score that students' eligibility to the final examination is to be determined. If laxity is shown and an error is committed, the clerk might have to pay it through his nose. Therefore, he is got to be very careful. In addition, the clerk also handles numerous queries of the students that they make, *inter alia,* about the delay in evaluation of their response sheets. Thus, the administrative handling of the response sheets is not only enormous in size but multi-faceted in nature. It keeps a number of officials on their tenter hooks throughout the year.

Having not changed their nineteenth century work-culture, most of these Institutes still manipulate this enormous operation manually. The slow and cumbersome technique of doing things further compounds their problem of delay. In case they go in for modern technology, they would streamline this operation to a very great extent. The computer would then take care of all types of record-keeping, whether relating to the receipt of the response sheets, the maintenance of the record thereof or the disposal of evaluators' bills. When toward the end of the academic session, the departmental clerk is required to furnish a consolidated statement of the defaulters (whether on account of the number of response sheets or their score falling short of the required minimum), the computer would do the work. The clerk will no longer have to shuffle pages after pages and peep into the various columns carefully in order to collect the information. Instead, he would simply press button and the entire information in the fashion it is needed, will appear on the screen. Moreover, the information that the computer would furnish would not only be flawless but more authentic than the one he now prepares manually. These Institutes thus need to seriously think in terms of this change.

Evaluation of response-sheets is a difficult and time-consuming task. It is much more comprehensive and straining than evaluation of examination answer-books. In the case of the latter, a person is supposed to assess the performance of a student in terms of marks and grades. But in so far as the response-sheets are concerned, one is not only to do the assessment, but, as alluded above, one is also required to point out the mistakes as well as other deficiencies and to give profuse remarks how to avoid those shortcomings and how to improve one's performance in the future. Satyanarayana and Sesharathnam (1992) very aptly underline that "distance teacher's comments should be, such as to help the learners (a) to sustain interest in learning, (b) to get motivated and activated, (c) to facilitate learning, and (d) to assess his progress in comparison with others." This task makes it incumbent upon the evaluator that he should read the script thoroughly between the lines and not just glance it over. More importantly, he is sometimes required to give the correct answer of a certain question or to reproduce the right version of a point or explanation. A conscientious evaluator's remarks often run into a few paragraphs, for he is performing that job in writing which a classroom teacher does it orally at the face of his students.

This is indeed quite a difficult and challenging task. One who perceives his role as a 'friend, philosopher and guide' to his distance learners, is bound to derive pleasure and immense satisfaction by spending time on their response sheets, while those who are stung by the mercenary bug, would find this task monotonous and oppressive. Ironically, the former is a rare species whereas the latter rule the roost. Obviously, evaluation is not done as desired. It is widely observed that teachers do not take this work seriously and try to hurry through their daily quota of response sheets. As for the outside evaluators, their performance is perhaps a shade worse, mainly for the reason that most of the Institutes

(16 out of 20 as per Bakshish Singh (1994) have not devised any system of checking (even on random basis) their evaluation. As a result, the response sheets, as and when received from them, are straightaway mailed to the students by the departmental clerk. No one bothers to open the packets and give a glance to them. Only 4 Institutes make a provision for some sort of a random check of the evaluated response sheets. How far does that system work and what follow-up action is taken, no one knows.

It is an open secret that the quality of evaluation of the response sheets is far from satisfactory. Even the teachers of the Institutes/Open Universities are themselves not happy with it (Bakshish Singh, 1994, p.132) Inayat Khan (1989) also reports that "he collected some valued response sheet assignments from students and found to his dismay that the evaluation of these assignments was done in a lackadaisical manner. Some of the answers were not valued at all. There was no comment. Just a few ticks and crosses and then the marks were awarded." (p.165) Corroborating this fact, B.N.Koul (1988) also remarks, "There is no lack of evidence to establish the fact that not every teacher/tutor handles answer-scripts with the attention and devotion expected of him." (p.41). Quite often the students have been found complaining that their response sheets contain only a few ticks here and there and also such beaten-track remarks as: 'good', 'satisfactory', 'poor', 'elaborate', 'work hard' and so on and so forth. Some of them do not hesitate to come to the Institute in person with their evaluated response sheets under their armpit and ask the teachers to explain the wisdom of certain remarks or to give to them the correct answer to that question whose explanation the evaluator had struck off. On certain occasions, the teachers have to face a good deal of embarrassment at the hands of those dissatisfied students.

Poor quality of response sheet evaluation is too inimical for the growth of the system of distance education. For, it frustrates the philosophy and purpose of the two-way communication which is one of the basic planks of this system. Besides, it deeply hits hard psychologically those students who take this work seriously. How greatly let down these students feel can be gauged from the depressed and indignant faces with which they bang into the office doors of their teachers.

Another grouse of the students is that they do not receive back their response sheets, and whenever they do so, they get them very late. There is no denying the fact that every Institute endeavours hard to get the response sheets evaluated and send them back to the students as early as possible. They have also created an administrative mechanism to take care of this work. Thus there appears to be not much substance in the charge that response sheets are not returned to the students. There may be some Institutes which may not be able to fully cope with this work, especially toward the end of the academic session when the number of response sheets increases tremendously. In normal days, evaluation and return takes place smoothly.

As for the turn-around time, 6 Institutes out of 22 which furnished this information (Bakshish Singh, 1994) claimed that they send back response sheets within a month; 13 said 2-3 months and 3 did not specify any time limit, saying it is uncertain. (Question No.43.) Rathor's study based on the response of 592 students, puts the turn around time between 36 and 60 days. (p.109)

Our own impression is that an Institute normally takes one to two months. However the fact remains that evaluation consumes an unduly long time and that students receive them quite late. Taking into consideration the time that such administrative tasks consume as their transmission to the Institute and back, their shuffling and record-keeping in the office, and their evaluation, a response sheet should normally reach back to the student in three weeks. But this time span is seldom adhered to. It often stretches into five to six weeks, and sometimes even later than that as well. It may be pointed out that delay is a universal phenomenon. Mackenize reports that even the students of the British Open University also complained of the long turn-around time, although they appreciated their tutors' comments. Another study done in the same University in 1987 revealed that, on an average, it took a waiting time of 24 days for a student to get back his response sheet (both studies quoted by Satyanarayana and Seshrathnam, 1992). The biggest bottleneck of delay is the evaluator who, more often than not, takes this work casually and leisurely. Another bottleneck is the receipt and dispatch clerks. Unfortunately, they do not appreciate the urgency involved in this task.

However, it goes without saying that one who has written the response sheet seriously is quite keen to hear back the comments of his teacher. Here is an account (very graphically given) by one John Stivenson a student of a the National Extension College. He writes in his college magazine, *Home Study*:

> "I sent off my first assignment with many doubts. I waited patiently for the results. Days passed, a week passed, two weeks passed. I wondered if I had done anything wrong? Maybe, they won't bother with me, after seeing my first assignment? Then, finally

the day came when I received my first result and comment. I asked my father to open the letter for me. My heart thumped and thumped harder while my father was opening it up. What would be the result? What lay in it? Was it bad news or good news? These thoughts went through my mind that moment. First, I asked my father to give me my course card. He laid it on my desk. I turned my head down toward it. My eyes.fell on bright red fell-tip writing. Then I saw on (A). Could this be right? Was I seeing right? Yes, I was. I had got a top mark for my first piece of work. Then I read my tutor's comment and that was all praise. Well, from that day I knew that I was on the right path for my future. My work had become easier to me and more enjoyable. I have really enjoyed working through the WEC courses." (ICDE *News Bulletin*. p. 13).

Conversely, delay blunts the edge of student's keenness and further (incessant) delay may rob him of his entire interest and enthusiasm in this work. He may also lose respect for his teachers and , may be, for the system at large. Holmberg (1989) rightly bemoans, "An evident weakness of normal distance study is the delayed feedback provided by tutors comments......" He meaningfully adds, "Students seem to accept and profit from comments and corrections given within 7-10 days after an assignment has been completed, but are usually dissatisfied if delay is of a longer duration. Students on the whole are highly appreciative of the two-way communication element and expect rather full comments on their submitted works within as few days as possible."

Obviously, the question arises, why do the teachers do not do justice to the student's response sheets ? B.N.Koul (1988) identifies five major reasons for 'teachers' indifference to this work (a) he is working under some kind of compulsion; (b) his tendency not to read the answer scripts, but grade them to record an overt evidence of having done his duty; (c) lack of time on his part to write his comments; (d) his ignorance to appreciate the significance of his comments from the pedagogic point of view; and (e) his inability to write appropriate comments." (p.41)

The arguments that a teacher does not have time to read the scripts or that he does not know what to write or how important his comments are for his students do not appear to provide the right clue to his indifference to this work. As per the system that operates in all Institutes, the internal faculty members who do this work, are conceded enough time for it. The norms of work as determined and given by the U.G.C. to the various Institutes of the country, prescribe that a teacher would evaluate in the course of a day 16 response sheets. This number was determined after a good deal of thought. If objectively analysed, this is an optimum number. It provides to an evaluator enough time to go through a script thoroughly and give his comments in detail. As far as the outside evaluators are concerned, time is no consideration for them because they voluntarily contract themselves for this work.

As for the other two arguments, a teacher who is the master of his subject is competent enough to know how and where a particular answer to a certain question is wrong—deficient. What remarks he is to give by way of correction and guidance is not difficult for him to conceive. In the same manner, one who has worked in an Institute of Distance Education and rubbed his shoulders with distance learners can very well feel the pulse of his students, and understand how keenly do they look for his guidance and instruction. Therefore, the question does not arise of his not knowing the importance of his remarks.

The actual reasons of his being indifferent toward response sheets are : first, that this work is too monotonous and boring. By nature, teacher is a creative being. He is in the profession because he finds that teaching by nature is a creative activity whether it is in the form of writing a lesson for distance students or lecturing to a class. As regards response sheets, their evaluation is undoubtedly a highly challenging job. By giving his comments, a teacher is doing great service to a distance learner to improve his performance. But compared to classroom teaching or even writing a lesson, response sheet evaluation is a listless job, particularly when one is supposed to repeat that exercise day in and day out. One gets tired and is prone to do justice in diminishing returns. This is one big reason of a teacher getting indifferent to this work.

Second, those who are working in these Institutes are, by and large, a disgruntled lot. Having been overwhelmed by a deep sense of alienation and apathy, they do not find charm in any aspect of their work, much less in the evaluation of the response sheets. Obviously, the quality of evaluation at their hand would be far less satisfactory.

The issue of our immediate concern however is, how to improve the quality of evaluation of response sheets and also how to cut down the element of delay in this work. To this end, the Institutes need to adopt a two-pronged policy. On the one hand, they will have to bifurcate the entire academic work, as suggested earlier, into two halves. Accordingly, this work will fall to the share of the junior faculty. They would be accountable for its performance to their senior colleagues, who would exercise supervision over them somewhat more strictly in view of their casual way of doing things. One the other, the system of getting the work done from the outside evaluators need to be radically improved. Instead of allowing them to do this work at their respective homes and convenience, they should be required to do the evaluation in the premises of the Institute itself. As the secrecy branch of the university conduct on-the-spot evaluation of the examination answer-books, the Institute should also make these evaluators sit together in large halls and evaluate the response sheets under the supervision and guidance of the departmental teachers. At the end of the day, they should be paid their remuneration in cash. In addition, some modest provision should also be made for their daily allowance. This provision along with handsome remuneration would attract a number of seasoned and retired teachers for this work who would also do it in a more conscientious manner.

This two-pronged policy would help the Institute not only to improve the quality of evaluation but also in cutting down the evaluation time considerably. This system further supported by computerised recordkeeping service would effect radical improvements in the discharge of this work. It may furtheron be added that the disposal time of the response-sheet can also be considerably cut down if evaluation process is also computerised. This is a very wide-prevalent practice the world over. However, it requires that response sheets be designed purely on the basis of the objective questions. But as mentioned above, the requirements of the graduate degree (testing of their analytical and critical faculties) demand that besides the objective type questions, they should also include essay-type questions. Since the computer cannot evaluate essay type questions, this technique is of little assistance to us.

The issue that further needs to be probed is, why students do not write response sheets ? As mentioned earlier, the general experience of all the Institutes is that their students tend to avoid this work and, as a result, a situation has come to be created whereunder the Institutes are obliged to allow all their students to take their terminal examination, irrespective of the consideration whether or not one has fulfilled the condition of submitting the prescribed minimum number of response sheets. Various studies, conducted from time to time by different Institutes as also by individual research scholars, have brought out the following three reasons :

First, the inhospitable response of the Institutes. The students generally complain that whenever they submit response sheets, they do not get them back soon, and whenever they receive them, they find them casually marked. If the desired purpose of their getting guidance from their teachers through the medium of the response sheets is not duly served, they feel that there is no use of spending money to mail them and then wait indefinitely for their return. If their Institutes extend full co-operation to them, they would not mind submitting as many response sheets as they receive alongwith their lessons, they add. This is quite a valid reason, for there is no denying the fact that our teachers do not take this work seriously. It is they who have disillusioned the students, by their apathetic attitude to this work. As far as students are concerned, most of them appear to be serious in their studies and are also keen to submit the response sheets. It has been observed that a large number of students who bring their response sheets to the Institute for evaluation, if get a sympathetic attention of their teachers (which they invariably do), they repeat this exercise time and again. In fact, it is this section of the satisfied students who send their response sheets in large numbers.

The second reason adduced by an equally large number of students is that they do not get time. Their argument is that their day is so heavy, on account of their being in employment, that it often becomes difficult for them to find time even to glance through the lessons, not to speak of the writing of the response sheets. This argument too does not seem to be devoid of reason. The routine of daily work is undoubtedly too much back-breaking for those who are employed. The plight of those who are also married and have children is still worse. There is no denying the fact that they are too much hard pressed with work and that they do not get time. But since they have offered themselves for study, they must discharge its attendant obligations, whatever be their limitations.

Thirdly, some of them question the wisdom behind the response sheets. They are of the view that this is a futile exercise having absolutely no relation with their performance in the examination (we will examine this issue a little later in this chapter).

These reasons may be valid. But they do not explain the whole truth. It appears that the students of these Institutes have developed the habit of evading this responsibility. Who doesn't know that when this system was instituted for the first time in the country/region, people had many misgivings about it and one of them was that it did not entail any obligation or responsibility on the students. 'Enroll yourself with an Institute and get away with the eligibility to appear in the examinations' was the big impression that was let loose about these Institutes. (Earlier too people could appear in the university examinations privately. But this privilege was restricted to a few select categories only. Now these Institutes would allow everyone to come to their fold and avail of the facility of the university examination). This impression was confirmed by the lax discipline of the Institutes when they connived, willy nilly, at the non-fulfillment of the condition of response sheets. When the Institutes themselves would not bother whether or not any of its student submitted response sheets, why should the students bother for them. The students became all the more averse from them, particularly because writing a response sheet is quite a taxing task involving a lot of time which they would have to squeeze from their otherwise heavily-packed routine. Thus, it is the habit of shirking this work which lies at the root of the problem.

While this author was the Director of the Chandigarh Institute, he initiated the drive to wipe out the incidence of recalcitrance with respect to the response-sheets. Right from the beginning of the academic session, he began to impress upon the students the vital importance of the response sheets in their scheme of studies. He would shoot out letters from time to time, persuading them to write the response sheets in as great a number as possible. Besides, whenever he would get the opportunity of meeting the students and addressing them, especially when they assembled for their personal contact programmes, he would dwell upon this theme at length. The response of the students began to show improvement but very gradually. When the session headed toward its close, he changed the tone of his letters, from persuation to intimidation. Those who failed to discharge their obligasion to submit the required quota of response sheets, would be debarred from the examination, he warned them. This warning shattered the stubbornness of a sizeable number of students. What most of them would do is that they would scribble a few lines and submit them, thereby fulfilling the eligibility condition. Despite these efforts, the number of the recalcitrants at the end of the session remained too formidable to allow him to translate the threat of detention in practice, he fell too depressed and small to continue to drive any longer.

Even though this experiment failed to hit its objective, it did, however, establish, first, that students shirked discharging this obligation, and second, if adequately forced by actual implementation of the threat, they would take this work very seriously. This fact is corroborated by the experience of the Open Universities and the others which made their students to adhere to this condition meticulously. That they do not get time or there is no wisdom behind the response sheet are all but lame excuses of not doing the things. 'Be tough and they would yield', this should be the motto of all these Institutes. As suggested earlier, they should work in unison to wipe out the incidence of recalcitrance in this respect in order to achieve hundred per cent success.

That there is little wisdom behind the response sheets is a proposition which too needs to be probed in depth. A number of studies have also been conducted in order to establish a correlationship between response sheets and the performance level of the students in the examination. None of these could however clearly establish whether those who write and submitted the response sheets in sufficient numbers show a better performance than those who do not submit any. In certain cases, the 'obedients' obtained high marks while in certain others the 'recalcitrants' fared better. How one fares in the examination depends not on one factor (writing of the response sheets) but on many (e.g. one's level of the I.Q., one's background knowledge, one's art of putting across things, one's expression, one's writing habit and so on ).

One thing, however, is very clear and unambiguous that whatever may be the correlations between the two, the institution of response sheets is not going to be dispensed away. Instead, it needs to be strengthened further, for it is not only a channel of the feedback as said earlier, but also an instrument of control over the students. Above all, this is the only method to bestow respectability on the system of distance education.

## REFERENCES


Bakshsish Singh, Saroj Mullick and Neelam Chaudhary, *Correspondence/Distance Education in India: An Indepth Study Covering the Year 1989-90.* Koul, B.N. (Ed.) New Delhi, Indira Gandhi National Open University, 1994.

Erdos, Renee, *Teaching by Correspondence.* UNESCO Source Book, London, Longman, 1967

Holmberg, Borje, 'Communication and Study Success—Quality in Distance Education', in Bakshish Singh (Ed.) *New Horizons in Distance Education.* New Delhi, Uppal, 1995

Holmberg, Borje, 'On the Organisation of Distance Education', in Khan, Inayat (Ed.) *Teaching at a Distance.* Delhi, Amar Prakashan, 1989

Khan, Inayat, 'Why Should we train our teachers in the system of Distance Education', Khan, Inayat (Ed.) *Op.Cit.*

Koul, B.N., 'Tutor-Comments: A Distance Teaching Technique', Koul B.N., Bakshish Singh and Ansari, M.M.(Eds.) *Studies in Distance Education',* New Delhi, Association of Indian Universities and Indira Gandhi National Open University, 1988.

Mary. Thorpe, Quoted by Satyanarayana, P. and Sesharatnam, C. 'Student Assignments for Submission in Distance Education'. *Kaktiya Journal* (Warangal, India) Vol. I, No.2. (1992)

Mackanizie, M. Quoted by *Ibid.*
Satyanarayana, P. and Sesharathnam, C. *Ibid.*
Stevanson, John. *I.C.C.E. Bulletin.*
Summary Report of the Recommendations of the National Workshop on Academic Counselling in Distance Education (20 June to 3 July, 1992). Organised by Dr. B.R.Ambedkar Open University Hyderabad.

CHAPTER VIII

# FACULTY

TEACHERS constitute the backbone of an educational institution. Besides developing courses and curricula, creating knowledge and disseminating that knowledge among the incoming generations of the mankind, the teachers mould the minds of the youngmen and the youngwomen and often leave an indelible imprint of their personalities on them. This is as much true of distance education as the conventional system. Even though the distance system is managed non-formally with the help of the written and the audio-video lessons, yet the teachers have an immense role to play. They write lessons for their students, prepare audio and video programmes, evaluate their home assignments, give counselling and do a number of other odd things for them. Their importance is further enhanced by the demanding nature of the distance learners. Being grown up adults and having a lot of life's experience (unlike the youngsters of the conventional system who are mostly empty vessels) and, above all, being seekers of knowledge/skills, they expect of their Institutes a reasonably good quality of the study material (Moore, 1987). Thus, teachers are as much central to this system as they are to the class-room based conventional system.

Unfortunately, many universities in India do not appreciate the need and relevance of a whole-time faculty for their Institutes of Distance Education. To illustrate, while the Barkatula and the SNDT provide for as small a faculty as 3 teachers each. The Madras Institute which has on its rolls 1,12,740 students, carries on with a faculty of just 21 teachers. (Bakshish Singh, 1994). These Institutes prefer to get their academic work done by the outside faculty on small contract basis. In justification of their position, these Institutes may advance high philosophical arguments. However, the underlying reason is that a whole-time faculty is too costly an institution which they cannot afford. (Inayat Khan, 1989 and Chan Dang Kim, 1988). In sum, these Institutes do not want to forego a part of their profits in order to create that facility which they can easily buy in the market at a far lesser monetary and administrative cost.

That distance education can be provided in a 'better' and more economical a manner seems to have led away many an Institute elsewhere in the world as well. Morrison and Saraswati, (1988) relate to us the Athabasca experience . To begin with, that University had decided to engage a faculty on hire and not to have one on permanent basis. "But operational difficulties developed none too soon. Some established academics of other institutions declined to write Athabasca courses because of commitments in their institutions. Of those who agreed to write failed to meet the deadlines. And for quite a few outside authors, the concept of distance was foreign and the course materials that they wrote were not acceptable to the institution. The University realised that it had to have a reasonable number of academics to its staff to write and produce courses" (p. 26). The experience of the IGNOU was none too different. It also had to go in for its own faculty sooner than later. Today, it has on its rolls a faculty of 137 teachers comprising, Professors: 20, Readers:29 and Lecturers:88. (Bakshish Singh, 1994).

Most of our Institutes which do not have a whole-time faculty are, however, unmindful of these difficulties. To them, not the quality of instruction but growing profits is a dominant concern. The chances of their revising the present position in favour of a full-fledged internal faculty of their own seem to be quite bleak unless they are compelled to do so by outside academic or funding agencies.

It may further be pointed out that those Institutes which maintain a very small internal faculty (as for instance Barkatula or SNDT) would perhaps have gone without this semblance even, had they not been driven to such a situation by certain administrative difficulties. This is evident from the nature of duties that the faculty performs. It is an open secret that the persons, who constitute the faculty, function less as teachers and more as liaison officers. Their job mainly consists of the indentification of the outside teachers and to assign to them lessons for writing, response sheets for evaluation and PCP classes to teach, and to ensure further that they complete their assignments in time. After the manuscripts have been received, these are then to be passed on to the printers and so on and so forth. Thus, they move back and forth between the outside teachers, on the one side, and the Institute's administrative office, on the other. Very seldom are they found either writing a lesson or teaching a class. Thus, they are teachers only in name.

Parallel to these Institutes, there are a few others which maintain a full fledged faculty of their own, comprising university professors, readers and lecturers. Besides catering to the manifold academic needs of these

Institutes, these teachers lend dignity and grace to them. For, an Institute's reputation depends upon the calibre of its faculty.

However, the bulk of their faculty comprises lecturers and readers, whereas professor's positions are comparatively very few. (See Table 8.1) It may be pointed out that if the number of the readers is somewhat impressive and if there also occur a few professor's positions, here and there, it is largely due to the U.G.C. sponsored merit-based promotion scheme under which many a lecturer has been promoted to a reader and the reader to a professor. But for it, there existed only lecturers and readers. (The number of the latter, as compared to the former was very small) The original scheme had provided mainly for lecturers and even junior lecturers.

**TABLE 8.1: Table showing the Faculty Position in various Institutes**

| Name of the | Total | Profes | Readers | Lecturers | Others |
|---|---|---|---|---|---|
| Delhi | 91 | 1* | 57 | 33 | — |
| Chandigarh | 71 | 3 | 27 | 37 | 4 |
| Patiala | 56 | 3 | 27 | 26 | — |
| Shimla | 38 | — | 4 | 34 | — |
| Kurukshetra | 14 | — | 2 | 12 | — |
| Jammu | 23 | — | 3 | 20 | — |

* Head of the School, bearing the designation of the Principal.

*Source*: Records of the respective university.

The question arises, when all these Institutes belonged to the universities, why were these faculties loaded with lecturers and junior lecturers only and why no provision was made for the professor's position and very meagre for reader's position? No one in authority has any explicit explanation to offer, nor have the office records of the universities or the Institutes anything to reflect. Nonetheless, it appears that the vested interests of the conventionalists may alone be held responsible for providing junior-grade teaching positions to these Institutes.

To dilate upon these vested interests, it is now an open secret that the introduction of correspondence education in India (which in fact had taken place as a result of some broad-based socio-economic compulsions of the nation as also of some difficulties of the local nature) was perceived by the conventional educationists as an encroachment upon, and a distortion of, that system of education which they had so diligently nursed over the decades and centuries. They resented, though in vain, that the opening of the portals of higher education to every Tom, Dick and Harry would denude the system of all that was good and worthwhile in it. Thus, irked over this development, they accorded to these Institutes the status of an ordinary degree college. They had thought that the new system was so much academically unsound that not many people would come forward to buy it and, as a result, these Institutes would end up as arts degree colleges at best. Since the concept of a university professor was then foreign to the college structure, the U.G.C. (which had come in due course of time to be the overall guardian of this component of the higher education as well) did not provide for professor's positions in the guidelines that it issued for the efficient functioning of these Institutes

On the contrary they made a lavish provision for lecturership. Ironically, some of these Institutes were robbed of the benefit of even the lectureships thanks to the vested interest at the local level. The opening of these Institutes provided to these vested interests a rich crop of lucerative faculty positions. Obviously, they were tempted to oblige their friends and relatives by accommodating on their faculty as many of them as possible. Since lecturer's positions did not provide much scope for back-door entry, they so manoeuvred the situation that they got many of these positions down-graded to junior-lecturerships and then got their henchmen adjusted against these positions. To begin with, 'their' persons were recruited on an ad hoc basis. With the passage of time, the services of these incumbents were regularised. Later on, when the Fourth Pay Commission effected a revision of the status and salary structure of the university and college teachers, all these junior lecturers stood automatically elevated to lecturers' status.

The predominance of lecturers and readers in our Institutes marks a serious contrast with many Institutes and Open Universities in India and abroad. The IGNOU, as stated above, has 20 professor and 29 Readers. The Y.C.Maharashtra Open University has 16 Professors in a faculty of 35 teachers (Bakshish Singh , 1994) The Japanese University of the Air had on its faculty 51 Professors and associate professors in 1982 which number was expected to rise to 75 by 1987 (Yoshiya Abe, 1988).

The prejudice of the conventionalists against this system is further manifest in their stubbonness not to grant higher academic positions to these Institutes even when most of them have added post-graduate sections to their existing study programmes. Instead of appreciating that these Institutes would then onward be doing teaching upto the same level and administering the same syllabus as the university departments did and should have thus made a provision for professors' positions, the U.G.C. continued to adhere to its older position. The staff structure that it suggested in its new guidelines (as revised in the mid-seventies) comprised three lecturers (assistant directors) and two readers (associate directors). They would exclusively take care of the post-graduate section. (Guidelines para 10.02). Again, professor's positions were left out .

All these factors combined together to conspire against the calibre of the faculty of these Institutes. Most of the teachers working in them are not as qualified as the requirements of distance education demand (Satyanarayana, 1992).

More deplorable than the attitude of the higher level decision-makers, is the step-motherly treatment that the parent universities give to the faculty of their own Institutes of Distance Education. In this context, we cite two instances. First, when the U.G.C. sponsored the Promotion Scheme, most of the universities (the Panjab, for instance) were reluctant to extend it to their Institutes' faculty, even when the latter was part and parcel of the general faculty of the university concerned and had been recruited in accordance with the established mode and pattern of the university and on the same basis and qualifications as the rest of the university faculty. A long and sustained battle had to be waged to persuade the decision-makers to bring the Institute's faculty under the purview of the Scheme.

Second, the universities do not treat the Institutes faculty at par with the rest of its faculty. The latter wear a halo of superiority around them and treat the latter as untouchables. These conventionalists never tolerate if any member of the Institute's faculty is transferred to their department and vice-versa. This touch-me-not attitude of the university faculty has resulted into water-tight compartmentalisation of the faculty. Though the departmental teachers lean heavily upon the Institute for providing to them teaching assistance whenever there is a temporary vacancy or a new course is introduced or any such contingency arises, they would otherwise look down upon the Institute's teachers.

In this way, we find that the conventionalists, whether operating at the higher echelons of decision-making such as the U.G.C. or at the lower levels of the universities, do not see kindly to this system. It appears that they are not going to relent their attitude in the near future. No wonder then if these Institutes might one day think in terms of severing their relationship with the conventional universities.

The Institute's faculty is generally given a separate entity within the overall frame-work of the university faculty. It is specially recruited for the Institute and sometimes on qualifications somewhat different from their counterparts in the university teaching departments. The latter practice is in vogue in those universities which accord to their Institutes the status of a degree college, whereas in those universities where their status has been elevated to that of a university department, this distinction has ceased to exist. However, the separate character of the faculty of the insti- tute continues to remain intact even after the elevation of its status, for the principle of either the inter-departmental transfers or the joint cadres (for the purpose of determining seniority of the teachers for the chairmanship of the subject departments) is generally not conceded. (The Shimla Institute may perhaps be the only exception in this case.)

But for these two distinctions, the Institute's faculty is completely at par with the rest of the university faculty. It is governed by the same nomenclature (lecturer, reader and professor), salary structure and the other service conditions. The departmental status has also fetched to them the membership of the various academic decision-making bodies of the university, such as the boards of studies, the joint research board, faculties and the academic council, which membership had been denied to them earlier under the college status.

As regards the nature of their work, the Institute's teachers, being distance educators, are supposed to perform three main functions, namely preparation of the study material, evaluation of response sheets and teaching at the PCP. Of these three, writing, vetting and updating of lessons form the main component of their responsibility. For, the Institutes having not so far fully adopted the modern electronic instructional technology, they continue to impart distance instruction through the medium of the written lesson-scripts only. As a result, they keep themselves occupied with this work for the better part of the year. As per the guidelines of the U.G.C. (or as modified by the various Institutes themselves in order to suit to their local needs and requirements) a teacher is given one week to write a lesson, irrespective of the level of the course (under-graduate or post-graduate) and again three days to vet the lesson (Guidelines Annexure: para 1). One week-period is too short to do full justice to develop from the scratch a full-length lesson, particularly for the post-graduate classes. Though teachers invariably take a longer time, there is a case for the formal revision of this particular guideline.

Those Institutes which enjoy the hospitality of the All-India Radio (AIR) also require their teachers to write and broadcast talks to their students. Since these radio broadcasts are primarily the AIR show, this activity does not form an obligatory part of their responsibilities. The

AIR offers contracts to those individual teachers who willingly accept this offer. Sometimes the outside teachers are also roped in by the AIR either on its own or at the instance of the Institutes authorities. Some of the Institutes, as mentioned in an earlier chapter, have also gone in for the TV and the video technology (though in a restricted manner). They also expect their teachers to involve themselves in developing and producing video lessons for their students. By and large, the teachers are not very enthusiastic to accept this responsibility.

The second major activity of the Institute's teachers is to evaluate students' response sheets. The U.G.C. prescribes 16 response sheets of the under-graduate classes as a day's quota of each teacher (Guidelines Annexure: Para 5). As far as the post-graduate classes are concerned, these guidelines are silent. However, the various Institutes have developed their own norms within the framework of these Guidelines. The response sheets that exceed a day or week's quota of the departmental teachers are got evaluated from the outside teachers on a payment basis. In certain Institutes the teachers have staked their claim to this remunerative work. The Jammu and the Patiala Institutes are reported to have conceded this demand of their teachers. On the theoretical plane, the case both for and against this demand/suggestion, is strong. These teachers' argument is that their commitment to the students, their expertise in this field and their availability on the spot for this task will go a long way in improving the quality of evaluation as also in cutting down the delay quite considerably. On the other side, doubts are expressed whether such a practice may not lead to some sort of bungling and corruption. These doubt apart, this 'back-door method' of lining the pockets of the Institute's teachers would be highly resented by the rest of the faculty of the university. The critics also wonder whether the quality of the work would improve or gets degenerated. These arguments on either side notwithstanding, no uniform policy has so far emerged. Only a few Institutes have adopted the practice of entrusting the work to their own teachers, whereas most of them get it done from outside.

The third aspect of the teachers' responsibility is the teaching in the PCP's. On an average, a teacher is required to do teaching for a month or so and that too in two or three short spells. As for their day's quota of teaching, it generally consists of one to three periods of 40 minutes to one hour duration each. When on PCP duty, they are not supposed to do any other work. In other words, a teacher is supposed to do one thing at a time. He may write/vet a lesson, evaluate response sheets or teach in the PCP.

As highlighted earlier, these Institutes do not make a distinction among professors, readers, lecturers and the others in so far as the allocation of work among them is concerned. Everyone is treated alike and must perform the same duties that his colleagues, junior as well as senior to him, perform. This practice is not very conducive for the overall health of the Institute. For, the expertise and experience of professors and readers is wasted on such pedestrian activities as evaluation of response sheets and teaching in the PCP. On the other hand, the involvement of the junior faculty in the preparation of the study material is to risk the quality of this work. Granville Rumble (1992) rightly points out, "As course numbers increase... the teaching role has to be divided between teachers who plan the courses and develop the materials, and those who tutor the students." (pp.17-18). It is high time that these Institutes consider the suggestion of bifurcation of the roles of their teachers into developing the study materials and the evaluation of response sheets and teaching in the PCP's.

## II

With the passage of time, it is being increasingly realised that distance education is a highly specialised task and thus those teachers who are inducted into it need to be given pre-entry training and in-service refresher courses, summer schools and periodic seminars. It is pointed out that not only is the technique of lesson writing for distance learners is different from either the conventional classroom teaching or the writing of a text-book, but evaluation of response sheets is an equally difficult task, requiring the expertise of a specialist. The ushering in of the era of modern electronic-based instructional technologies has further drawn the distance educator away from the conventional teacher. In the Indian context, the need for training is felt all the more acutely in view of the far-from satisfactory study material that these Institutes have been producing (Arun K.Gupta, 1988).

Keeping these hard realities in view, the U.G.C. has of late been impressing upon these Institutes and their parent universities that "staff development is of utmost necessity for the teachers and administrators of CCI/DDE's", which area has unfortunately "been neglected and (hence) calls for serious attention." In a recent communique to the Vice-Chancellors of some of the universities, the U.G.C. has commended to them the recommendations of a high power Working Group, constituted by it to look into the working of the distance education system in the country. Being the first-ever comprehensive set of recommendations, made in this behalf, its relevant excerpts need to be reproduced at length. They are, as follows.

1. 'Now that we have regular courses like the IGNOU Diploma and M.A. in Distance Education, the staff members should be required to do one of these courses... Now that IGNOU has decided to set up a Distance Education Training Institute (STRIDE) we can expect extensive staff training facilities in due course of time'.
2. 'As short-term measures to meet the immediate needs of staff development' steps should be taken to organise 'intensive orientation programmes to familiarise teachers with the various aspects of distance education system'.
3. 'As long-term measures, there is an urgent need for ..organising intensive workshops in different regions for providing comprehensive orientation and skills to the CCI teachers, concerning the various aspects of distance education system with special emphasis on the transformation of printed course material into selfinstructional distance education format and improvement of the contents of the lessons. At each of these workshops a few lessons of the participating institutes could be improved upon so that these might serve as model lessons....'.
   (Letter of the Deputy Secretary ,U.G.C., December, 1993).

Though some action has begun to be taken on these recommendations (as is evident from the workshops that are being currently organised in the various Institutes to convert the existing study material into self-learning distance education format), the requisite degree of earnestness with which the training programme ought to have been taken up, is somehow missing. Both the Institutes and the teachers thereof take this exercise very casually. As for the pre-entry training courses, plenty of which are now available in the country, but they go largely unutilised. Unless the various inhibiting factors are removed, the need for training would remain a wishful thinking while the various training facilities would go a begging. What are those inhibiting factors?

Those persons who are already in the employ of these Institutes do not feel the necessity for any such training. On their own, they are little conscious that the work that they have been doing is deficient in any way and requires any type of improvement. They have developed such an attitude partly because of the deep-rooted sense of complacency on their part and partly because of the non-existence of any such system of the feedback about the quality of the lessons as their review by outside subject specialists or their pre- testing on a random sample of students. If anyone dares to offer some comment on the study materials that they produce many of them would either laugh it away or brush it aside scornfully; only a very few of them would lend their ear to him. With this given attitude of complacency who would buy the idea of training or even of periodic refresher courses?

In this context, the experience of the Panjab University Department of Political Science with the U.G.C. sponsored CHSSIP (College of Humanities and Social Sciences Improvement Programme) is worth relating. Under that Programme, the University faculty of the Department concerned (with which this author had also had the privilege of being associated) would organise from time to time a series of refresher courses, sometimes at the headquarters and sometimes in other towns. It would take due care to ensure that these courses were held at a time when the teachers were not busy with their class-work or were not vacationing at home lest they should have a valid reason for their non-participation. In the course of five years that Programme lasted what we witnessed was that the same old faces of the young and the newly-recruited lecturers would show up in the class room, time and again. On the other hand, the older persons, occupying senior positions on their faculty, would seldom take the trouble of attending those courses. In fact, these courses had been designed more for their benefit in view of their non-familiarity with those concepts which had been introduced in the discipline only too recently. But they on their part would consider it beneath their dignity to sit on the benches and listen to the teachers like school children. Moreover, where was after all the need for them to suffer the 'humiliation' of that exercise of learning these new concepts, when whatever little knowledge they had acquired in their good old school and college days could help them carry on their work without any loss or disadvantage of any type to them.

The moral of the story is that our college teachers have, by and large, lost the zeal to learn. Nothing supports this conclusion better than the demand of the Haryana College Teachers (put up in 1994-95) for the waiving of the condition of their participation in refresher courses/summer schools for their promotion to the higher position. It appears that distinctive trait which had put the teachers on a pedestal higher than the rest of the society, appears to have faded out. The 'student' in them is gone, leaving behind a lifeless and inert soul capable of pursuing only that which fetches to them immediate gains in monetary terms. Ironically, whatever little urge to read and write that they had, has been mercilessly curbed by the new promotion policy whereunder one moves up the professional hierarchy (comprising such levels as lecturer, senior lecturer, selection-scale lecturer, reader and professor) less by hard work and more on the basis of one's seniority in service. Why should one forego exhilarating social activities and sit in the dark and isolated cabins of the library and pour oneself over books for hours together when one is going to be rated at par with the marry-go-round lot? This policy has thus done greater harm than good to the profession.

A mention also needs to be made to the much trumpeted course on Distance Education that the IGNOU has instituted. There is no gain saying the fact that the course has been imaginatively conceived and comprehensively designed. But the tragedy is two-fold, those who are in the profession already do not buy it while those who join it are not suitably rewarded. As pointed out earlier, the distance teachers of our country do not feel the need for any such training/refresher course, partly because of too much complacency on their part and partly because of the misplaced priorities of the profession. However, not all the teachers have become corrupt and perverted. The number of those who are committed both to the profession and to their own academic betterment is still large. Many among them may like to go in for this IGNOU course. But the question arises, what would they gain out of it? They would neither get any additional increment in their salary, nor would this additional feather in their cap be given any recognition at the time of their promotion to the next step in the professional hierarchy. No one would ever take note of their having done that course. Instead, if one goes in for M.Phil or Ph.D. in his parent discipline, he would be amply rewarded for it. These priorities of the profession thus make one think increasingly in terms of investing one's time in Ph.D. than in the IGNOU course on Distance Education.

The experience of the freshers who completed this course is no different. In a country like India where unemployment is rampant, any course which gives even a faint idea of providing to its takers some employment sells like hot potatoes, especially in its initial stages. When the IGNOU advertised this course on Distance Education a large number of students felt attracted towards it with the hope that it would brighten their prospects for teaching jobs in the Institutes of Distance Education. But when they passed out, they discovered to their great chagrin that jobs even in these Institutes were given to those who have distinctive qualification (master degree in first or high second class, M.Phil or Ph.D.) in their respective disciplines rather than to the degree holders in Distance Education. The latter qualification might at best be rated as subsidiary or complementary in nature. The course thus lost its initial luster.

If we are keen to provide training to our distance educators, the only way we can hope to achieve this objective is to institute suitable incentives for those who go in for it. In the first instance, we should provide one or two additional increments in the salary of those who successfully complete a course in Distance Education, may be from of the IGNOU or any other such reputed institute or university. Secondly, such qualifications as participation in one or two refresher courses or workshops relating to distance education should be linked with one's promotion from one position to another on the same pattern as subject-related refresher courses. Finally, these should be organised from time to time subject workshops of two to three weeks duration at regional level and participation of all teachers should be made obligatory may be on a rotational basis. Unless steps on these lines are urgently taken the situation may deteriorate fast.

## III

The issue that needs to be further looked into at some length is why do most of the teachers working in these Institutes feel alienated from the system? (A reference to this fact has already been made). The issue assumes importance in view of the fact that the degree of contentment of those who work the system determines the level of their morale and, in turn, the overall efficiency of the system concerned.

One main reason of their unhappiness is that almost all the teachers of these Institutes have come from the conventional system. Their having been bred and brought up in that system has provided to them an orientation which ill-fits into the new system of distance education. The demands that the latter system makes upon them are different from those of the conventional system. Obviously, those who presently work in this system were not initially familiar to the responsibilities that it entails. Even now they are not mentally prepared to fulfil them. This chasm between their orientation and the nature of their responsibilities lies at the root of their unhappiness. They may write lessons (perhaps not very satisfactory), evaluate response sheets, and teach in the PCP's. But beyond that the interest of the rank and file among them appears to be just marginal.

Pandey (1992) complains, "Teachers do not generally evince a high level of involvement in the programme and most of them are not quite naturally drawn towards the various assignments and activities associated with planning, designing and implementing educational process in this channel".

However, this is not a peculiar feature of the distance teachers of India only. Elsewhere too such situations of unhappiness on the part of the teachers were noticed when they switched over from the conventional system to distance education system. Otto Peters (1988) tells us how they confronted the problem of dichotomy in its instructional system when they started the Fernuniverstat in Germany. He says, "Scientific knowledge was to be taught according to the same regulations for examinations and according to the same standards as at the other universities of our country.... Now in the new institution, the Professors were expected to adapt their teaching to an entirely new situation. In order to be able to increase the availability and accessibility of academic teaching, they were to accept new systems of organising and communicating. In other words, they had to get acquainted and actually learn to deal with important aspects of instructional technology. The structural antagonism inherent in such a plan is obvious—as most professors disregard and reject activities such as curriculum construction, the use of technical media, tests and systematic evaluation. I believe the real accomplishment of the Fernuniverstat is that this antagonism could be overcome to a large degree." (p.82).

Apart from their being new to the system, the method of evaluating the performance of distance teachers, particularly for the purpose of their promotion from one level of their hierarchy to another, also contributes in no small a measure to their sense of divided loyalties to this system. Like their counterparts in the conventional system, their performance is also judged by the contribution they make to their respective disciplines by doctoral and post-doctoral work. On this account, they generally tend to be weak and hence prone to lag behind the others. In justification of this weakness, they adduce the argument that their being too much occupied with the work of designing and preparation of the courses and interaction with technical consultants for the preparation of multi-media packages leaves but little time with them for their professional development in (their) own discipline." (Rudra Datt, 1993).

The inhospitable treatment that their parent universities meets out to them further adds to the woes of these teachers. As highlighted earlier, most of the universities accord to these Institutes the status of a degree college which status if judged in the context of the Indian university system, is considered somewhat inferior to a university department. The psychological dimensions of this distinction apart, the benefits accruing to the teachers of the departments (as for example automatic representation on various academic bodies) are denied to the teachers of these Institutes.

Thus, the causes of unhappiness of the teachers are rooted in the organic nature of their relationship with their parent universities. Compared to them, the teachers of the Open Universities do not appear to be as unhappy as the Institutes' teachers are and, as a result, the morale of the former is also comparatively high. For, the Open University teachers are neither required to compete against those who belong to a different stream, nor does their parent university give a raw deal to them in such matters as membership of the various academic decision-making bodies or overlooking their difficulties. Being the only one on the faculty of their university, these distance teachers are the master of their own affairs. They do not play a second fiddle to anyone else. Thus the question of their being slighted or hoodwinked by anyone else does not arise. On the contrary, the main problem of the Institute's teachers is that being marginal in strength on the overall faculty of the university, they are to depend upon the goodwill (albeit, mercy) of the conventionalists who predominate every aspect of the university's decision-making. They cannot, therefore, ever hope to turn a corner so long as they live under the 'benign' dominance of the conventionalists. Is then deliverance from the conventional system the only solution of their present woes? (We examine this issue at length in one of the subsequent chapters).

However so long as these organic linkages remain intact, it becomes obligatory on the part of the university authorities that they should take some steps to mitigate the sense of discrimination that has seaped into the soul of the teachers of these Institutes. In the first place, they should review the issue of the status of these Institutes. Since the college status is perceived by them as inferior to their dignity and nature of work, it should be withdrawn and some other status which may meet the demands and aspirations of their teachers should be granted to them. A note of caution may however be added that while reviewing the issue of the status consideration must also be given to the needs and requirement of the institute at large. (We discuss this issue as well at a later stage).

Secondly, the criterion of their promotion from one cadre to another should also be given a second thought. The merits of their argument that they do not get time for research notwithstanding, there is a strong case for giving due weightage to the literature that they produce for distance students in the form of written lessons, audio talks and video programmes (which literature is also invariably used very profitably by the students and even by the teachers of the conventional system). There is no denying the fact that writing a lesson is not only a difficult task but time-consuming as well. Granville Rumble (1992) quotes Sparkes who says, "Developing a teaching text which takes the equivalent of one hour's student work require 50 to 100 hours of academic time; an hour's broadcast quality television require 200 hours of academic time" (p.55).

Another fact that cannot be overlooked is that some of the literature produced by these academics is of a very high standard, and in certain cases, it is quite original. Not to take this literature into consideration is to do great injustice to the teachers. It may be emphasised that once this literature begins to be taken due cognisance for promotion purposes, the teachers of the Institute would begin taking greater interest in its preparation. Incidentally the quality of the study materials would also improve.

Thirdly, the principle of inter-departmental transfers should be conceded. Not only the deep-seated grievance of these teachers will be redressed but they would also be exposed to class-room teaching, which, in turn, would goad them to extensive reading and research. At the same time, the class-room teachers would get to know how to transcribe their oral knowledge into written lessons, thereby sharing their wisdom and experience with distance learners. Thus, this system of rotation would prove to be beneficial to both the wings of the university. The standard of instruction in the class-rooms as well as in the distance mode would improve. To a question about the desirability of the exchange of teachers between the Institute and University Departments and Open Universities and Conventional Universities, "66 per cent of the Institute's teachers and 83 per cent of O.U.teachers who favoured the idea, opined that the transfers/exchange would enhance efficiency in teaching at both the places." (Bakshish Singh, 1994). Such a healthy practice is already in vogue in many universities of the world. The most prominent example is that of the Deakin University (Australia) which combines on-campus teaching (class-room based) with off-campus teaching (distance mode). The same academics who teach the classes also write lessons for off-campus students.

Finally, representation should be given to these teachers in various academic bodies of the university (such as Board of Studies, Joint Research Board, Faculties, Academic Council and Senate) on the same pattern as to the departmental teachers. Besides redressing yet another grievance of theirs, such a step would enable them to look after the interests of their system and of the distance learners in a better way.

These small steps will go a long way in toning up the teachers' psychology, thereby creating healthy environments of work for them. Then there is no reason why their morale and consequently their performance does not show improvement. However, it must be underlined that these steps in themselves would fall short of an ideal solution which perhaps lies in the overall reorganisation of the system of distance education in the country as a whole.

## IV

The argument that teachers of these Institutes advance in defence of their being weak in research activities also needs to be objectively examined. As alluded above, these teachers put forward the plea that distance teaching, and more specifically writing of lessons, is so demanding in nature that they are not left with enough time to do research and such like other academically fruitful activities. The question arises, is it really a valid argument?

There are no two opinions that writing, compared to reading, is both a difficult and time-consuming task. To produce a first-rate lesson requires the author, first, to prepare a bibliography of literature on the subject and then to get those books and learned articles. Poor maintenance of our libraries makes the tracing and procuring of the literature a difficult task. After the literature is procured, the author will scan through it and brush up his knowledge. The stage is now set for him to construct the broad outlines of the script. At this stage, he might like to have consultation with his colleagues. Once all these preliminaries are over, he will set himself to writing and develop the script step by step. He will take his own time, depending upon the nature of the subject, level of the course, his own competence and the mood. In this way, we find that writing a lesson involves a good deal of hard work, extensive reading, concentration of mind and, above all, desk work. Thus these teachers are not wrong in their assertion that the time and energy that they spend on this work, if invested in research, they too can produce as good research papers and theses as their counterparts of the conventional system do.

These critics, while not doubting the difficult and the time-consuming nature of the lesson-writing work, do, however pose certain questions. They ask how many lessons does a distance teacher produce every year? Does he keep himself busy with this task all through the three hundred and sixty-five days of the year? They further point out that since the syllabi of the various courses (language courses may be an exception) do not undergo changes so frequently, lessons once written can be (and in fact are) serviced for a number of years, with minor changes/modifications here and there. It is only rarely that the existing lessons are vetted whole-sale or discarded altogether. Thus to maintain that these teachers remain too occupied in the writing of lessons is not too convincing an argument.

As regards their submission that writing a lesson requires a good deal of hard work, the critics do not deny this fact as well. But again their rejoinder is that if a teacher proceeds as systematically as described above, he would produce a first-rate lesson. But the type of lessons that these Institutes service to their students do not bear a testimony to the fact that enough time and labour has gone into their production. They are a sad commentary of slipshod work, done by a casual and indifferent mind. The critics do concede that there are some lessons which are undoubtedly outstanding in nature, and they do speak of the high caliber and hard work of their authors. But the number of such lessons is far too small. Thus, the gist of the critics' counter-argument is that the Institute's teachers, by and large, do not utilize their time in a worthwhile academic manner and that their plea for not doing research is not very sound and valid.

We do not go into the merits of these arguments and, instead, dilate upon the nature of the work that Institute's teachers do. As highlighted earlier, there are two major duties that they perform — lesson-writing and response sheet evaluation. Lesson-writing, even if done in a half-hearted manner, is undoubtedly difficult and takes a lot of time and labour. But this is a work which everyone does not do all the time. Lessons are written only when either the syllabus changes whole-sale or the subject matter of an existing lesson becomes too stale and out-dated. What a distance teacher does every year and which ties him down for a better part of the academic session, is the vetting and up-dating of the existing lessons. This is a work the intensity of which ranges from fundamental changes to simply appending the remarks 'vetted and may be printed'. A conscientious teacher may read it between the lines and may bring about changes and modifications, wherever he finds the need for them. In the process, he might substitute paragraph after paragraph with new subject matter, with fresh data, with new commentaries and so on, thereby giving to the script a new look altogether. On the other hand, a 'care-free' person may not open the script and even cut its edges and yet pass it on for printing. The former who spends the two or three weeks, allotted to him for this work, in a highly busy manner, may not find this period short, but the latter would certainly do, for he is 'too busy' with many other activities. The lack of accountability in the system breeds the number of the latter.

Thus, a distance teacher can conveniently evade his responsibility which his counterpart in the conventional system cannot afford to do. The latter must take his class every day and must go thoroughly prepared for it, lest some student may create some embarrassment for him in the class. As for the distance students, their being new to the system as also their being shut in remote, isolated hamlets, renders them too incapable to create embarrassing situations for their teachers. Their mature and respectful nature further inhibits them from indulging into any such unbecoming activity. They mutely accept the lessons without any murmur or objection.

The second aspect of distance teacher's duty is the evaluation of response sheets. Here too the quality of evaluation varies from teacher to teacher. A committed person may give profound remarks, pointing out the deficiencies in the script and also helping the student to overcome them. His remarks may run into a few paragraphs even. On the other hand, there may be a teacher who dismisses a response sheet in less than five minutes. He would put a few ticks here and there and may give such stray and out of the context remarks as 'good' 'satisfactory', 'work hard', etc.etc. In this way, we find that the nature of their work is such that it leaves a wide scope for the Institute's teachers to do their work in a slipshod manner if anyone of them so chooses.

The wide scope for shirking their responsibilities when viewed in the context of such other factors as sub-standard recruitment, absence of the challenge of active class-room teaching, lack of accountability in the system at large, etc.etc. generates a climate more conducive for gossip than for research. Obviously most of the teachers tend to be polluted by that climate. This is the reason why most of our Institutes of Distance Education reflect the atmosphere of a typical under-graduate college rather than of a university teaching department. Seminars, learned lectures, academic discussions and such other activities as are characteristic of a teaching department are conspicuous by their absence in the Institute.

Notwithstanding the image of the Institute that is thus tarnished, what should actually worry the authorities as well as all other well-wishers of the system is the growing tendency of academic sluggishness on the part of its teachers. They have lost the urge to learn. It is an open secret that a teacher is goaded to extensive reading partly because of his urge for research and partly because of his desire to face his students effectively with a good grip on his subject. The Institute's teachers are lucky not to face the inquisitive students. As for the urge for research, the Institute's atmosphere does not allow that urge to take birth in their mind. Those teachers of the Institute who conduct research (luckily there is no dearth of them) owe this interest to their pre-Institute days. If early steps are not taken to curb this rising tide of academic sluggishness, distance lessons will be deprived of good and the latest knowledge and the Institute may have then to seek an increasing assistance from the outside teachers. It is in the context of this situation that the suggestion of inter-departmental transfers calls for a serious thought.

It hardly needs to be emphasised that research has a very close bearing on one's quality of teaching and, more specifically, in the writing of lessons for distance students. Not only does research inculcate in a teacher the undying habit of reading and writing but also goes a long way in continuously reinforcing his knowledge on the subject. Above all, he learns the art of processing and interpreting the data, and arguing his viewpoint in a more cogent manner. Thus, research is all the more necessary and useful for distance teachers. This is the reason why we recommend that the work of the preparation of the study material should be entrusted to the exclusive care of the senior faculty of readers and professors. It may further be relevantly pointed out that those lessons which are rated very high in quality are invariably the product of the labour of the professors and readers and those who have the credit of having done extensive research in their respective fields. Thus, it becomes all the more imperative that healthy conditions conducive for research should be created in these Institutes.

We may further venture to suggest that the qualifications for the recruitment of teachers for these Institutes in particular should be made more stringent than for the departmental teachers and that the universities concerned should take due care and caution to keep the vested interests at bay lest they should play with the destinies of these Institutes. The present attitude of treating them as the 'pocket boroughs' of the Institute's director, syndics, senators and the governmental high-ups should be given a good-bye as early as possible. Already much harm has been done to these Institutes.

## V

Finally, the issue that needs to be considered at length is whether or not an Institute should have an independent whole-time faculty of its own. That both these practices of having and not having their own faculty have been in vogue all over the world and, further, that those who have one and those who do not have any are satisfied in their own way, makes this issue both interesting and controversial, hence demanding an in-depth analysis.

First to look at those Institutes which do not maintain their own faculty. As mentioned earlier, they get their lessons written, response sheets evaluated and PCP taught by the outside teachers on contractual basis. They assert that "the system that we use, by necessity gives (us) the flexibility to find the best author, editor and tutor for the job and it also enables us to meet deadlines by placing work with freelance people who can handle it in the time allotted." (Ros Morpeth, 1990). Conversely, they do not bind themselves with one set of permanently employed teachers. The freedom that they thus enjoy to hire any teacher whom they find competent for their work, further enhances their scope for adopting the team approach in the development of the study materials. This freedom is somehow not available to those institutes which engage a whole-time faculty. For, they are to depend, *ipso facto*, on their own faculty and, further on their distribution pattern of work. Invariably, the distribution pattern makes for the individual author approach. The non-faculty Institutes, thus, have an advantage of adopting the team approach, which, as mentioned earlier, has an edge over the individual author approach.

It is further contended that persons when permanently employed (may those be the teachers or anyone else) become more assertive of their rights and dues and comparatively less conscious of their obligations toward their Institute. Besides creating problems of administrative nature to the employer, they tend to neglect their work, thus jeopardising the quality of the study material. This type of a situation is not to be confronted by the non-faculty Institutes. Above all the latter also save a sizeable chunk of their finances, for a whole-time faculty is far too costly an institution.

The full-fledged faculty Institutes, on the other hand, assert their independence and self-sufficiency. They further emphasise that the faculty constitutes the back-bone of an educational institution and that those Institutes which do not have a faculty of their own do not deserve to be described as such. Undoubtedly, there is a weight in this viewpoint For, social respectability of an educational institution is directly correlated to the calibre and status of its teachers. If the university departments have an edge over the post-graduate colleges, the reason is that the faculty of the former consists of professors and readers, and further these teachers, more often than not, are such persons who have carved out for themselves by their hard work and research a dignified place in the world of academics.

Public image apart, there are a number of academic and administrative problems which an internal faculty is alone competent to handle. One such problem relates to the timely preparation of the study material. Lack of control over the outside teachers, on the one hand, and the tendency of the higher decision-making bodies of the university to delay the finalisation of syllabi of the various courses, on the other, expose the non-faculty Institutes to the danger of delay in the timely preparation of the study material. If the Institute has its own faculty, such contingencies can be overcome easily.

As has been repeatedly emphasised earlier, lesson-writing for distance learners is a highly technical job which teachers of the conventional system cannot do it with that degree of fineness and competence as those who have been in the system for some time. Apart from being technical, a lesson must also meet the requirements and aspirations of the distance learners. Only those teachers who maintain a continuous touch with distance learners and get a regular feedback from them alone qualify themselves to write lessons for them. It has often been observed that lessons written by the outsiders are either too tough or too soft for distance learners. Before these are administered to them, these are toned up/ down so as to answer their needs suitably. If an Institute does not have its own faculty, who would judge the quality of those lessons? That is the reason why in most of the non-faculty Institutes of this country, lessons are straightaway mailed to their users as soon as they are received from their authors, thus reducing the role of the Institute to a mere administrative agency. Such lessons especially when go unscrutinised by any responsible person, generally ill-fit into the needs of the distance learners, forcing them to depend on other extraneous sources for help.

Yet another problem which non-faculty Institutes are incapable to handle suitably is that of academic guidance or individualised tutoring to the students. As highlighted earlier, besides PCP, students seek the personal guidance of their teachers especially when the examinations draw close at hand. During that period tens of students pour into the teacher's cabins everyday, seeking their help and guidance. More often than not, they come without any prior intimation to them. It is only the Institute's teachers who being the employees of the Institute, can make themselves available to the students at all hours of the day and, more importantly, who being fully conversant with the study material, on the one hand, and the student's needs, on the other, can alone satisfy them. The outsiders are too ill-equipped for the job.

The argument that the non-faculty Institutes are better placed to employ the corporate method for the preparation of the study material, is not supported by the practice and tradition of this country. As pointed out earlier, the team approach is just foreign to us. All Institutes, whether with a faculty or without it, assign their lesson-writing work to individuals only. If the non-faculty Institutes are also to adopt the individual author's approach, then there is hardly a point for their not having a faculty of their own.

Concludingly, it may be observed that no clear-cut judgment can be passed about the merits of the one system and demerits of the other. Arguments on both the sides are weighly and cogent. However, the argument of the non-faculty Institutes that their method of getting the various academic activities performed by the outsiders, gives to them the freedom to adopt the corporate approach in lesson-preparation, cannot be refuted at least on theoretical grounds. In the same manner, there also appears to be a lot of truth when they point out that permanently employed persons become after some time more assertive of their rights and that they also develop tendencies to neglect their work. On the other side, the immense benefits accruing from a full fledged faculty of its own cannot be denied. Keeping all these facts in view, the method of 'the golden mean' needs to be adopted . An Institute should have a core faculty comprising preferably two senior and one junior teachers in order to review the lessons and to provide on the spot guidance to the students. They should not, however, be goaded actively in the performance of either the preparation of the study material or the evaluation of the response sheets. These activities should be left for the outsiders. However, a rider must be put that the Institute would employ the corporate method for the preparation of the study material. It is only on this condition that the Institute should be exempted from the burden of the faculty. This type of an arrangement appears to be the only viable solution.

## REFERENCES

Abe, Yoshiya, 'The Japanese University of the Air', Reddy, G. Ram. (Ed.) *Open Universities, Ivory Towers Thrown Open.* Delhi, Sterling. 1988.

Bakshish Singh, Saroj Mullick and Neelam Chaudhary, *Correspondence/Distance Education in India, An Indepth Study Covering the Year 1989-90.* B.N.Koul (Ed.) IGNOU. 1994

Dutt, Ruddar, Open Universities versus Distance Education Directorates. Keynote address to a seminar on distance education, organised by the Punjabi University, Patiala. October, 1993.(Unpublished)

Dutt, Ruddar, Distance Education versus Traditional Higher Education. Koul, B.N., Bakshish Singh and Ansari, M.M. (eds.) *Studies in Distance Education*. New Delhi, Association of Indian University and IGNOU, 1988.

Gupta, Arun K. and Gupta, Annu. 'Training of Distance Educators Progress and Prospects.' *Indian Journal of Distance Education*. Vol.II.(1988).

Khan, Inayat, 'Why Students Dropout from Correspondence Courses' Khan, Inayat (Ed.) *Teaching at a Distance*. Delhi, Amar Prakashan. 1989.

Kim, Chan Dong, The Korean Air and Correspondence University, Reddy, G. Ram (Ed.) *Op.cit.*

Letter of Dr. R.P. Gangurde, Additional Secretary U.G.C. to Vice-Chancellors, D.O. No.F-3-14/93 (NFE-II), December, 1993.

Moore, Michael G., 'Learners and Learning at a Distance'. *ICDE Bulletin* No.14. (1987).

Morepeth, Ross, 'How the National Extension College Approaches Course Development. *ICDE Bulletin* No. 23. (1990).

Morrison, Terrance R. and Saraswati, Deepak, 'Athabasca University-Responding and Adapting to Change', Reddy, G. Ram (Ed.) *Op. cit.*

Pandey, K.P., 'Distance Education, A new scenario and the problems with reference to quality of Distance Education.' *Report of the NIEPA Workshop* (1992).

Peters, Otto, 'Tradition And innovation - the Fernuniverstat in Hagen', in Reddy, G. Ram (Ed.) *Op. cit.*

Rumble, Granville, *The Management of Distance Learning System*. Paris, UNESCO International Institute of Educational Planning 1992.

Satyanarayan, P., 'Distance Education in India, Some Concerns'. *Kaktiya Journal*. Vol.1, No.1. (1992).

U.G.C. Guidelines for the Introduction of Correspondence Courses, 1976.

CHAPTER IX

# FINANCES AND FINANCIAL ADMINISTRATION

FINANCIAL administration of an ordinary educational institution is simple accounts-keeping of a typical routine nature. It is neither elaborate in size nor technical in operation. Whatever little income accrues to it by way of the student fees (the only source of its income) is credited to the government exchequer/institution's bank account and the deficit (a normal feature) is met by the state, irrespective of the consideration whether or not the institution concerned is owned by the government. In a welfare state, education of the citizens is the responsibility of the state; finance and its management do not, therefore, cause much concern to an educational institution. However, the Institutes of Distance Education are somewhat differently oriented. The general impression that this system is capable of providing low cost education, in view of its being based on the economies of scale, forces the Institutes to devise ways and means how to limit the expenditure to its bare minimum and enhance their income to the maximum, so that they may be able to generate at best some income or at worst be self-supporting in nature. Though it has clouded the vision of every Institute, this perception is not only ill-founded but also deeply harmful to both the Institute and the system at large. For, this pursuit makes the former compromise with the quality of its instruction and the latter lose its credibility.

## II

The annual budgetary turnover of an Institute of Distance Education generally runs into a few hundred thousands of rupees. However, there are some Institutes (as for example Madras, Delhi, and Anamalai) whose budgets cross even eight digits. (Table 9.1)

These Institutes derive their income, mainly, from two sources—student fees, and sales and savings. If the income from these sources falls

**TABLE 9.1: Income, Expenditure and Savings/Deficit of some of the Institutes**

| S.No. | Institute | Year | Income | Expenditure | Surplus/ Deficit |
|---|---|---|---|---|---|
| 1. | Chandigarh † | 1994-95 | 162.36 | 270.40 | — 108.04 |
| 2. | Delhi † | 1994-95 | 220.89 | 474.40 | — 253.51 |
| 3. | Patiala † | 1994-95 | 84.97 | 126.77 | — 41.80 |
| 4. | Kurukshetra † | 1994-95* | 90.56 | 26.91 | + 63.65 |
| 5. | Shimla † | 1994-95 | 200.36 | 176.25 | + 24.11 |
| 6. | Madras‡ | 1989-90 | 1,401.85 | 993.83 | + 408.02 |
| 7. | Annamalai‡ | 1989-90 | 679.97 | 663.89 | + 16.08 |
| 8. | Bombay † | 1989-90 | 94.56 | 47.02 | + 47.54 |
| 9. | Venkateshwar‡ | 1989-90 | 14.92 | 6.53 | + 8.39 |
| 10. | Madurai Kamraj‡ | 1989-90 | 263.45 | 275.50 | — 12.05 |
| 11. | Barkatulla‡ | 1989-90 | 42.71 | 60.21 | — 17.50 |

* This statement pertains to the courses started upto 1993-94.

*Sources:* † Unpublished Annual Financial Statements of the Institutes
‡ Bakshish Singh, *et al*, Research Report.

short of their expenditure, (which in most of the cases it does), the deficit is met by the parent university out of the maintenance grants that it receives from the Government. As for their own individual contribution, the student fees account for a share, ranging from 53.84 per cent of the whole (Chandigarh) to 100 per cent (Kurukshetra) (Table 9.2). Ansari's study also corroborates this fact. It reveals that, on an average, the student fees contribute 80 per cent (as based on the 1980-81 statistics), the lowest being 29 per cent in the case of the Delhi Institute and the highest 100 per cent in the Cochin Institute. The position remains, by and large, intact even in 1986-87 with the average of 74.10 per cent, he adds (Ansari, 1992).

The second internal source comprises the sale proceeds of the Institute's prospectus, study materials, waste paper and the like, and the interest on the securities and the other savings. The contribution of this source is rather insignificant. In 1994-95, it was 2.50 per cent in Chandigarh and 6.52 per cent in Patiala. Ansari puts it at 9.14 per cent (1980-81).

As regards the external support, some Institutes have so managed their internal resources that they do not need any assistance at all either from their parent university or from the Government. Instead, they generate so much of income from within themselves either by charging exorbitant fees or by efficiently manipulating the economies of scale that they contribute huge piles of money to their parent universities. The Institutes of Madras, Rohtak and Kurukshetra are the glaring examples of this

**TABLE 9.2: Break-up of the Institutes Income by its Sources**

| S. No. | Name of the Institutes | Tuition Fees | Other Fees | Total (2+3) | Sales | Saving | Miscel- neous | Total (5+6+7) | Total Inter- Income | Uni. Share | Grand Total (9+10) |
|---|---|---|---|---|---|---|---|---|---|---|---|
| | 1 | 2 | 3 | 4 | 5 | 6 | 7 | 8 | 9 | 10 | 11 |
| 1. | Chandigarh* | 64.55 | 81.04 | 145.89 | 6.76 | Nil | 10.00 | 16.76 | 162.36 | 108.04 | 270.40 |
| | 1994-95 | (23.87) | (29.97) | (53.84) | (2.50) | | (3.70) | (6.20) | (60.04) | (39.96 | (100) |
| 2 | .Patiala* | 32.99 | 46.44 | 79.43 | 5.54 | Nil | Nil | 5.54 | 84.97 | Nil | 84.97 |
| | 1994-95 | (38.83) | (54.65) | (93.48) | (6.52) | | | (6.52) | (100) | | (100) |
| 3. | Kurukshetra* | N.R. | N.R. | 90.56 | Nil | Nil | Nil | Nil | 90.56 | Nil | 90.56 |
| | 1994-95 | | | (100) | | | | | (100) | | (100) |
| 4. | Delhi | 1,18.94 | 79.43 | 1,98.37 | 7.72 | Nil | 14.80 | 22.52 | 2,20.89 | 2,53.50 | 4,74.39 |
| | 1994-95 | (25.08) | (16.74) | (41.82) | | | (4.74) | | (46.56) | (53.50) | (100) |

*Note:* 1. N.R: Not Separately Reflected.
2. Kurukshetra's Budgetary Statem_nt reflects the position of the Courses instituted before 1993-94 and not of those instituted thereafter.
3. Figures in parenthesis indicate percentages.

*Sources*: *Budgetary Statements of the relevant year.

category. At the other end of the continuum, there are a number of Institutes which sustain themselves only on the maintenance grants of their parent universities/Government, as for instance Chandigarh which depends upon its university for as much as 39.96 per cent of its expenditure Delhi, 53.44 (1994-95, Table 9.2) Kashmir 50 per cent (1980-81), Allahabad 41 per cent (1980-81) (Ansari. 1992).

## III

To come to the expenditure part of the budget, its main heads are salaries and the other perquisites of its establishment, printing, paper and stationery, preparation and production of personal contact programme, study material, response sheet evaluation, postal expenses, and the maintenance of its buildings and estate. Of all these items, salaries of the staff devour a large chunk of the Institute's budget. The size of the staff and correspondingly the expenditure on its establishment varies from Institute to Institute.

As highlighted in the preceding chapter some Institutes engage a very small faculty and thus incur a comparatively less expenditure on its establishment. The outstanding examples of this category of Institutes are: Madras (which spends just 1.7 per cent of its overall expenditure), and SNDT, Bombay (4.6 per cent). In comparison to these Institutes, there are a number of the others which support a large faculty of professors, readers, lecturers and the others. They spend a lot of money on the maintenance of this large contingent of teachers. Their salary bill consumes nearly 1/3 of their total expenditure. (Annamalai 31.3 per cent, Delhi 25.33 per cent, Shimla 30.9 per cent). As regards the Chandigarh Institute, its establishment expenditure on the faculty as officially reflected in the annual budgetary statement for 1994-1995 is 35.03 per cent. It is by far the largest. But if we take a realistic view, we find that as against the sanctioned strength of 122 member of the academic staff (on the basis of which the budgetary estimates are framed year after year), the Institute actually employs a faculty of 75 teachers. The difference in the number (47) obviously leads to a decrease in the establishment cost. If we take into consideration this decrease in the overall expenditure of the Institute, the salary bill of this component of the staff comes down to 28.9 per cent, thus almost falling in line with the other Institutes.

The other category of the Institute's staff consist of the ministerial officials, technical hands, para-academic personnel, class four employees and the like. Keeping in view the staff nature of these officials, we bracket them together and describe it as the non-academic wing of the

Institute's staff. No organisation can function without this category of the personnel. That is the reason why every Institute must make a provision for this category of the staff, irrespective of the fact whether or not it provides for the academic staff. However, those Institutes which manipulate their administrative operations in the same old stereotyped manual way tend to employ a larger staff, whereas those Institutes which have switched over, wholly or partially, to the machinisation of the administrative operations, have succeeded not only in cutting down the number of their officials but also in handling their managerial operations more efficiently. If Table 9.3 reflects some degree of variation in the quantum of expenditure on the non-academic wing of their staff, machinisation is the underlying reason. The expenditure under this head ranges from 14 per cent (Madras) to 40.08 per cent (Chandigarh).

If we club together the establishment cost of the two wings of the Institute's staff, we find that both of them combinedly eat away two-third of the total expenditure of the Institute. Ripley Sim's study (1962) also assessed the establishment cost at two-third of the whole. (p.88). Yet another startling revelation with respect to our Institutes is that this cost has shown a marked escalation during the past few years. Gupta and Sharda's study (1984) reveals that "between 1972-73 and 1982-83 the total expenses on the salaries of teaching and non-teaching staff increased six times." They observe, "While during the early 1970's the expenses on salaries constituted about 40 per cent of the total expenditure, this proportion has shot up to 75 per cent." (Pandey. p.37). Endorsing this fact, Ruddar Datt (1994) says that in the Delhi Institute "the salary component (both academic and non-academic) accounted for 55 to 60 per cent (in mid-seventies) but it has increased thereafter and ranged between 64 and 70 per cent of total costs" (p. 34). This steep rise can be attributed partly to the upward revision in the salaries as also to the periodic release of the instalments of dearness allowance for all categories of employees and partly to the expansion and proliferation of the study programmes almost everywhere, necessitating the employment of more and more staff.

The next important head of expenditure is 'Printing and Stationery'. The cost of printing the lessons in bulk and the paper and other stationery articles needed for this purpose make this head significant both from the fiscal and the academic points of view. Though nowhere near the salary head, it does claim a sizeable part of the budget. It ranges between 4.84 per cent (Chandigarh) to 30.6 per cent (Bombay). In the case of the SNDT, it consumes as much as 60.5 per cent of the budget. (The reason

**TABLE 9.3: Break-up of the Institutes Expenditure under Various Heads**

| S. No. | Institutes | Year | Salaries | | | PCP | Resp. Sheets |
|---|---|---|---|---|---|---|---|
| | | | Ac. Staff | Non-Ac. Staff | Total | | |
| 1 | 2 | 3 | 4 | 5 | 6 | 7 | 8 |
| 1. | Chandigarh† | 1994-95 | 94.73 (35.03) | 108.38 (40.08) | 203.11 (75.11) | 0.60 (0.22) | 0.30 (0.11) |
| 2. | Delhi† | 1994-95 | 1,20.17 (25.33.) | 1,70.40 (35.91) | 2,90.57 (61.24) | 20.5 (4.32) | — |
| 3. | Patiala† | 1994-95 | 56.13 (44.27) | 43.65 (34.43) | 99.78 (78.70) | 0 88 (0.69) | 0.65 (0.51) |
| 4. | Kurukshetra† | 1994-95 | N.R. | N.R. | 21.94 (81.53) | 0.10 (0.37) | 0.005 (0.002) |
| 5. | Jammu† | 1993-94 | N.R. | N.R. | 24.93 (55.76) | 3.15 (7.05) | 0.46 (1.03) |
| 6. | Annamalai‡ | 1986-87 | 22.39 (31.3) | 13.30 (18.6) | 35.69 (49.9) | 0.95 (1.3) | N.R. |
| 7. | Madras‡ | 1986-87 | 7.49 (1.7) | 60.20 (14.0) | 67.69 (15.7) | 16.17 | N.A. |
| 8. | Bombay‡ | 1987-88 | 6.34 (21.5) | 10.42 (35.2) | 16.76 (56.7) | N.R. | N.R. |
| 9. | SNDT‡ | 1988-89 | 1.32 (4.6) | 8.09 (28.5) | 9.41 (33.1) | N.R. | N.R. |

**TABLE 9.3 (*Contd.*)**

| S.No. | Lesson writing | Paper & Prining | Postage | Publicity & Adver. | Miscl. | Total |
|---|---|---|---|---|---|---|
| | 9 | 10 | 11 | 12 | 13 | 14 |
| 1. | 0.26 | .13.10 | 3.97 | 0.60 | 48.45 | 270.40 |
| | (0.10) | (4.48) | (1.47) | (0.22) | (17.92) | (100) |
| 2. | 1.0 | 69.0 | 22.0 | 9.0 | 62.32 | 474.39 |
| | (0.21·) | (14.56) | (4.64) | (1.89) | (13.14) | (100) |
| 3. | 1.20 | 13.24 | 3.78 | 0.81 | 6.44 | 126.78 |
| | (0.95) | (10.44) | (2.98) | (0.64) | (5.8) | (100) |
| 4. | 0.75 | 2.40 | 0.90 | 0.165 | 1.33 | 26.91 |
| | (2.78) | (8.92) | (3.34) | (0.61) | (4.94) | (100) |
| 5. | 0.63 | 9.46 | 1.02 | 0.32 | 3.74 | 44.71 |
| | (1.41) | (21.15) | (2.28) | (1.20) | (8.36) | (100) |
| 6. | 0.64 | 20.06 | N.R. | N.R. | 17.09 | 71.43 |
| | (0.9) | (28.1) | | | (19.8) | (100) |
| 7. | NR. | 96.42 | 25.48 | 20.90 | 220.0 | 446.66 |
| | | (22.8) | (5.9) | (4.8) | (50.9) | (100) |

*(Contd.)*

**TABLE 9.3 (*Contd.*)**

| S. No. | Lesson writing | Paper & Prining | Postage | Publicity & Adver. | Miscl. | Total |
|---|---|---|---|---|---|---|
| | 9 | 10 | 11 | 12 | 13 | 14 |
| 8. | N.R. | 9.06 (30.6) | N.R. | N.R. | 3.75 (12.7) | 29.57 (100) |
| 9. | N.R. | 17.21 (60.5) | N.R. | N.R. | 1.32 (6.4) | 22.44 (100) |

*Note*: N.R. = Not Reflected separately.

*Sources*: † Annual Budgetary Statement of the Institute (Unpublished).

‡ Rudra Datt. Cost of Distance Education in India. *op.cit*.

of this bill being so heavy in the case of this Institute is that it also includes postal and publicity expenses).

The other heads of expenditure are, writing, vetting and review of the lessons, response-sheet evaluation, PCP conduct, printing and paper, postage, maintenance of buildings and estate, advertisement and publicity, etc. etc. Even though most of these items constitute the critical inputs of the Institute's academic programmes, they do not consume much of its budgetary outlays. (Table 9.3) This may be due to the reason that in those Institutes which possess sizeable faculties of their own, most of these academic activities are performed by the internal teachers themselves, whereas in those Institutes which having no teachers of their own are thus supposed to get them from outside, do not appear to bother for the same. In both the cases, the level of expenditure on account of these services is bound to be low.

## IV

Comparative statement of their incomes and expenditures brings out the fact that these Institutes fall, broadly, into two categories which (in the absence of any other more appropriate terminology) may be described as the Deficit Institutes and the Surplus Institutes. Because of the lack of adequate internal resources, the former sustain themselves on the maintenance grants of their parent universities, whereas the latter are financially so well-off as to provide huge funds to their parent universities. We may now analyse the problems and the other allied issues of each one of these two categories of Institutes.

To take up the Deficit Institutes first. Inadequacy of internal resources on their part makes these Institutes run, time and again, to their parent universities for making good their financial deficit. The latter though left with no option but to provide the required support, feel quite sore while doing so. They consider these Institutes a liability on their depleting resources. If given an option, many of them may not hesitate to close them down (NIEPA Workshop. 1987 and Ram Reddy, 1988).

The fact of the matter is that distance education in this country was originally conceived to be an institutional contrivance to generate some income for the conventional universities so that they might be able to overcome a part of their budgetary deficit (NIEPA Workshop, 1992). High-sounding objectives such as : 'distance education will help spread education among the masses', 'it will share the responsibility of the conventional system to absorb the surging crowds of education-seekers', it will help improve the working skills of the people', 'it will be able to edeploy the workers from one trade/occupation to another', and the like, are the development of the later years. In earlier years, whichever university instituted this system, it aimed, overtly or covertly, at making some money out of it in order to improve its financial position. The Delhi institute which is the outcome of a high-level committee of the Government of India, was perhaps the only exception to this rut.

Though much water has flowed under the bridge since then, these universities still expect their Institutes to be at least self-supporting if not yield an income for them. That is the reason why they look down upon them and heap condemnation upon their Directors the moment the latter approach them for the maintenance grant.

In order to lessen their own burden, these universities force their Institutes to enhance their income by such means as increase in the existing student fees and the levy of certain new charges. As a result, these Institutes have imposed a variety of such charges which in most of the cases are totally irrelevant in so far as the needs and requirements of distance students are concerned, as for instance the University Holiday Home Fee, University Sports Fee, Infrastructure Fee, Building Fund and General Development Fee. Interestingly, these fees fetch much more income to the Institutes than the tuition fee (Table 9.2). Recently, the U.G.C. has tightened up its belt with regard to its monetary support to the universities. The resultant financial stringency has further hardened the attitude of the latter toward these Institutes compelling them to further enhance the fees. To cite the case of the Chandigarh Institute. It used to charge in 1990-91, Rs.700 and Rs.770 as fee, respectively, from the B.A. and M.A. students. In 1994-95, it increased these fees to Rs.1550 and Rs.1905, respectively (Table 9.4). In other words, the fees marked an

**TABLE 9.4: Showing the Increase in Fees at the Chandigarh Institute**

| Course | 1990-91 | 1993-94 | 1994-95 |
|---|---|---|---|
| Annual fee | Rs. | Rs. | Rs. |
| B.A. | 700 | 710 | 1550 |
| M.A. | 770 | 845 | 1905 |
| Diploma | 756 | 781 | 1770 |
| *Prospectus:* | | | |
| At the counter | 10 | 10 | 100 |
| By Post | 18 | 18 | 110 |

*Source*: Institute's prospectus (Handbook of Information).

increase by 2.21 times for B.A. and 2.47 times for M.A. classes in the course of just five years. Equally surprising is the cost of the prospectus. In 1990, it cost Rs.10 at the Institute's delivery counter and Rs.18 by post. In 1995, its cost has gone up to Rs.100 and Rs.110, respectively. The case of the Chandigarh Institute is just illustrative, the others are no exception. Thus, it is painful to find that these universities/Institutes spare no effort to frustrate the basic objective of distance instruction, namely of providing low-cost education to the people.

On their part, the universities too have a point. Way back in the sixties, distance education was looked upon the world over as an extension service of the conventional system. Inspired by that philosophy, many universities of this country set up, one after another, Institutes of Correspondence Education. To begin with, they started a few degree-oriented conventional study programmes and roped in their departmental and college teachers to provide to them the requisite academic assistance. In this way, thev managed to keep the recurring cost of distance instruction low. Their task was further facilitated by the heavy enrolment of students that they could then attract in view of the reason that a large number of people had been keenly looking forward for an opportunity to improve their educational qualifications. Highly favourable situation that was thus created, made these Institutes earn fabulous incomes both for themselves and for their parent universities.

However, that situation was not to last for long. A number of developments occurred which badly told upon the Institutes' financial health. To begin with, the enrolment began to shrink, bringing in due course an end to the euphoria of the initial years. Side by side, the demand for more and more of new study programmes of both conventional and non-conventional nature increased. On the top of it, the working of the system for a few years brought to the surface some of the shortcomings of the way we had been running it. To remove those shortcomings some improvements had obviously to be made, the most important of which was the staffing of the Institutes by their own separate whole-time faculties. Yet another development was that the system had acquired in the meantime new philosophical dimensions. These too had mounted fresh demands on it. The cumulative impact of all these factors and forces was that the system no longer remained a mere extension of the conventional universities. Instead, it had carved out a distinct entity for itself, claiming to provide a new type of education through the newer technologies. This changed perspective not only led to the evaporation of the phenomenon of surplus funds but also pushed many an Institute into the red. In this way, the universities which had patronised the new system so enthusiastically, had to face a good deal of disillusionment especially when the U.G.C. did not come to their rescue and they had to face the brunt on their own. Their resentment knew no bounds when they were forced to starve their 'own departments' in order to keep this illegitimate offspring of theirs (as they would describe their Institute) surviving. Keeping this developmental sequence in view, it is not very fair to hold the universities exclusively responsible for either perpetuating the notion that distance education is a source of income or for debasing the standards of its instruction.

One wonder why the U.G.C. has not spared any funds for the development and growth of this system? Instead, why has it shown utter indifference towards it? An analysis of the distribution pattern of its grant-in-aid of the past few years reveals that the U.G.C. grants to distance education for any single year have seldom exceeded 0.5 per cent of its total budgetary outlay. Ansari (1992) says that it was 0.66 per cent in 1980-81. It may further be underlined that whatever little grant has been given to it, it has gone out in the form of a specific grant for the introduction of new courses. In other words, no grant whatsoever was provided to the system by way of its maintenance or to make up the deficit in the budgets of the various Institutes. Had this supreme funding authority assisted the universities concerned in maintaining their Institutes properly in the manner it monetarily helps the various departments of the conventional system, the former would have neither themselves faced such a serious situation nor had they given a raw deal to their Institutes.

In comparison to such an utterly broken state of the Institute's health, the Open Universities are flourishing, not to speak of just pulling on. The IGNOU, for instance, received grants totalling Rs.75 crores during the first six years of its inception.In the same manner, Dr. B.R.Ambedkar Open University, Hyderabad was given by the IGNOU (which is the chief funding authority for open universities) Rs. 22 lakhs for staff development and computer facilities.

It is really a pity why the U.G.C. does not take a holistic view of the situation and treat distance education as an integral part of the university system. It is only in recent years that distance education has come to be perceived as a different system, quite distinct from the conventional system. Way back in the late sixties, when the destinies of this system were entrusted to the care of the U.G.C., it was universally regarded as part and parcel of the conventional system, or at best a sub-system of the larger system of education. Even then the U.G.C. did not look very kindly to it. This is something which puzzles distance educators.

It is painful to learn that when in the late seventies these Institutes began to face the financial crunch and their parent universities turned their back against them, the U.G.C. came out with a suggestion that these Institutes could explore the possibility of levying development fee on their students. It was this suggestion which made the various Institutes to levy a variety of non-tuition fees which have become over the years an undue burden on distance students.

The issue is why should the students of the Institutes be penalised for the inhospitable attitude of the universities and be required to provide for the maintenance of their Institute? One fails to understand that when the state can subsidise conventional college education to the extent of 92.47 per cent (Ruddar Datt, 1994) or even 95 per cent (Punjab State pattern of financial support to the colleges), why cannot the state treat distance education likewise?

Taking an objective view of the whole situations, we feel that even the canons of social justice demand that distance learners should not be treated differently. As highlighted in Chapter III, the bulk of the Institutes' students consists of those youngsters who mostly hail from the humbler homes and who prefer to pursue their higher studies through this mode in view of the facility of 'learning while earning' that it offers. It also comprises those persons whose comparatively low placement in offices and factories makes them struggle hard to improve their status in life. Their social conditions as well as their zeal to improve their living conditions demand that instead of penalising them by heavy fees, they should be encouraged to achieve their objective by making distance education less costly for them.

There is yet another reason to keep the cost of this education low. The fast-growing rush of education-seekers in colleges and university departments, on the one hand, and our inability to put up educational institutions of the conventional nature (on account of their cost-prohibitive nature) on the other, have already made us take a policy decision to divert at least 50 per cent of the new aspirants of higher education to distance education. (*Eighth Five Year Plan*. Para. 11.7.2.3). If we are to fulfil that objective, we must keep the cost of this education as low as may suit the pockets of even the poorest sections of society. Conversely, there is a very strong case for adequate financial support to this system. The present attitude of indifference on the part of the Government and the U.G.C. towards this system thus calls for an immediate review.

However, the argument of the Government and the U.G.C. that they are not obliged to share the burden of the second-chance education of the grown-up adults, is tenable but partially. There is no denying the fact that distance education is a pastime for certain sections of the people, as for instance house-wives, high civil and military officers, the super-annuated persons etc. etc. who take up studies through this mode in order to while away their time. Though there is nothing wrong in this in so far as they are concerned, the state is certainly not obliged to dole out the tax-payers' money on them. However, this is not a sufficient ground to deny the state grant to this system. There are a number of methods by means of which we can ensure that the benefit of the state grant are not frittered away on the fulfilment of the superfluous needs of these sections of the distance students. We can, for instance link the fee structure of the various study programmes with age, profession, status of those persons who enrol themselves with these Institutes. In this way, those who need the support would not be deprived of it.

Instead of burdening the students unduly, we can make the system economically viable, by applying the principle of the economies of scale upon which it is based more effectively. Presently there are too many Institutes/Open Universities in the country to allow this principle to operate meaningfully. Unless their number is drastically pruned by such methods as fusion or merger of the various Institutes with one another, this objective cannot be attained. Elsewhere we suggest that this number can be brought down to half a dozen of regional open universities. We are confident that such a step would not only ensure quality education but also reduce its cost quite considerably.

To examine the issue of external monetary grant to the system further. If the argument for not assisting distance education is that it is comparatively a less costly system, hence not requiring any external support at all, again the answer is that the U.G.C. does not take an objective view of the needs and requirements of this system of education. Even Prime Minister, P.V. Narasimha Rao is convinced that all these arguments "are based on fallacy", (Bakshish Singh, 1995). We dilate upon this argument in the section to follow; suffice it to say at this stage that by denying financial support to this nascent system, the U.G.C. is indirectly aiding and abetting the debasement of the standards of its instruction.

Now the whole structure providing financial support to distance education is in the process of a radical change. The U.G.C. is being relieved of this responsibility and in its place, the IGNOU is being vested with the authority of co-ordinating, developing and funding the entire system of distance education. This is being done in accordance with the provisions of the parliamentary statute governing the IGNOU. This change is welcome to the extent that distance education would be released from the stranglehold of those persons who are both indifferent and hostile towards it. Its services as well as its needs would be better appreciated, for its destinies would then vest with those persons who belong to it and are very well conversant with its 'ins' and 'outs'. They would certainly not give a raw deal to it.

However, the principle of vesting the authority of funding the open universities and the Institutes with the one which itself is a member of the flock and competes against the others for providing distance instruction, does not appear to meet the canons of justice and fairplay. For, it implies the danger of the donor-dispenser of the grants assuming the role of a big brother and may not, therefore, be able to do full justice to them in the allocation of either the resources or the courses of study. These hard realities of the day-to-day world make us come out with a suggestion (spelled out in detail in one of the subsequent chapters) that there should be created an altogether new institution, to be named as Open Universities Grants Commission (OUGC) which may be vested with the authority, presently given to the U.G.C., namely, that of co-ordination, development and funding of distance education. Having been accorded a status higher than all the institutions, and (thus) not having been locked in competition against anyone of them, the OUGC would be able to do full justice to all, (including the IGNOU) without fear or favour to anyone. It is only in this way that the problems of the system would be tackled smoothly and successfully.

## V

The second category of Institutes comprises those which 'earn' to their universities huge piles of money (refer to Table 9.1) These Institutes are the outcome of the psychology that if distance education is managed prudently, it can turn out to be a highly 'lucrative business', (Sheath, 1969, p.121). This psychology appears to be deep-rooted in such characteristic features of the system as that an Institute neither needs class-rooms to house its students nor is there any ceiling limit on the enrolment of its students. Besides, there are a number of other in-built avenues which can yield substantial amounts of savings. Ironically, a few 'enterprising individuals' have translated this psychology. The upshot of this tragic development is that many of our universities which are supposed to be the guardians and trend-setters of the academic standards have already plunged themselves deep into the quagmire of profiteering. Their number is 20 out of 27. Bakshish Singh (1994) put it at 18 out of 26 (Question No. 96, p.147). That such a large number of university-sponsored Institutes harness distance education for purposes of making money is something to be seriously pondered over.

The secret of their profits lies in the low profile nature of their expenditure. The main head of expenditure where they effect a sizeable saving is faculty. None of these profit-making Institutes employs a whole-time full-fledged faculty of its own and, instead, engages teachers from colleges and university departments in order to dispense the various academic services to their students. They hire these teachers on small contract basis and pay very little remuneration to them. By employing such cheap methods, they manage to effect large savings. How much money do they actually save on this account can be gauged from the fact that on one side there is the Chandigarh Institute which spends Rs.94.73 lakhs on account of its faculty and, on the other, there is the Madras Institute whose faculty costs to it barely Rs. 7.48 lakhs. Further, compare the Delhi Institute with its expenditure of Rs.61.04 lakhs with SNDT, Bombay spending only Rs.1.32 lakhs on its faculty.

That an Institute may not have a whole-time faculty of its own and may manage its various student services through the instrumentality of the outside teachers hired on small contract basis, is by no means an academically unsound practice. A large number of well-reputed Institutes the world over adopt it. But the problem arises when an Institute is led away by the ulterior motive of making money and starts economising on those essential academic services which contribute to the quality of its instruction. Unfortunately, most of our Institutes that fall in the non-faculty/profit-making category tend to pay very little to the contracted teachers and, further, they do not engage them in an adequate number and thus try to save money in every possible way.

While it is expected that these Institutes which do not maintain their own internal faculties would employ a large number of outside teachers for the conduct of the PCP and the evaluation of the response sheets so as to make good the absence of the internal faculty, sadly enough, the quantum of expenditure under these heads, as reflected in their budgets, does not provide any evidence to this effect. This highly counter-productive tendency gets a further fillip from the lack of any in-built mechanism which may compel the system to discharge these obligations properly. On the contrary, the system leaves a wide scope for the Institutes to dilute these services to any extent. Once the study materials (the printed lessons) are received, the students do not bother whether or not the Institute holds any PCP or asks them to submit the response sheets. The latter are in fact taken by them as an unwarranted interference in their freedom to self-study. As for the teachers, they too feel immensely relieved if they are not bothered either to organise PCP's or to evaluate response sheets. Thus, in the absence of any in-built mechanism, these Institutes feel free to maintain the PCP, the response-sheets, library services and the like just in a skeleton form (if not to skip them over completely), thereby indulging in the unholy game of making profit in such a noble venture as education.

Yet another indicator of their lust for profit is their deliberate attempt to keep the per capita expenditure on students as low as possible. Ruddar Datt's study (1994) reveals that the per head student expenditure of academic services in the non-faculty profit-making Institutes is comparatively far less than the faculty Institutes. While the Madras and the SNDT, Bombay (non-faculty Institutes), respectively, spend Rs.8 and Rs.11 per head, the Delhi and the Chandigarh Institutes' cost respectively is Rs.180 and Rs.706. Equally wide variations are noticed with respect to the per head non-academic cost. Annamalai Rs.32, Madras Rs.64, Delhi Rs.212, Shimla Rs.329, and Chandigarh Rs.693. (pp.140-141).

Yet another evidence of this lustful tendency and corresponding lack of concern for the quality of distance instruction is manifest in the policy of their parent universities which grab the whole or a lion's share of the revenue surplus of their Institutes, leaving but little with them either for the creation of the capital assets or for the improvement of student services. To quote the case of the Madras Institute again. In the year, 1988-89, it was coaxed to part with nearly half of its total earnings (i.e.Rs.359.57 lakhs out of Rs.749.73 lakhs). (Ruddar Datt, 1994) How unjust it is for the University to take away such a large chunk of the total revenue income of the Institute and ask it to manage the various sundry expenses of as large a student population as 1,12,000. The balance amount left with the Institute is hardly sufficient to meet its day-to-day expenses. How would it be possible for it to bring about any qualitative improvement in its academic and administrative services? That is the reason why it has not been able either to expand its faculty or enhance the remuneration of the outside teachers ever since it has started earning profits. How can it do so?

Thus we find these Institutes are so much obsessed by the profit mania that they do not hesitate to enrol students in hundreds and thousands without the least regard for either their managerial capabilities or the absorption capacity of the market. At the same time, they do not mind curtailing the essential academic services to their minimum and thus leave no stone unturned to ruin either the quality of their instruction or the reputation of the system at large. Some of the Institutes do not hesitate even to enhance their fees. It is of little consideration for them that many of their students come of the poorer homes. They are concerned only with their profits.

There has hardly been any regional or national level meet of distance educators where a concern might not have been expressed over this ugly practice of the various Institutes. On their part, the Directors plead their helplessness and blame their parent universities. They grind their teeth with chagrin while telling us that the money that they so 'painstakingly' save at the cost of their own and their Institute's reputation is utilized on the development of the conventional departments which happen to be the arch critics of their system. They further bemoan that instead of feeling obliged, these conventionalists heap condemnation on them despite their being its beneficiaries. The Directors are not far wrong in making such a submission. Only recently the Vice-Chancellor of a university boastfully remarked in the course of his interview to a press correspondent that by just one policy stroke (of instituting the B.Ed. course by correspondence) he had transformed the financial health of his university from the state of an utter deficit to that of a respectable surplus. No longer would he have to look to the extraneous sources for either meeting the day-to-day expenses of the university or for effecting qualitative improvement in the instructional services of the various departments, he added (*Yugantar*, Chandigarh, May 22, 1995). The Vice-Chancellor concerned does not appear to have any qualms of conscience when his crusade to improve the financial health of the university makes him trample over the nascent system of distance education.

Deploringly, these universities do not pay any heed either to the entreaties of their Institutes or to the advice of the higher level authorities and organisations. The U.G.C., NIEPA, the NCDE and many others have repeatedly impressed upon these Institutes though in vain, "to desist from using these surpluses to meet the needs of the conventional system". In December, 1993, the UGC again suggested to them that "they should ensure adequate investment/ploughing back of surplus for the development and upgradation of DDE's to the distance education mode. A part of the surplus may be kept as a reserve/endowment fund of the Institute for meeting unforeseen expenditure." (Additional ecretary UGC, letter to the Vice-Chancellors). This communique too had little impact. Neither the

Madras University stopped exacting its levy from its Institute nor did the Kurukshetra University desist itself from joining the rat race with its neighbouring sister university in producing trained graduates in thousands.

It may again be emphasised that distance education is not a hen laying golden eggs. This impression is not only erroneous but ill-founded also. There is no denying the fact that an Institute of Distance Education does not need class rooms and that there is no ceiling limit on the enrolment of students. But at the same time it can also not be denied that it needs to be well-staffed with professors, readers and lecturers in order to produce first rate study materials. Or alternatively, it must engage an equally competent part-time teachers from outside for this purpose and must pay handsomely to them. Besides, it must have on its staff a sizeable contingent of editors, designers language experts, graphists, computer technicians and the like. Further, it must acquire the capability of supplementing its written lessons with their audio and video components. It must have access to such modern technologies as television, computer-mediated instructional system, audio/video tele-conferencing, etc. etc. Above all, it must have requisite will as well as the necessary infrastructure to effectively goad its students to such of the traditional academic services as PCP and response sheets.

The procurement of all these services requires huge capital investment. We must not lose sight of the fact that it is these distinct types of services (PCP, audio, video, computer, tele-conferencing, etc. etc.) which alone make distance instruction effective and meaningful. If today our Institutes are being denied the status of 'distance education', the underlying reason is their inability to diversify their instructional methodology into these newer technologies. Thus, it is a wrong impression that distance education is a low-cost instructional method. (Wurm, (1989), p.52). It is in no way less costly than conventional education. If the latter requires huge recurring cost, the former involves huge capital cost.

If after having procured the whole of this paraphernalia of the system and also after having developed its managerial capacity to run it efficiently, the Institute earns some profit none would raise his little finger by way of criticism. But the manner in which this system is being craftily tamed for business purposes, it has become an eye-sore for everyone.

The only way we can save both the Institutes and their parent universities from the embarrassment of this profit mania is to provide to them grant-in-aid on a lavish scale. It may be noted that much of this grant-in-aid would be a one-time assistance to them for the creation of such essential services as audio-video hardware component, computerisation, desk top publishing system, composite study centres, library facilities, etc. etc. Once these facilities are provided, the quality of distance instruction would improve which, in turn, would attract a larger enrolment of students. Since this system functions on the basis of the economies of scale, there is no reason why these Institutes may then become self-supporting, thereby offsetting the need for greater maintenance grant of a recurring nature.

It may also be underlined that if the Government provides to these Institutes recurring grant, it should not treat it as a burden on it, for the reason that education whether it is for the young or for the old, is the responsibility of the state. This principle has received universal recognition. In U.K. the Open University was supported by the Government to the extent of 73.4 per cent in 1985 and 69.6 per cent in 1987 (Blowers, 1989, p.57). Riplay Sims' study (1962) discloses that 85.2 per cent of the total cost is borne by the central authority, 0.3 per cent by the provincial authority and 14.5 per cent by the student. (p. 89). In our own country we find that the IGNOU is being provided with lavish grants. When grants can be managed for it why can't these be made available to the other Institutes? Thus there is a very strong case for the U.G.C. allocating to the Institutes grants in proportion to the number of students that they enrol for higher education to the total population of students in the universities and colleges of the country. Presently, no less than 10 per cent of the students receive higher education through this stream. If the UGC agrees to give 10 per cent of its grant to them, their needs are eminently served.

## VI

From the fiscal management point of view, the Institutes fall into two broad categories. There are some Institutes (whose number incidentally is very small) which have not been conceded any financial autonomy at all. The entire financial power is concentrated in the hands of the Registrar. As a result, the Director runs to him every now and then, seeking his approval for all types of expenditure. These universities also do not provide for any separate fund for the Institute which may be operated by the Director. Incomes accruing to the Institute from the student fees, sale of the prospectuses and the other sources are credited to the Registrar's fund. Likewise, moneys are drawn out of it to meet the day-to-day expenditure of the Institute. Such a situation, besides being humiliating for the Director, hampers his functioning a good deal. It is obvious that when a person is required to submit his proposals to another person of an equal status and tender an explanation to him to clear the proposal, his managerial initiative is curbed and the Institute suffers in the long run. The Directors of these Institutes have expressed their unhappiness with an arrangement of this type at every available occasion, may it be a conference of the distance educators or a meeting of some high level body/authority.

Compared to them, there are a number of other Institutes where a substantial degree of autonomy is conceded by providing to them a separate budget and a separate fund and wide discretionary powers to their Directors. In their case, the Institute's budget, though forming a part and parcel of the general budget of the university, is accorded a distinct place. Its enactment, passage and operation constitute a part of the Director's responsibilities. To explain the mode of its enactment and passage at some length. The process begins with the Director formulating the proposals and then informally discussing them with the Vice-Chancellor. After the latter has given his nod, the former proceeds ahead and gives to these proposals a formal shape of a full-fledged budget. Thereafter the budget is presented to the Governing Body of the Institute. Consisting of the Vice-Chancellor, the university deans, the representative members of the syndicate and the Institute's faculty, the Registrar, the Finance Officer and distance education experts, this supreme policy-making body of the Institute discusses it thoroughly and puts its seal of approval at the end. The budget then gets tagged with the general budget of the university and its receipts and expenditure also like-wise come to be reflected in the latter. Now commences its final journey. Gradually winding its path through the Board of Finance and the Syndicate, it finally arrives at the floor of the Senate, where it is again subjected to close scrutiny and serious discussion at the hands of the university fellows. After it emerges from the Senate Hall with the final seal of approval, it is now ready for operation.

The Institute's budget is operated by the Director. He draws money as and when need arises and spends it in accordance with the lines indicated in the budget. He can incur expenditure independently but upto a certain specified limit, beyond which the prior approval of the Vice-Chancellor is obligatory. However, wide variations are noticed even within this category of Institutes with regard to the discretionary powers of the Director. Bakshish Singh (1994), study discloses that in 27.6 per cent of the cases, the Director's powers ranges between Rs.50 and

Rs.500. There are however Institutes where the Director can spend on his own any amount ranging between Rs.3,000 and Rs.6,000 (Question No.103, p.154). By and large, the Directors enjoy a fair degree of financial autonomy, which the chairmen of the other departments sometimes feel jealous. However, it has been observed that wherever the status of the Institute was converted into that of the department, the hawks sitting in the Registrar's office do not take a moment to withdraw the excess powers of the Director and pull him down to the level of the Chairman of the other departments of the university. Their efforts to obliterate the autonomous/distinct entity of the Institute do not stop at that point only. They further seek to rob it of the separate character of its budget as also of its (Director's) fund. Above all, they seek to merge the Institute's office, more specifically its accounts section, with the Registrar's office. Their argument is that the Institute, after having been put at par with the other teaching departments of the university, should be treated like them for all administrative and financial purposes. That the Institute, even though a teaching department, is different from the rest is of little consideration to them.

These wide variations with regard to such vitally important issues as the internal administrative framework of the financial set-up of the Institute, budget making and the financial powers of the Director call for an intensive study which may suggest an arrangement beneficial to all.

## VII

As hinted at the outset, heads of expenditure of an Institute are precisely defined and there is not much scope for economy in the overall expenditure. The educational nature of the Institute further underlines that it must, *ipso facto,* draw its sustenance not so much from its internal resources as from the state grants. These facts notwithstanding, there always exists in every organisation a constant need as also scope (large or small) for applying a cut here and plugging a hole there. A prudent manager is one who is ever in quest of the ways and means how the efficiency of the organisation he presides over can be enhanced, preferably not by taxing its resources any further but by conserving them as much as he can.

As for the Institutes, there is no denying the fact that they suffer from the paucity of resources. But at the same time, it is also true that most of them are ill-managed. Having been created in the image of the Registrar's office, they exhibit the stereo-typed work culture, typical of the bureaucratic concern for rules and regulations rather than for economy and efficiency. This culture is no longer in tune with the times and it can therefore be held mainly responsible for the mismanagement of these Institutes. The industrial orientations of distance education, provided to it by its philosophical and technological moorings, demand that the Institutes should bid good bye to this culture and substitute in its place a new work culture which may help them achieve their goals speedily and effectively.

As already discussed at length earlier, our old habit of manually manipulating our office and other operations has not only fetched for us the stigma of being backward, but has also made us lose pace with the fast-changing world. If we want to cast off this stigma and make our Institutes to fit into the new perspective, we must adopt 'efficiency' and 'economy' as our watch words and make computerisation and 'privatization' as our driving force towards the goals.

There is not an iota of doubt that computer alone holds out a hope for the future. If this technology is suitably harnessed it can induct into our administration economy as well as efficiency which phenomena have thus far been elusive to us. There are numerous areas in the Institute's administration where we spend a lot of money, yet we fail to do things to the satisfaction of our clients. To name a few of them: printing of lessons, prospectuses and various types of forms; response sheet record-keeping; students profiles and performance rolls; accounts-keeping; library services; and day-to-day correspondence with the students and the others. If all of these operations are computerised, we can effect sizeable savings in terms of both money and man-power. Functional efficiency, a by-product of this modern technology, would be in addition to this direct saving.

Likewise, there are various other areas of our administration which if opened to private enterprise can also further contribute to the saving of resources. There is, for instance, the work of packaging of study materials. Presently, we entrust this work to the permanently employed whole-time personnel of our administration. The non-technical and seasonal nature of this operation makes this arrangement unviable both financially and administratively. It can be entrusted very profitably to a private contractor.

As discussed earlier, faculty is the only dominant variable whose presence or absence makes an Institute either save or lose a very large chunk of its monetary resources. Those Institutes which engage a whole-time faculty of their own generally run into a huge budgetary deficit, whereas those which carry on their work with the help of the outside part-time teachers, save piles of money and earn 'profits' for their universities. In Chapter VIII we have pointed out that both these extreme positions are unsound, academically as well as administratively. The 'golden mean' alone can ideally serve the needs of the Institute. The Institute should engage only a core faculty of a few professors, readers and lecturers who may be able to look after the various types of academic needs of the students in an effective and dignified manner and leave the rest of the things to be taken care of by the outside part-time faculty. Such an arrangement would further help the Institute to save some of its precious little resources.

Then there is the set of two more institutions (study centres and audio-video or educational media centres) which too hold out a scope for economy. The former, though maintained at a heavy cost, provide qualitatively too poor a service. Lack of both the will and resources on the part of the Institutions has made them neglect these centres. Similar is the case with the audio-video centre. Growing desire on the part of the Institutes to supplement their study materials with audio and video components, further coupled with their political manoeuvrability, has made some of them set up these centres. But the unavailability of suitable soft-ware and fast obsolescent nature of the hardware and, on the top of it, the incapability of these Institutes to raise resources to meet the contingencies arising out of the former two situations make these centres functionally ineffective. Keeping these hard realities in view, one is apt to suggest that it is far more desirable if these Institutes do not go in for such shabbily maintained audio-video centres. It is high time if the U.G.C. assumes to itself the responsibility of providing composite study centres as well as the educational media centres, on the lines already suggested earlier. Such an arrangement would not only save these Institutes of the heavy expenditure that they presently incur on their creation and maintenance but would also provide qualitatively much better services.

Finally, if the universities are too keen to see their Institutes turn a corner financially, they should stop students taking their examinations privately. The institution of private appearance has otherwise too lost its relevance and justification particularly in view of the availability of methodically-sound academic guidance through the Institutes of Distance Education. If this institution is abolished, thousands of students who adopt this route to satiate their hunger for higher education, would divert themselves to the Institute, thereby boosting its enrolment tremendously, which, in turn, would imply more money for the Institutes. This is an urgently called for measure of educational reform.

These are some of the areas of the Institute's financial administration where there occurs some scope for pruning the expenditure. But it may once again be emphasised that too much concern for savings and income might prove to be counter-productive for the overall well-being of the Institute. Any policy that the Institute might develop to plug the loopholes with a view to conserving the precious little resources must be in consonance with the laudable objectives of the Institute, most important of which is the maintenance of the qualitatively high academic standards of its instruction. The latter is of a paramount consideration; all else must be subservient to it. If sometimes economy is effected, it should aim at enhancing the standards rather than lowering them.

## REFERENCES

Bakshish Singh, Saroj Mullick and Neelam Chaudhry, *Correspondence/Distance Education in India: An In-depth Study Covering the Year 1988-90*. New Delhi, Indira Gandhi National Open University. 1994.

Blowers, Andrew, 'The Open University of the U.K.-Ideals under challenge ' *ICDE Bulletin* No.20, (1989).

Datt, Ruddar, *Cost of Distance Education in India*. New Delhi South Asian Publishers and National Institute of Educational Planning & Administration. 1994. *Eighth Five Year Plan*., (1992-97) Vol. I. Government of India, Planning Commission New Delhi.

Gupta, S.K. and Sharda, N.K., 'Financial Dynamics of Distance Education with reference to Autonomy and a Central Agency', Pandey, K.P., Gautam, O.P., and Gupta, S.K. (Eds.). *Distance Education: A Reappraisal. (Report of the Fourth National Seminar of National Council of Correspondence Education)*. May, 1984). H.P. University, Shimla.

Letter of Dr. R.P. Gangurde, Additional Secretary, U.G.C. to Vice- Chancellors. D.O. No. F-3-14/93 (NFE-II) December, 1993.

Rao, P.V. Narasimha, Address delivered at Dr. B.R. Ambedkar Open University reproduced by Bakshish Singh (Ed.) *New Horizons in Distance Education*. New Delhi, Uppal. 1995.

Reddy, G. Ram, 'Open Universities, the new temples of learning', Reddy, G.Ram (Ed.) *Open Universities, Ivory Towers Thrown Open*. New Delhi, Sterling 1988.

Sheath, H.C., 'External Studies at the University Level—Some Recent Development,' Erdos, Renee (Ed.) *Proceedings of the 8th International Conference of the International Council of Correspondence Education*. UNESCO House. Paris. 19-23 May, 1969.

Sims, Ripley, *An Inquiry into Correspondence Educational Processes*. International Council for Correspondence Education, 1962.

Wurm, Fackie, 'A User Perspective on Distance Education in Australia'. *ICDE Bulletin* No. 20 (1989)

*Yugantar* (Chandigarh). 22 May, 1995.

CHAPTER X

# ADMINISTRATIVE SET-UP OF THE INSTITUTE

ADMINISTRATIVE set-up of an organisation is that arrangement of its offices and officials which enables it to achieve efficiency, on the one hand, and effectiveness, on the other. While efficiency is measured in terms of the relationship between the inputs and the outputs. (which relationship is conceived and developed in a manner that minimises resource cost), effectiveness refers to the attainment of the goals of the organisation. (Granville Rumble, 1992). The non-static nature of these objectives makes this set-up an on-going and dynamic process. It needs to be reviewed and reordered every now and then in the light of the feedback of its functioning as also the new demands that are occasionally mounted on it. Thus, the administrative set-up constitutes the kernel of the organisation from where the necessary force to achieve the targets is generated.

The administrative set-up of an Institute of Distance Education needs to be developed in a manner that helps it to provide distance instruction to a large clientele of students which may be spread over the length and breadth of the globe, (not to speak of a country or a region thereof). Further, it must also ensure that the quality of instruction that it imparts is second to none and that these are given at the bare minimum cost and as efficiently as possible. The absence of a constant face-to-face interaction between the teacher and the taught adds a peculiar dimension to its organisational set-up, thereby making it pretty different from a conventional educational institution. (Ripley Sims, 1962) Its organisational pattern, therefore, needs to be imaginatively conceived and diligently developed lest the students at the other end do not feel disillusioned by the sluggishness of its services.

The peculiar nature of its goals demands that the administrative set-up of an Institute of Distance Education must provide, among other aspects, for: (a) information and publicity; (b) students' admission;

(c) evaluation of response-sheets; (d) printing and despatch of lessons; (e) conduct of the PCP; (f) postal aspect of the library services and (g) production of the non-conventional type of study materials. The other areas of typical concern of an organisation, which too need to be efficiently managed are: (a) establishment; (b) accounts-keeping and (c) the maintenance of the estate and buildings. We may now take up these administrative aspects, one by one, and see how these Institutes manage them.

**Information and Publicity**

That it enrols students from far and wide makes it incumbent upon every Institute that it provides for as wide and repeated publicity to its study programmes as may be possible. Any laxity on this account may make the Institute lose a sizeable part of its clientele. Apart from the newspapers, there are also available such other media of publicity as radio and televisic As for the Institutes of Distance Education of this country, the IGNOU is perhaps the only one of its kind which harnesses all these three media, whereas the conventional-university sponsored Institutes still confine themselves only to the newspapers. Even on this account, their approach is conditioned by frugality, partly because of their deep concern for economy and mainly because of the lack of appreciation on the part of the university authorities that distance education is clientele-oriented in nature. To make up the deficiency on this account, a number of other methods have been tried by various Institutes with varying degrees of success. These are: holding short-duration camps for an on-the-spot admission, seeking through letters the good offices of such local influentials as panches and sarpanches, school teachers, retired civil and military officers and the like, display of posters and films. However, the fact remains that the study programmes of most of these Institutes remain ill-advertised, with the result that the common man in the sprawling countryside is not much aware of the vast new avenues that are now available to him to improve his educational skills. These Institutes, therefore, need to pay greater attention to this side. In its latest communique to the Vice-Chancellors, the U.G.C. has also impressed upon them to set up such a cell in their Institutes. It has further advised the Institutes to make efforts in "collaboration with the State Public Relations Department to reach people in remote areas and tribal areas and to attract larger number of women and backward sections of society." (Additional Secretary's letter to Vice-Chancellors, December, 1993).

Another aspect of the information and publicity work is the disposal of innumerable enquiries that pour into the Institute day in and day out. A number of students, present and prospective, seek by mail, through telephone and even by their personal visits varied types of information regarding the courses of study that the Institute offers, the eligibility qualifications thereof, the mode of instruction and so on and so forth. Due care needs to be taken to ensure, first, that all these letters are promptly answered, and, second, the telephonic calls as also the visitors are courteously attended to. Further, the letters that are addressed to the outsiders on behalf of the Institute are nicely drafted and beautifully printed. This little care makes a profound impact on the addressee, thereby projecting a good public image of the Institute.

But what is widely observed is that the clerk-in-charge of the enquiry cell drafts out a general comprehensive letter, couched in a typically officious tone and tenor, containing the stock replies of all possible types of enquiries, and gets it cyclostyled in advance in hundreds of copies. As soon as an inquiry drops in, he pulls out of the file one copy of that answer letter, tick marks the number/column relevant to that inquiry and shoots it out. When that half-faded and casually answered letter reaches its addressee who has been very keenly waiting for it, he is thoroughly disillusioned. All his enthusiasm saps. However, in the absence of an alternative, he may join the Institute but with a deep sense of despondency on his part.

In the same manner, the telephone bell goes on ringing for minutes at a stretch, but nobody attends to it. And whenever someone picks it up, he answers the call in a far from satisfactory manner. His stock reply is 'send the inquiry by post', 'I don't know', and so on. This kind of discourtesy and officiousness needs to be avoided at any cost if the well-being of the Institute is of any concern to its authorities. Holmberg (1989) rightly stresses that every Institute must make administrative arrangements to provide for "correct, competent and courteous treatment of all letters... and proper reception of students calling in person or on the telephone...", p. 4).

Yet another aspect that needs the particular attention of the Institute's authorities is the prospectus and other brochures that they bring out every year with a view to acquainting the prospective students and the others with the type of the study courses that the Institute offers, the requisite entry qualifications for each one of them, the mode of instruction and study, the fee structure and such other relevant information. These are very important documents, for on the basis of the information that they give to a person that he decides whether to join the Institute and which course to offer. Distant location of the students and their inability to come over to the Institute in person further enhances the importance of these documents. It is, therefore, very essential that these informatory handbooks are produced in an easy language and a lucid style so that the students may not face any difficulty to comprehend the various conditions of eligibility of admission to the Institute. We must bear in mind that those who seek admission are (in certain cases) children in their teens or adults in lowly placed professions who may not have much knowledge of English. Long distances further render them incapable of seeking elucidation in person of any clause or paragraph of the prospectus. If it is possible, these documents may also be brought out in Hindi and also in the language of the region concerned. That would further facilitate the task of the candidates.

It may be pointed that the common práctice all over the country is that all public documents (Institute's prospectus is no exception) are produced in a highly difficult legal parlance. Long groovy sentences, replete with juridical provisos, make their comprehension even by fairly well-educated persons difficult. That is the reason why admissions of a large number of students are scratched by the Institute every year only because they fail to make out correctly whether or not the qualifications they possess fit into the Institute's requirements for the various courses. In this way, innumerable students lose one precious year of their life as well as a few hundred rupees. It is therefore advisable that the Institutes should bring out their prospectuses in the American style of 'what', 'where' and 'how'.

The whole of this work of information and publicity should be assigned to a separate administrative cell. The vital importance of this role as well as the public relations involved in it demands that this cell should preferably be put under the direct charge of the administrative head of the Institute's secretariat, who, in the present university structure, generally wears the designation of a deputy registrar. He should personally ensure that the well-trained, soft-spoken and courtesy-loving persons are put on such sensitive seats as receptionists, telephone operators and the like, so that outside visitors and telephonic calls are nicely attended to. Similarly, the letters are well drafted and promptly acknowledged. He should also develop an efficient monitoring service to keep him in constant touch with how things are managed in the various cells of his office.

**Students' Services**

Though the entire administrative set-up of an educational institution is student oriented, the distance nature of the Institute's instructional system calls for the creation of a special section/branch/division exclusively devoted to the student's services. It has to handle such administrative aspects as are of crucial importance to the students. To spell them out, a bulk of the students who seek admission to the Institute transmit their admission forms, fees and other relevant documents by post. As soon as these are received, the Institute's office is required to deposit the fee in the bank and simultaneously verify whether or not he is eligible for admission to the course of study, he has offered. In case he fulfils all the conditions and his admission is through, he is informed, accordingly. The certificates and other documents that he has submitted in proof of his basic qualifications are also returned forthwith. Simultaneously, the other sections of the office, namely the lesson-mailing section, library, educational media centre, etc. etc. are communicated his enrollment number and postal address for further communication on their part. In case he is not found eligible, his documents too are sent back immediately alongwith the letter of regrets. At the same time steps are also initiated to refund his fees. This is the normal procedure that the Institutes office generally adopts. But many a time considerable delay and deviation takes place which tendency on the part of the officials needs to be drastically curbed in the interests of the Institute's efficiency.

It is widely observed that the officials do not take the work of the verification of eligibility with as great a sense of earnestness as they ought to do with the result that the work goes on accumulating while the candidates at the far off end are put to a great suspense quite unduly. It may once again be emphasised that the reputation of an Institute of Distance Education is closely hinged with the promptness with which it handles the various affairs of the students. To ensure promptness in this particular area of the Institutes administration, the authorities may reinforce the strength of this section by temporarily drafting officials from other sections. Even then if some accumulation takes place on account of the great rush for admission, the Institute should not hesitate to get the accumulation cleared by paying the over-time allowance to the officials concerned. But it must ensure at all costs that the forms that are received each day are cleared by the following morning, lest the vicious circle of accumulation sets in.

Another allied aspect is the co-ordination between the admission branch and the lesson mailing cell of the Institute. The latter needs to be promptly apprised as to which student has been granted admission so that the first packet of the study material is released to him without any delay. This co-ordination is of vital importance, for (as said earlier) a distance student who has applied for his admission in the month of June or July, expects that his studies also commence almost simultaneously with the class-room based collegians. But in most of the Institutes this co-ordination is weak with the result that the delivery of lessons gets unduly delayed.

Next to the verification of the admission forms comes the adjustment of the admission fees. In order to attract a larger number of people to this stream of education, every Institute gives an option to its students to pay their fees in instalments (preferably two) if they so choose. Many of them do prefer this course. The general practice is that such students are required to pay a certain fixed amount at the time of their admission and the balance by a certain subsequent date. What generally happens is that quite a large number of students do not remit the balance in time, may be for the reason that their interest in studies by then gets worn out or there may be certain other compulsions. If co-ordination between the fee collection section and the lesson dispatch section is not effective, which generally happens to be the case, the Institute is put to a great financial loss. It is, therefore, essential that the fee-collection section should keep the lesson-dispatch section constantly informed as to which of the students in this category has cleared his dues and which has not, so that the lesson delivery work may be tuned accordingly.

It is in this particular area that there is a great need of a computer. If one is installed in the Student's Service's Section, not only will the work of the verification of the documents and the preparation of the consolidated lists of the admitted students become easier but the accounting of the fees, issuance of reminders to the defaulters and co-ordination with other branches of the office will also be streamlined. The incidence of mistake as also of delay will be eliminated altogether.

Another administratively sensitive issue is the refund of the fees of the rejected candidates. As mentioned above, the fees once deposited in the university treasury can be withdrawn only when the candidate concerned puts up his claim to it on the prescribed form. The system, as it operates, is that the candidate is supplied this claim form alongwith the communication of his having been found ineligible for admission. It is on the receipt of this form that the process to release that amount. is initiated. Since every dealing official is busy with the clearance of the admission cases, no one has time to attend to this work. It is only toward the end of the academic session that these refund cases are taken up. More deploringly, some of these rejected candidates who have either not received the refund form or have misplaced it and have thus not put up the claim go on anxiously waiting for the refund. Their enquiries generally fall on deaf ears. This system thus needs to be improved upon so that these unlucky persons are not put to hardship on this account as well and (more importantly) the image of the Institute is not tarnished.

The work of the admissions commences sometimes in July and continues till the end of October. By the time, the admission work draws to a close that of the terminal examination begins. Though this examination is to take place in April-May the following year, yet a good deal of preparatory work is to be gone through. The Institute's office will sort out the university examination forms. These are then thoroughly scrutinised in order to ensure that each candidate has duly filled them up and has also discharged all other attendant obligations. In case a deficiency is noticed in any form the candidate concerned has to be informed accordingly by post. Sometimes even reminders have to be issued to them. Then the forms are arranged in a certain prescribed order and transmitted in bulk alongwith the fees to the university controller of examinations. This work too is time consuming in nature and thus keeps the clerks busy.

As for its organisational pattern, this Section is generally put under the exclusive charge of an assistant registrar. The branch is then divided into a couple of sections, each under the charge of a superintendent. Each section is divided into a number of cells which, in turn, are manned by assistants and clerks. Each cell is assigned a certain number of students, say 250 or 300. It would handle the cases of this number of students, right from the verification of eligibility and their enrolment to the declaration of the results of their terminal examination and the dispatch of their result cards. In this way, the responsibility is clearly defined and the work is precisely earmarked to each functionary. Thus, this pattern is suitably geared up to ensure a smooth and efficient discharge of the work..

**Response-Sheet Evaluation**

Evaluation of response-sheets constitutes another facet of the student's services division of the Institute. The response sheets as received from the students are generally enclosed in packets. Instead of putting each individual response sheet in a separate cover, students tend to bunch a few of them together in one single packet perhaps with a view to saving the postal expenses. Obviously these packets contain an assorted lot of response sheets of various different subjects and papers. Their sorting out in separate lots thus constitutes the first aspect of this operation. The subject and paper-wise bundles that are then prepared are transmitted to the offices of the subject departments for their evaluation by the department teachers or by the outsiders as the case may be. After the evaluation is done, the performance of each student is entered into the master register and the response sheet is mailed back to the person concerned. In the case of the outside evaluator, their remuneration bills are also prepared and passed on to the accounts section for payment.

This work too is highly time-bound. Response sheets if expeditiously evaluated and sent back to the student as early as possible, he feels encouraged and is further inspired to write and send more of them. If, on the contrary, he has to wait for the response sheet for months together, his whole enthusiasm towards his studies is sapped. But what actually happens is that this work is neither done efficiently nor effectively. This is one major scar on the face of this system. While the quality of evaluation needs to be tackled in a different way, the administrative organisation of this work should be patterned in a manner that not much time is spent either at the pre-evaluation stage or at the post-evaluation stage.

As far as possible, this work should be wholly assigned to the exclusive charge of the subject departments. They should receive them directly from the students, get them evaluated, maintain their record and despatch them back directly to the students. Thus patterned on the principle of undivided responsibility, this type of an organisation would result into a good deal of the saving of time, otherwise wasted in transmitting the bundles of response sheets from one section to another. But to assign the responsibility of this work to the subject department may not be possible in all cases. This is particularly so with regard to the under-graduate classes wherein a student is required to study three/four different subjects. The work of sorting out the response sheets of the various subjects would pose difficulties. It is, therefore, essential that there is created a separate section in the students services division to receive and sort out the response sheets. The rest of the work may be left to the care of the subject departments. In view of the correlation of the students' performance in response sheets with their eligibility to the terminal examination, this section should form part and parcel of the students services division.

**Personal Contact Programmes (PCP's)**

With a view to enhancing the efficacy of its instruction every Institute organises a series of Personal Contact Programmes. Though of a short duration of a week or ten-days each, PCP is an elaborate affair, involving organisation on a large scale. All types of arrangements for full-fledged teaching and counselling of a few hundred students are to be improvised. In the absence of its-own infrastructional facilities in mofussil towns, the Institute is required to hire buildings from local college/schools, to transport either its own faculty or to arrange one locally, procure all other equipments necessary for this exercise. Not to speak of these on-the-spot arrangements, a good deal of planning and programming is gone through before these series are actually organised.

To smoothly and successfully conduct these PCP's, the Institute needs to set up a separate department for this work. Its job would comprise fixation of the dates for these PCP's, their timely notification to all students through circulars, press releases and the like, answering students' inquiries, making suitable arrangements for their actual conduct and, above all, to handle the accounts of varied types of activities associated with them. Since this work commences generally from October onward by which time the rush of information seekers considerably alleviates, it is administratively prudent to entrust it to the care of the information and publicity division of the Institute. Apart from providing work to the latter during the lean period, its expertise in public relations would prove immensely useful for the efficient conduct of the PCP.

**Lesson Production**

No other administrative activity of the Institute is either so multi-faceted in nature or voluminous in size as lesson production. Again, this is the activity which imparts to distance education an industrial touch. Basically, it is performed at two levels— editing and printing. The former concept, though comparatively somewhat foreign to our Institutes, is of crucial importance in so far as the presentation of the subject matter and the resultant comprehensibility of the students is concerned. Editing is a very broad concept. It refers not only to editing of the subject matter *per se* but also to designing, lay-out, preparation of the diagrams, tables, charts and such like other illustrative aids. Conceived as such, the editing section should comprise editors, language experts, designers, cartographers, draughtsman and the like.

Every well-reputed Institute/Open University does maintain such an elaborate technical personnel. As soon as a lesson-script is finalised by the subject specialists, it is passed on to this cell where everyone of

such case) from adopting the registration mode of lesson packets. In view of the close affinity of this work with that of the production of the study material, it would be administratively viable if this cell is put under the charge of the assistant registrar/superintendent of the production branch. Two to three assistants and a few clerks would be quite sufficient to cope with this work.

## Accounts-Keeping

Accounts-keeping of the Institute too is an elaborate affair, for it is required to maintain accounts of a number of different things. On the receipt side, it handles fees of thousands of students which amount runs into lakhs of rupees. More significant than either the mammoth number of students or the large volume of the fees, is the wriggling nature of this work. As hinted earlier, fees continue pouring in throughout the course of the year, thus necessitating the creation of a permanent mechanism for it. As for the payments, the range of activities on account of which these are made, is bewilderingly large. The major heads of expenditure are, first, the salary of a large number of employees who manipulate the Institute's manifold operations. Then comes the payment of the bills relating to the purchase of a number of articles that are purchased day in and day out. Most prominent among which are, paper and stationery, library books, equipment for the educational media and the computer centres and the laboratories and various other sundry articles. The activities of this department thus far described are typical of every educational institution. The extra-ordinary nature of the accounts department of the Institute of Distance Education lies in the payment of such unusual types of bills as those of the printers, lesson writers, response-sheet evaluators, PCP teachers and such other institutions/functionaries as are engaged in the production of the study materials or the imparting of distance instruction In this way, we find that the accounts branch is quite a busy section of the Institute's office. More importantly, the efficiency level of this department determines the reputation of the Institute to a very large extent.

One of the ugly aspects of the accounts-keeping of our society in general and of the Institutes of Distance Education in particular is the tendency on the part of those who handle the payments to delay them as long as possible, sometimes even till the end of the financial year. Besides bringing a bad name to the Institute, this delay breeds corruption. When the suppliers of the goods and services know on the basis of their own or the other's experiences that the payments would be unduly delayed, they quote the prices of their goods/services at a premium, providing a cushion for the interest on the capital that would thus be locked, risk involved and also for the speed money required to grease the palm of the dealing officials to obtain an early release of the payments. Conversely, if payments are released promptly, the quotations tend to come down. It is, therefore, important that the chief executive of the Institute must ensure that all the suppliers submit their bills alongwith each and every consignment and further that each bill is promptly processed, passed and paid. He must have a very sound and efficient monitoring system and must take to task all such officials who show sluggishness on this account.

Another unhappy feature of our accounts-keeping is not to make any payment unless a proper claim for it is filed. This is an in-built flaw of our system. It is too out-moded to ensure efficiency in the system. To give an illustration. Every Institute gets lessons written and response-sheets evaluated from the outside teachers on small contract basis. Before making assignments, written requests are made to them and their consent obtained. Once the assignment is completed and the lesson-script is received from the writer concerned and, similarly, the response sheets are received back after evaluation and the head of the department certifies to this fact in writing, where is the need for the author/evaluator concerned to put up his claim in writing for the release of the payment? If someone fails to file his claim (a number of such cases are noticed every year) he loses his remuneration. The case of such persons notwithstanding, the system is irritating. This author had to wage a long battle against the die-hard, ultra-cautious formalists in order to get rid of this unwarranted requirement of filing claims in writing. Now the system is fairly streamlined. As soon as the assignment is complete, steps are automatically initiated to release the payments without the loss of much time.

Varied types of bills and accounts-keeping thereof gives one an impression that the work of this department is gigantic in nature. There is no denying this fact as well. However, if all those departments which make purchases or procure the different types of services are assigned the responsibility to process their own bills and after the necessary procedural formalities are complete, they transmit these bills to the accounts branch for payment, the work of this department can be reduced considerably. If such a decentralised system is evolved and enforced, the accounts department can be assigned to the care of just one superintendent who can conveniently cope with this work with the help of a few assistants and clerks. In addition to this department, this superintendent can also be given the charge of the establishment section, dealing with the salaries and other monetary perks of the employees, their postings and transfers, their leave account, their disciplinary conduct and so on and so forth. Patterned thus, this organisational set-up of accounts-keeping can ensure a reasonable degree of efficiency. If this orgnisational arrangement is further supported with a good monitoring system, it can help the Institute to permanently cast off the stigma of delayed payments and other allied ills.

## Academic Wing

The academic wing of the Institute comprises the various subject sections (better known as departments). The specialised nature of each discipline and its distinct academic and administrative needs and requirements, demand that each departments is accorded a separate, autonomous status and organised accordingly. Patterned on the lines of their counterparts in the conventional wing of the university, each one of them is provided with a well-defined office with clerk/clerks who function under the overall supervision of the head/co-ordinator of the department (a senior teacher). This office caters to all the needs of the department concerned. Besides maintaining its records, it communicates directly with script writers, response sheet evaluators and the others who render services to the department. It receives response sheets, get them evaluated and despatches them back to the students. It also processes all types of bills and organises the PCP. In order to lessen the botheration of the departmental clerk in typing the lesson scripts, record-keeping of the students' response sheets, bill-making, correspondence and communication with outsiders, etc. etc. he should preferably be provided with a portable computer. This will add immensely to his efficiency.

## Para-academic Departments

Library, Educational Media Centre (which undertakes the work of preparing the audio and the video components of the study material) and the Computer Centre, are those sections of the Institute which can be labelled neither strictly academic nor administrative in character. The services that they provide are in fact staff in nature, contributing to the efficient performance of the work of the academics, on one side, and the students, on the other. Like subject departments, they too should be treated as autonomous, separate entities and should thus function under the over-all supervision and control of their respective heads. Compared to the Library staff which would consist of a librarian, a few library assistants, restorers, clerks and the others, the Educational Media Centre would necessarily be a larger organisation, comprising producers, cameramen, graphists, maintenance engineers and such like other technical experts, provided, of course, the Institute has the will and resources to have a full-fledged audio-video unit of its own. The Computer Centre would like-wise be a small organisation, again depending upon the Institute's perception of this technology. All these departments should also be conceded the autonomy to operate their own budget without the interference of the administrative wing of the Institute. It hardly needs to be emphasised that the bureaucracy, of all sectors of our public life, is the least progressive in nature. Too much rule-worship and ultra-cautious attitude that they are trained to develop, make them perceive all modern progressive developments as an encroachment on, and an erosion of, their well-guarded and carefully nursed administrative system and the values thereof. They adopt the new technology and other modern concepts but very gradually and cautiously. If, therefore, the administrative office is conceded any role in the management of these wings, that might prove to be counter-productive for the efficient functioning of these department. Their heads should be directly responsible to the Director.

## Director's Office

Being the office of the chief executive, the Director's Office is the nerve centre of the Institute. It is from here that all policies emanate and all strings are pulled and everyone is therefore kept on his tip-toe. This office might not require many officials but those who are posted here should be quite proficient in their job and well-versed with all rules and regulations so that they may be able to tender sound advice to the Director, thereby justifying their posting at this nerve centre. Above all, they should be quite courteous and polite in their public dealings in view of the large number of the visitors who visit this office every day.

As for the requirements of this office, it would need to be staffed by a personal assistant (PA) who should not only be an efficient stenographer but also a good confidant of the Director. Besides him, there is needed an office assistant who would deal with the files and papers, received from the lower echelons of the office and are meant for the perusal and approval of the Director. He too plays a very crucial role in view of the fact that all types of files and papers pass through his hands.

Yet another person required is the one who would deal with the faculty on behalf of the Director. In the course of the performance of their role, the faculty comes across various types of problems, relating to the different facets of the Institute's administration. To allow them to sort out these problems directly with the functionaries concerned would imply, on the one hand, an unwarranted interference in the work of the latter, and, on the other, exposing the former to unwanted humiliating situations. It is, therefore, administratively prudent to provide a channel through which all the problems of the faculty are funnelled to and from the functionaries concerned. It is for this purpose that an office assistant needs to be stationed in the Director's office who should help the faculty to sort out their administrative problems. He should also act as a liaison between the office and the subject departments, receiving from them the files, lesson-scripts and the like and forward them to the other sections of the office and vice versa. Thus, this functionary too would play a very important role.

It may once again be emphasised that the major job of this office is to get the feed-back from the various departments about their day-to-day functioning. No separate official is required for this work, for all the above-named three functionaries if work with their eyes and ears open and with an element of commitment on their part, they can provide sufficient feed-back. Besides them, there is the deputy-registrar who is supposed to oversee the functioning of his office in a wide-awake manner and also to keep the Director duly posted with the day-to-day progress of work of the other departments. The Director on his part should also whole-heartedly devote himself to the well-being of his Institute. He should keep on pricking all these officials for more and more of information. Any slackness on his part would provide to the others an excuse to sleep over their work. It has been observed that those persons who have extra-institutional interests as that of the university politics, have taken but little care to develop their Institutes. Their divided loyalties have landed their Institutes into dens of corruption, inefficiency and nepotism. Much therefore depends upon the personality of the one who dons this chair.

## Administrative Set-up—An Integrated View

The foregoing discussion and description of its managerial needs and requirements leads us to the conclusion that the Institute's administrative set-up would comprise, at its grass-roots, nine major sections, each under the charge of a superintendent. These sections would then be clubbed together into three branches, which would be headed by assistant registrars. These would be as under:

1. Establishment and accounts branch :
   (a) establishment section;
   (b) accounts section, and
   (c) buildings and estate maintenance section.
2. Students' service branch :
   (a) admission and examination section;
   (b) information, publicity and PCP section, and
   (c) response-sheet section.
3. Production Branch:
   (a) lesson printing section;
   (b) editorial section, and
   (c) delivery section.

Further onward, these branches would be put under the charge of a deputy registrar who would act as the head of this administrative set-up. He would exercise the powers of superintendence, direction and control over the entire office. While he himself would be responsible to the Director, he would ensure an expeditious and smooth execution of the policies and other decisions taken at the levels of the Director, Governing Council and other policy-making bodies of the University.

As for the subject departments and the para-academic divisions (library, educational media centre and the computer centre) these would be directly accountable to the Director. They would channelise their administrative needs to the sections concerned through the agency of the Director's office.

## II

### Efficiency Inputs

Every organisation, like a human being, functions in a given environment. Both act and react upon each other. To make an organisation successful, we therefore need a healthy environment which may ensure to it unhindered functioning. Conversely, if the environment is not conducive to its smooth progress, howsoever well-designed an organisation may be, it would not come upto its expectations. This is precisely the reason why our Indian

## ORGANIZATIONAL SET-UP OF THE INSTITUTE

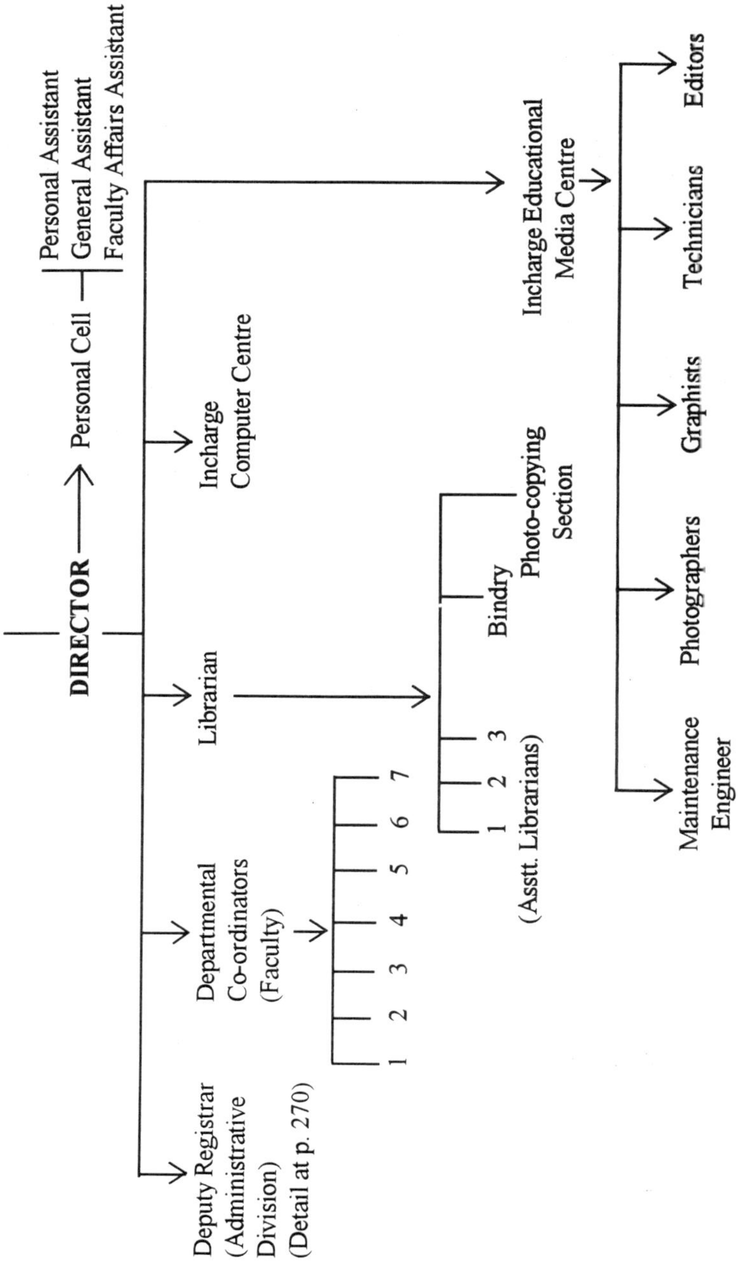

**ORGANIZATIONAL SET-UP OF THE INSTITUTE (Contd.)**

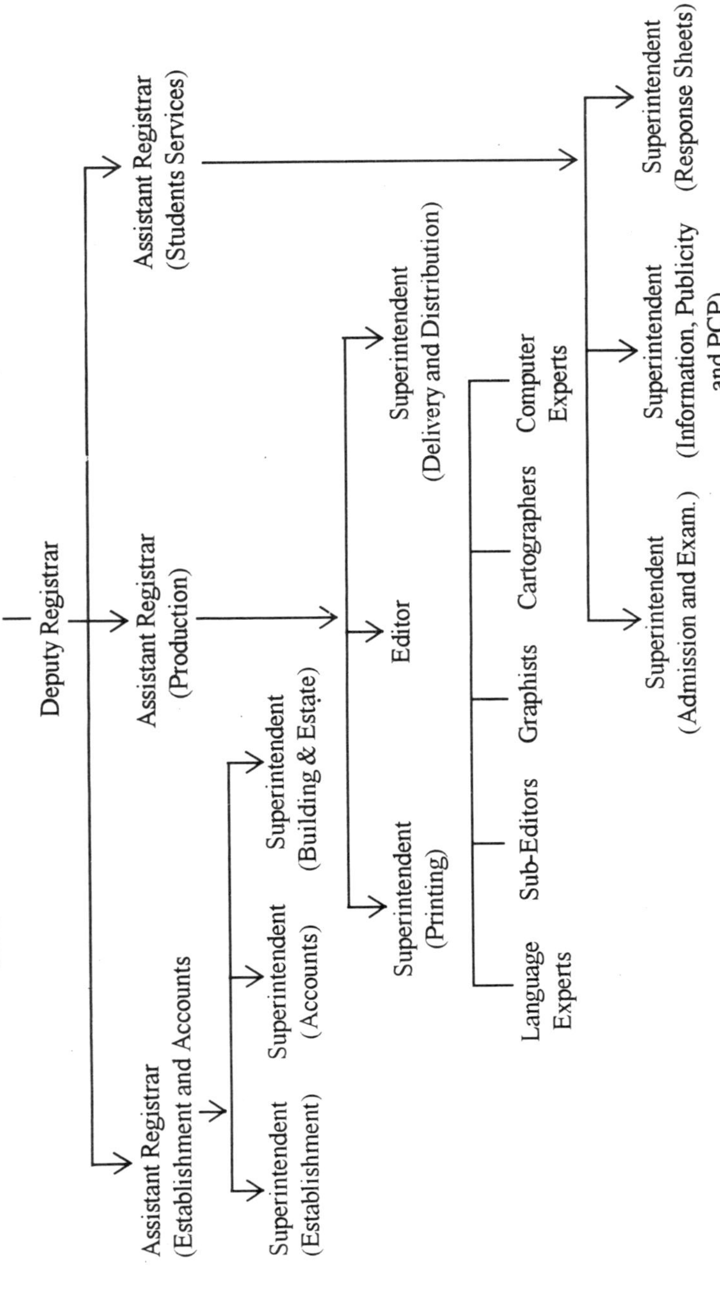

administration has, by and large, failed to serve the society as ideally as both people and its planners and designers had expected of it.

Broadly, the environment has two components — psychological and sociological. The former refers to the psychology of those men and women who work in the organisation. How do they perceive their role, what is the degree of their commitment to the organisation and, above all, what is the work culture that they and their predecessors have developed over the years ? As for the sociological component, it consists of those structural, social, cultural and economic factors that condition the psychology of the workers. Thus this component has a very a broad sweep, both in its range and impact. If this component is suitably taken care, it can go a long way in toning up the psychology of the workers, enhancing their morale in the long run. Keeping in view its importance, we confine our discussion to this component and identify some of those factors as are of vital importance in so far as our limited objective of the overall well-being of the Institute is concerned. It may also be mentioned that these factors are not very difficult to be taken care either.

1. *Curb on Frequent Transfer of the Employees*

The Institute, being one of the many departments of the university, draws its employees from the Registrar's office. All those who work in the university are borne on one common administrative cadre, which is at the behest of the Registrar. It is he who allocates them to the various offices of the university (the Institute included) and also transfers them from one place to another. Transfers and postings are, more or less, discretionary on his part; very seldom he may consult the head of a department.

This system has proved to be highly inimical for the smooth and progressive functioning of the Institute. As has been repeatedly pointed out earlier, the Institute is pretty different from the other departments of the university both in its objectives and the nature of its functioning. While the other departments deal with the students on the spot, the Institute's students live at far off places and have to be contacted only through the medium of post. Further, while the university is concerned either with the imparting of instruction or with the conduct of examination and it must discharge these obligations whatever may be the cost, the Institute, on the other hand, must always ensure that while discharging its obligations, its administration remains cost-efficient. Above all, there are numerous facets of the Institute's administration which need a trained personnel and not novices. Such however is not the case with the other departments of the university.

These differences apart, the overall progress of the university as also the canons of courtesy demand that the Registrar should take the Director into confidence before effecting any change in the personnel make-up of the Institute. But unfortunately such has not been the case. Complaints of arbitrary action on the part of the Registrar have been received from all over the country. As early as 1982, a concern to this effect was expressed in the national meet of the NCDE. The resolution that it passed, *inter alia,* said, "The present position about administrative staff working in some institutes, but controlled by the Registrar, bristles with difficulties. Frequent transfers without consultation with the Director, new recruitment and constant changes from branch to branch render it difficult to train an ordinary office assistant with a clientele-oriented functioning of the Institute." (NCDE Second Seminar). Things have not improved since then. On the contrary, these might have deteriorated further.

The Institute is thus confronted with the problem how to run its administration smoothly and efficiently when it does not have control over its employee ? It has been frequently noticed that whenever an official has earned for himself a good reputation of a sincere and hard-working person, the Registrar picks him up for posting in a more favourite office, and, conversely, all the inconvenient persons are dumped into the Institute. The poor Director remains a helpless spectator of all these changes. No amount of pleading makes the adamant Registrar retrieve his position.

This system needs to be improved upon as early as possible. The Director's consent for any change must be obtained before any transfer or posting in the Institute is made. Besides, certain departments of the Institute should be identified which need a trained personnel, such as students' admission and examination section, computer and educational media centres, production department and the like. Transfers should not be effected in them so frequently. A via media of this type can alone save the Institute from the vagaries of this cancerous disease of frequent, arbitrary postings and transfers.

## 2. *Officer-oriented Administration*

The clientele-oriented nature of the Institute demands that its structural pattern should be cast slightly differently from the rest of the university. It should be manned more by the officers than by the petty clerks. The seniority and experience of the former make them more competent to handle the varied types of inquiries that pour into the office day in and day out. Those enquiries which are received by post need to be answered in writing. As said earlier, the letters answering clients' queries should be well-drafted and politely-worded so that they create a good impression on that distantly situated person who seeks the information/clarification. A superintendent, rather than a clerk, is more well-versed with the art of writing such letters. In the same manner, if a superintendent attends to a visitor or an in-coming telephone call, he would not only provide correct and comprehensive information but would also project a good image of the Institute/University by his sincerity and courtesy. It is therefore important that the Institute's administration should be officer-oriented.

This objective has already been achieved not only in the little world of the Institute but in the wider realm of the universities of the country and for that matter in other government offices as well. The new ratio between assistants and clerks (1 :1.5) and between superintendents and assistants (1:3) that now forms a nation-wide norm of the administrative structure, makes the administration more officer-oriented than bottom heavy. Now the number of the superintendents has gone up quite considerably. But unfortunately this increase has not created any dent in the tradition-hardened office routine. The desks of inquiry are still manned by the clerks and the noting on the files and drafting of the letters continues to be initiated again by the clerks. The office assistants and superintendents still confine their role to initialling the files and letter drafts with their signatures. Thus, the administration still continues to be run by the petty clerks. The winds of change seem to have eluded it. The Institute's authorities in particular should take necessary action to change this approach and provide a new orientation to it by making their officers assume greater responsibility of running the day-to-day administration.

### 3. *Monitoring and Feed-back*

As has already been emphasised, the Institute should develop an efficient and well-designed comprehensive system of monitoring so that the men at the top are kept regularly posted with the day-to-day progress of the administration and how far the targets are being achieved. The pre-requisites of this system are, first, clearly-defined channels for the free flow of information, and, second, pre-determined department-wise targets. While the latter provide measures to judge the progress of the Institute at any given point of time, the former expedite the feedback process.

There are certain departments in the Institute whose work is target-bound. It is all the more imperative to keep a track of their progress, failing which the Institute may run the risk of earning a bad name. These departments are: eligibility (to enrolment) preparation, printing and delivery of the study material; disposal of the inquiries and complaints of the students and the others; the payment of the bills, etc. etc. The fixation of the targets in their case is comparatively easy. Pre-determined schedules/time-tables can provide a convenient index to judge the performance of these departments. However, it is somewhat difficult to determine precisely, how long a complaint or an inquiry would take to be answered, or the eligibility of a candidate to be determined. In such cases, the Institute's authorities should take pains to work out the optimum time-limit for such a type of cases, and then ensure that those time limits are strictly adhered to. The officers-in-charge of these sections are got to be quite vigilant on this account.

Way back in the sixties, the Administrative Reforms Commission of the Government of India (1967) and of the Government of Punjab (1968) had also stressed the need to make each and every aspect of the work of the government offices target bound, especially at the grass-root level where the incidence of truancy and delay is perhaps the greatest. The former had recommended that the "work norms for various posts in Government.....should be evolved urgently. A target date for completing this work should be fixed for each Department." (Recommendation No.67).

The feedback, as received from the branches below, should be properly processed and analysed so as to find out the sources or causes why certain targets had failed to be achieved. Periodic meetings of the officers can go a long way in overcoming the incidence of delay/lapse and thereby the efficiency of the administration can be geared up suitably. Needless to repeat that the Institute, of all other departments of the university, should be made to function at a fairly high level of efficiency so as to serve the interests of distance students to the best of their expectations. A good system of monitoring the feedback is an effective bulwark against delay and inefficiency.

### 4. *Simplification of Procedures*

Long, circuitous office procedures also constitute another very important cause of delay and inefficiency in government offices (university or the Institute is no exception). This is a legacy of the good, old colonial administration. The deep-rooted psychology of the imperial rulers to look down upon the 'natives' of this land as dishonest rascals, had made them cleverly devise such long and difficult procedures so that the natives may be kept away from the state benefits as far as possible. Now when those suspicion-ridden rulers have gone away long since and (more importantly) efficiency and quick disposal of work has become the universal concern of the people the world over, there is hardly any justification to retain such procedures. It has been widely experienced that wherever rules and procedures have been simplified, not only the efficiency level has gone up but the output has also increased. In turn, the straightening and simplification of procedures has inducted into the administration an element of transparency which has further helped it to get rid of corruption.

In so far as the administrative set-up of the Institute is concerned, there is a lot of scope for the simplification of procedures. To identify some of the areas. In the first place, there is the prospectus (information hand-book) that the Institute brings out every year, for the guidance of the prospective students. As pointed out earlier, it is generally couched in a highly difficult juridical language. Its presentation needs to be simplified by softening its language, straightening its sentences and serialising the points in an easy-to-comprehend style. Similarly, there are numerous columns in the admission form which have become redundant. They are there more because of the tradition and less because of their relevance. These too can be deleted.

In the same manner, many of the requirements which a candidate is obliged to fulfil can be dispensed away. Besides, many a register that the Institute maintains to record the entries of numerous types of information also need to be given a fresh look. Their number and size too can be drastically pruned. A few years back, a farsighted Registrar of the Panjab University (Mr. D.P.Verma) initiated an exercise in collaboration with another expert (Mr. Shital Prakash) to simplify the record-keeping of the university. In the process, they successfully got rid of much of the dead wood. A number of forms and proformas and many columns in the fat registers were either deleted totally or their size was considerably reduced. This highly successful exercise resulted into enhanced efficiency, on the one hand, and economy of resources, on the other.

On his part, this author too made an effort in this direction in the Chandigarh Institute. When he took over, the Institute used to bring out two separate prospectuses, one for the M.A. classes and the other for the rest of the courses. Besides the duplication of effort and the consequent wastage of resources, this practice caused a good deal of confusion to the distantly situated candidates. To begin with, this author reduced the number of these prospectuses from two to one. Later on, he simplified its contents and the presentation thereof. Thereafter he paid his attention to the record-keeping and effected some economy there too. In this way, we find that there is an immense scope for a meaningful review of the procedures. But what is actually wanted is the requisite will to do so.

It may further be underlined that an effort, once made must not be construed as the dead-end of the exercise. Administration is an on-going, dynamic process, as hinted at the outset. It demands a continuous review and reordering of procedures and processes, structures and relationships. That is the reason why every big organisation maintains a separate wing, called R and D (research and development). Every Institute should try to work in that direction.

### 5. *Mechanisation of Processes*

In this age of technological advancement to carry on the office routine in the same old anachronistic fashion speaks very poorly of those men and women who sit at the helm of affairs of the organisation concerned. By doing so they project the image of their being either the rank conservatives or a highly ignorant lot of the fast changing and dynamic world. Why must not we try to get a leaf from the book of those organisations (may those be privately managed) whose efficiency we so highly emulate and harness modern technology in the conduct of our office operations. How long shall we continue rigidly sticking to the past traditions many of which have lost their relevance ? Why can't we be forward-looking and cast our lot with the future instead of letting the rotten past continue haunting us from behind.

Our thrust toward the simplification of the office procedures can acquire altogether a new look if we introduce computer technology in the day-to-day office operations of the Institute. There is hardly an aspect of its administration which may not be benefited by this technology. Record-keeping of all types, as for instance the students fees, response sheets, PCP attendance, varied types of purchases and payments, establishment details, etc. etc. will get streamlined. If the computer is efficiently managed and maintained, many a register can be totally dispensed away. Besides, the whole process becomes easy and smooth, particularly its retrieval aspect which under the manual system is highly irritating and time-consuming. Moreover, it is this aspect which is the main villain of the peace in so far as the efficiency level of the organisation is concerned.

The U.G.C. has also commended that "computerisation of office work and tutor-marked assignments should be introduced in the DDE's. This would add to their efficiency and eliminate certain cumbersome record keeping and other office procedures." (Additional Secretary's letter. 1993).

The second important area which computer technology can take care very effectively is the printing of lessons. As has been exhaustively explained earlier, a desk-top publishing system which is computer-based can help the Institute not only in cutting down the incidence of delay on this account but also in considerably reducing the cost of the production of the study material. Incidentally, these are the two-factors which bring a lot of humiliation to the Institute — delay in the estimations of the students and high cost in the eyes of the authorities.

In the third place, the computer can assist the Institute in upgrading the level of communication with the students and the others. Day in and day out, various types of letters and circulars are issued to its clients. Most of these letters are of a routine nature and are issued every year at one time or another. Instead of dictating them afresh every time to the stenographer and ask him to type and cyclostyle them, these could conveniently be fed into the computer and retrieved whenever need be and then sent to the students after proper printing on the DTP system. In this way, not only will the officers be saved of the annual exercise of drafting these letters, but the quality of these letters, both language-wise and printing-wise, would be considerably improved as desired above.

Besides the computer, the Institute should also go in for a good inter-communication system (inter-com). All important branches/ functionaries should be interlinked with one another through internal telephones. This scientific mechanism would expedite the flow of communications and, conversely, would reduce the need of the officials personally visiting one another either to give or to seek the information. Side by side, the habit to exchange information through this medium should be diligently cultivated. A new work culture, typical of private organisations, shall have to be promoted.

Then there are a number of other small machines such as those of franking the stamps and printing of addresses. These too should be installed. They would save a lot of botheration and the time of the officials. Above all, they would make their work neat and clean.

Thus, the Institute should adopt the modern technology in a big way and discard manual operations as far as possible. Such a bold change would radically improve its functioning and would also make the work of the officials more pleasant and dignified. But the adoption of new technology of computerisation, warns Ram Takwale (1995) is not an easy task. "It requires long term planning and enduring commitment .... (More importantly) the university has to develop an atmosphere that will promote application of new technologies in various university functions. "p.55). We must therefore be vigilant on this account.

6. *Physical Lay-Out of the Office*

One of the most neglected areas of our administration is the physical lay-out of the office. Wherever we find a little space we put a table and a chair and seat one official without the least regard to the distance he has to traverse and botheration he has to take in order to reach his boss or his record of books and registers. That is the reason why most of our officials tend to delay things because the records are located at an unduly far-off place from them. This is again the reason why most of them when wind up at the end of the day and go home, they leave their papers scattered on their desks and totally uncared by anyone. If we pay a little heed to the seating arrangement of our officials and the general lay-out of the office, we can induct a lot of efficiency to their conduct and can also, at the same time, bring to bear a more healthy and cleaner look to our offices. Compare the offices of the government with those of a private organisation, one would find a world of difference between the two. Recent researches have established that healthy and comfortable work environments contribute to the efficiency of an organisation in no less a measure than, say, the other service conditions. This aspect, therefore needs to be given due attention.

The offices should be so located that those of them which have a close interaction with one another (say students admission and response sheets), should be put on one and the same floor and as near to one another as possible. Secondly, those offices which are frequently visited by the students and the other general public (as for instance the Director, library, lesson-despatch, information and publicity bureau) should be located on the ground floor so that the visitor may remain restricted to that floor only and do not go beyond that. The faculty and the other staff are thus allowed to work undistractingly by the outsiders.

Further, each clerk should be provided with a desk, having a small cupboard by his side wherein he may put his entire record that he needs every now and then, so that he may not have to stand up every time he needs a paper or file and walk a few yards to reach his maga-sized almirah. What ought to be done is that there are built long rows of concrete, low-level platforms, under which there are provided small cupboards. Besides these platforms the clerks chairs and small tables are laid. These compact desks and side-cupboards make the functionality of these officials both smooth and comfortable. These cup-boards also do away with those tall steel/wooden almirahs which are generally put all around the walls of the room, obstructing light and fresh air, on the one hand, and giving an ugly look to the office, on the other. To make this proposed physical lay-out of the office look more elegant as also functionally more efficient, the services of the architects and designers may be requisitioned. In foreign countries, these desks are also connected with one another through conveyor belts for the onward transmission of files and papers. However, we do not need these belts for the time being.

A good lay-out can also lead to the conservation of office space which is so precious everywhere. This advantage is too important to be side-tracked.

*7. Bar on the Visitors*

Our university offices generally provide the look of a public place. Any one may come and any one may go at any time. That the outside visitors would disturb the highly paid public officials, engaged in an important state activity hardly forms the concern of anyone. This is too deplorable a state of affairs. This situation needs to be radically improved upon. To this end, we need to take three measures.

First, the visitors' entry beyond the reception counter is to be totally stopped. Those who want to meet anyone should be required to indicate the name of the official to be visited and the purpose of the visit. The receptionist would send the information to the immediate superior of the official concerned. If he is free, he may come down to the reception and meet his friend/relation. The number of the visitors that an official meets in the course of a day also needs to be restricted to the bare minimum. A strict vigil has to be kept both by the immediate superior of the official concerned and by the reception.

Second, in order to provide comfortable environments to the visitors while they are waiting for the official or talking to him, a nice waiting room needs to be set up at the reception so that one may not feel odd to be there. We must not overlook the fact that the Institute's reception is a very busy place. It is not necessarily true that only those who are to meet the officials alone come. Besides them, students come to collect their lesson packets, audio cassettes, prospectuses and also to pay the fees or to discharge various types of incomplete admission formalities. Then there are various other types of persons who come to seek one type of information or another. All of them are men of dignity who expect a nice treatment. Thus, it becomes all the more essential to provide for a well-furnished and elegantly maintained reception room. Needless to add that it too would also lend grandeur to the Institute.

Third, since we put a bar on the movement of the officials out of their offices, it also becomes incumbent on the administration that it makes a provision for in-session tea/coffee and snacks. Good arrangements should be made to serve the officials a cup of tea/coffee at their desks both in the forenoon and in the afternoon. If possible, this refreshment should be subsidised by the Institute. Such an arrangement would considerably tone up the morale of the officials and would also enhance their efficiency.

## Conclusion

As mentioned at the outset, the secretariat of the Institute constitutes the kernel of its organisational set-up. If it is well-organised and functions at a reasonably high level of its efficiency, it will radiate both light and fragrance, attracting everybody to its fold. If, on the contrary, this kernel is rotten, it will emit foul smell, keeping everybody at bay. Its clientele-oriented nature as also the interests of the distantly situated students demand that all-out efforts should be made to ensure that it provides the best of its service to its students. This is possible if efficiency inputs, as indicated above, are sufficiently fed into it. Besides, those who preside over the destinies of such Institutes are got to be more imaginative, dedicated and, above all, constantly vigilant about its day-to-day functioning. Howsoever well-planned the organisational set-up may be, it will go phut the moment hard vigilance is relaxed a bit. In the end, it may be observed that the responsibility of the managers of these Institutes increases all the more in view of the poor image that they have already been projecting. If things do not improve, this budding system of education will meet the fate of a promising child, crippled at birth.

## REFERENCES

Erdos, Renee F., *Teaching by Correspondence*. UNESCO Source Book. London, Longman. 1967.

Holmberg, Borje, 'On the organisation of distance study'. Khan, Inayat (Ed.). *Teaching at a Distance*. Delhi, Amar Prakashan. 1989.

Letter of Dr. B.P. Gangurde, Additional Secretary, U.G.C. D.O. No. F-3-14/93 (NFE-II) December, 1993.

Proceedings of Second Seminar of the National Council for Correspondence Education (Chandigarh), 1979.

*Report of the Indian Administration Reforms Commission.* Government of India, 1967.

*Report of the Punjab Administration Reforms Commission* (Personnel Administration). Government of Punjab, 1968.

Rumble, Granville, *The Management of Distance Learning Systems*. Paris, UNESCO International Institute of Education Planning. 1992.

Sims, Ripley, *An Inquiry into Correspondence Educating Process*. International Council of Correspondence Education. 1982.

Takwale, Ram, 'Application of New Technologies in Distance Education', in Bakshish Singh (Ed.) *New Horizons in Distance Education.* New Delhi, Uppal. 1995.

CHAPTER XI

# INTRA-UNIVERSITY STATUS OF THE INSTITUTE

IN India, distance education is imparted through the medium of the Open Universities and the Institutes of Correspondence Courses. The former are autonomous institutions and exclusively devoted to the promotion of this new system of education; as such they are the masters of their own destiny, untrammelled by any other institution or agency. As for the Institutes, they being the conventional university sponsored agencies, are totally dependent upon their parent universities. They are directed and controlled by the latter. What is the extent of this control and, conversely, what is the degree of autonomy of action that they enjoy, is that vital issue which seriously impinges upon the functioning of these Institutes. Ironically, it has not been settled so far. Even after nearly three decades of the inception of this system (incidentally this system was ushered in this country through the instrumentality of these Institutes rather than through the Open Universities), these Institutes are not very clear as to what is their relationship with other sister institutions of the university and what status do they enjoy within its institutional framework. It needs to be hardly emphasised that the lack of precision in this respect has done great harm to them and, more deploringly, to the well-being of the system at large. On one side, the decision-making bodies of the university ride rough-shod on them, and, on the other, the faculty and the others working in these Institutes nurse the grievance of their being given a raw deal, thereby sagging their morale. The status of these Institutes vis-a-vis the other departments of the university thus needs to be spelled out without any more delay.

To put the issue of the intra-university status of these Institutes in its proper perspective. Every typical Indian university provides instruction through two types of academic institutions, its organic teaching departments and the colleges affiliated to it. Devoted exclusively to teaching upto the degree level (bachelor's) and in some cases even upto the post-graduate level, colleges are set up and maintained either by the government or by some denominational organisation. They are affiliated to the universities for purposes of the standardisation of their instruction and the award of the degrees. In contra-distinction to them, the university departments are the organic offsprings of the university, created and maintained by it. They impart instruction mostly of the post-graduate level though their science departments also provide for undergraduate honours courses as well. Besides, these university departments undertake research activities which constitute their main function. Thus, the distinction between the two lies, first, in their parentage. While the departments belong to the university itself, the colleges are established and managed by the government or by private denominations. Secondly, the departments are organically linked to the universities, whereas the colleges are affiliated to them only for a limited purpose. Thirdly, the nature of their activities is also somewhat different, while the colleges confine themselves only to teaching, the departments also undertake research in addition.

However, the distinction does not end here. It stretches farther than that. In view of the teaching being a common factor between the two, all academic bodies of the university are managed by them jointly, though not on a parity basis. More comprehensive nature of the Department's academic activities, comparatively better qualifications and higher status of their faculty and, above all, the organic nature of their relationship with the university — are some of the factors that provide to the departments a dominant say in decision-making. Besides providing to them a numerical preponderance in various decision-making bodies (Boards of Studies, Faculties, Academic Council and Senate), the nominees of the departments hold the membership of these bodies (except the Senate) by rotation, in their ex-officio capacity. On the other hand, the limited number of seats allocated to the college teachers, are held by them through an open election.

Finally, the college faculty comprises mostly lecturers, who are generally masters graduates only. Very rarely does a college lecturer have to his credit a research degree, though the number of such persons is on the increase gradually. Of late, the U.G.C. has also sanctioned a few posts of readers to such colleges as provide for post-graduate classes. As for professor's positions, these remain conspicuous by their absence. Until recently, the salary structure of the college teachers was also different from the university teachers.

These are some of the differences between the two instructional components of the university. Though the colleges and the university departments, together with each other, manage higher education of the nation, the latter command an edge over the former in so far as their outward public image is concerned. The university departments are perceived by the public in general and by the students in particular as seats of higher learning.

In the context of this background, we examine the issue of the status of the Institutes of Distance Education. Way back in the late sixties and early seventies when most of the universities set up these Institutes, the concept of distance education was not very clear to anyone in the country. Induced by the idea of providing extension wings to their conventional system, the universities created these Institutes within their own structural frame and accorded to them the status of a constituent (in a way affiliated) college. The logic behind this decision was the under-graduate nature of their instructional level. Another underlying factor was the plurality of disciplines that these new institutes were supposed to cater. Compared to the uni-disciplined nature of the departments, college structure was thought to be a more suitable pattern to fit into the new institute's plural nature. Some of the universities however invoked the concept of the 'school' in order to accommodate these Institutes within the framework of their departments. But the number of such universities is too small, whereas those which accord the college status is too large.

Gradually as the implications of the college status unfolded themselves, the faculty of these Institutes discovered to their great chagrin that they were in no way better than the college lecturers and perhaps a shade worse. For they had to bear day in and day out such sarcastic remarks of their departmental colleagues as their being second grade teachers. It may be underlined that almost all those persons who had joined the faculty of these Institutes at the initial stages of their inception, were seasoned teachers who had put in a number of years of service in colleges. They had come over to the university because of the outward superior image of its service and also because of its better salary structure. At that time, the pay-scale of a university lecturer was Rs.400-40-800-50-950 whereas that of a college lecturer was Rs. 300-15-600.

Finding all their hopes and expectations dashing to the ground, the Institute's teachers rose in revolt and began to demand a parity with their departmental colleagues in all respects. The new horizons that distance education had by then beaten in the shape of the emergence of a number of Open Universities and the IGNOU in particular, made these teachers more vocal in their demand. New fora provided to them by such institutions as the National Council for Distance Education (NCDE) and the National Institute of Educational Planning and Administration (NIEPA) both of which held a series of national seminars on distance education provided to these teachers the much sought-after institutional support. The rising tempo of this demand, on the other hand, led to the hardening of the attitude of the university authorities. Nevertheless, a few universities conceded this demand. The Punjab, Punjabi and the Shimla Universities redesignated these Institutes as university departments, while the Kashmir University converted it into a faculty of distance education.

## II

The conversion of these Institutes from colleges to the university departments/faculties brought in its wake fresh issues. The new status made these Institutes gain in certain respects and lose in certain others. Consequently, a new debate started as to what is the ideal status that can preserve the distinct identity of these Institutes and pave the way for an unhindered development of the system of distance education, and also, at the same time, ensure dignity and parity to its faculty with their colleagues working in other departments of the university. The debate brings into a sharper focus the merits and demerits of all those institutional mechanisms — department, faculty and autonomous institutes— that are suggested as alternative to the college status. We may analyse these alternative solutions at length along with their attendant advantages and dis- advantages.

To begin with, we take up the college status. As mentioned earlier, there did exist colleges much before the establishment of the Institutes of Distance Education. But having been set up either by the Government or private denominational institutions, their relationship with the universities was just marginal in nature. It was limited only to their affiliation with it and the maintenance of the academic standards thereof. Consequently, they occupied but peripheral place in the university calendar. On the other hand, the teaching departments consumed the bulk of its space. When the Institutes of Distance Education emerged into existence, and the college status was conferred on them, the few provisions of the calendar relating to the affiliating colleges proved to be far too inadequate to deal with the various aspects of these Institutes. To meet their multi-faceted administrative and academic requirements a new plethora of rules and regulations relating to such diverse aspects as the norms relating to its faculty, functions of the Institute, admission norms, role of its governing council and so on and so forth, had to be inducted into the university calendar. What shape would these rules and regulations assume ultimately depended mostly upon the character of the new Institute, its administrative requirements and factors conducive for the effective and efficient discharge of its roles. However, personal equations that its top functionaries had built up at that given point of time with the powers-that-be also determined the shape of things from behind the scene.

Keeping all these factors into consideration, the new rules, as these were finally incorporated into the university calendar, provided for a reasonable degree of administrative and financial autonomy to these Institutes. Though there are variations from university to university, the Panjab University model, by and large, was comprehensive enough to explain the broad character of the powers and competence of these Institutes almost everywhere else. To spell out the details of this model, it is headed by the Director (this designation has received a nation-wide recognition) who is directly responsible fcr all his acts to the Vice-Chancellor. Like other faculty members of the university, he too is appointed by the Vice-Chancellor with the approval of the Syndicate and Senate through an open competition. Invariably, he bears the qualifications, designation and status of a university professor. He directs, superintends and controls all functionaries of the Institute — academic, administrative, technical and others. He presides over all their meetings and all policy decisions except those that require the approval of the Vice-Chancellor, are finally taken by him. The budget of the Institute, after it has been passed and approved by the appropriate fora of the university, is administered by him. The day-to-day expenditure upto a certain level (which incidentally was far higher in his case than that of heads of the university departments) is sanctioned by him, beyond which of course, the sanction of the Vice-Chancellor is obligatory. He is an ex-officio member of the Academic Council of the university, which is its highest academic decision-making body.

As regards the overall policy-making of the Institute, it vests with its governing council/standing committee. Being a small compact body of a few university deans, eminent distance educationists, representatives of the Syndicate and the Institute's faculty, Registrar and the Finance Officer of the University, the Vice Chancellor (its ex-officio chairman) and the Director (acting as its member-secretary). Holding its meetings from time to time, it passes the Institute's budget, reviews its functioning, take policy decisions and adopts various other measures necessary for the efficient functioning of the Institute. All its decisions lie straightaway with the Syndicate and Senate for their final approval. With these vast powers of review and decision-making, this small compact body provides to the Director (Institute) an ideal forum to present his problems and suggestions to these well-meaning persons in authority in as frank a manner as he can. These members too on their part get an opportunity to examine the various aspects of the Institute's functioning in as threadbare a manner as they may choose. In this way we find that the Institute derives the benefit of the wisdom and particular attention of all those who have a stake in university's decision-making, on the one hand, and eminent experts in the field of distance education, on the other.

The Institute, though being a college, provides for a faculty which for all intents and purposes is at par with the university department. It comprises lecturers, readers and (in certain cases) professors, who are recruited on qualifications as prescribed for the rest of the university faculty and in the same manner as the latter. The salary structure and other service conditions are also identical with the others. But in so far as their representation on various academic bodies, such as Board of Studies, Faculties, Academic Council and Senate, is concerned they are bracketed with college teachers. This is the biggest drawback of this model and it is this drawback which drove the faculty on the warpath.

In sum, the college model is conducive to the overall well-being of the Institute, on the whole, for it assures to it a reasonable degree of functional autonomy as well as the benefit of the wisdom and particular care of its governing body. But it is highly detrimental to the interests of its faculty. As explained in an earlier chapter, it not only creates hurdles in the way of its academic progress but it also subjected it to a good deal of degradation and humiliation.

To come to the Departmental Model. In simple parlance, this model obliterates the distinctive character of the Institute and merges it into the common institutional fabric of university departments. The change from the college to the departmental status is not confined to the change in its nomenclature only but it involves transformation of a fundamental character. In the first instance, the Director's place was taken over by the Chairman. There is a world of difference between the two. While the Director was appointed against a substantive post, quite distinctive and independent of the Institute's faculty, the Chairman holds his position because of his being a member of his faculty. While the substantive nature of the Directors' post conferred on him an element of permanence in his tenure, the chairman, being subject to the democratic principle of rotation, holds his position for a limited tenure of three years, at the end of which term, he must step down in favour of his immediate junior colleague. While the Director was directly accountable to the Chief Executive of the University, the Chairman submits himself to a comparatively lower-level functionary, namely the Dean, University Instruction. Above all, the Directors' powers were far more comprehensive than those of the Chairman.

The second focal point of the change was the administrative office of the Institute. Under the college model, it enjoyed an autonomous entity of its own, having such well-defined sections as students' services, establishment, accounts, printing, maintenance, etc. etc. All of them functioned under the overall direction, superintendence and control of the Director. But with the switch over to the departmental model, the whole of the establishment was taken over by the Registrar and these sections lost their autonomous character. They came to be merged with their respective counterparts in the Registrar's Office. Earlier, all moneys accruing to the Institute from the students' fees, amalgamated funds, and the like were accounted to the Directorate's Fund, separately maintained and operated by the Director. Now that Fund came to be abolished and moneys began to be credited to the Registrar's account.

Another major change related to the Institute's budget. It too had a separate entity and was first presented to, and passed by, the Institute's governing council and then considered by the Finance Board, the Syndicate and the Senate. Its presentation to the governing council provided to the Vice-Chancellor, the Registrar, the Finance Officer and the other high-ups of the university an occasion to have a closer look at the financial as well as the general state of health of the Institute. Out of the debate thereon many a constructive suggestion would flow out. With the transformation of the Institute to the Department, the budget has come to be merged in the general budget of the university. Now it is summarily considered alongwith the budgets of a number of other departments by a small committee of officials. The earlier privilege of its close and detailed scrutiny by a high level committee of the top brass of the university has lapsed in the process of change. In this way, the Institute lost its distinctive character as was manifest in the various aspects of its autonomy, in the high-powered institution of its director, and in the uniqueness of its governing council. Now it stands merged in the commonality of the departments.

Yet another area of change was the faculty. As mentioned earlier, the Institute's faculty was seriously discriminated against the departmental faculty in matters of representation on various academic bodies of the university. While in the case of some of these bodies, it had to rub shoulders with the college faculty, the doors of a few others had been completely banged against them. Under the new model, the faculty came to be fully delinked from the college faculty and was merged in the university faculty, discipline to discipline. Thus, the invidious distinction between the two faculties — Institute's and University's — stood totally abolished. Those who belonged to the Institute also acquired the privilege of membership of each and every decision-making body on the basis of their seniority in the cadre of their respective disciplines. No longer would they be required to contest elections for their membership. Instead, they would sit on them in their ex-officio capacity. Thus, the net gain of the change that accrued went to the faculty; the Institute on its own might have been a loser.

After having dwelt at length on the administrative and financial aspects of the Institute's functioning as also on the gains and losses of the faculty under the two models, we may now examine the academic facet of the Institute. For purposes of this discussion, it would imply only the courses and curricula of the study programmes that are given by the Institute through the distance mode. Whether the Institute is under the college model or the departmental model, its courses and curricula continue to fall in the purview of such academic bodies of the university as Boards of Studies, Faculties and the Academic Council. The Institute's faculty is no doubt represented on all of them, (earlier through election and now in their ex-officio capacity). Their say is marginal in the sense that the number of the conventionalists, hailing from the departments as well as from the colleges, is far too large. It is this preponderance of the conventionalists that seriously militates against the interests of the distance mode. Little appreciation of the Institute's difficulties in general and the withholding of the permission to institute's new courses, especially of the non-conventional nature in particular, are some of the manifestations of their step-motherly attitude toward the Institute. It is these academic bodies which can be held exclusively responsible for the stunted growth of Distance Education in these conventional universities. To substantiate this fact, we cite the following two cases.

A couple of years back, the Panjab University decided to institute through the distance mode a diploma course on environmental health and pollution. Keeping in view the multi-disciplined nature of the proposed course, the Vice-Chancellor constituted a well-representative committee, (drawing experts from such fields as bio-chemistry, bio-physics, microbiology, zoology, chemical engineering, sociology, economics and environmentalists) to draw out the details of the course. After a number of meetings, the Committee finalised the curriculum of the course, such other modalities as the mode of its instruction, (particularly its practical aspect), the duration of its PCP, the nature of the faculty to write the lessons and to conduct practicals, Everyone of the members whole-heartedly endorsed these details and assured his support for its final approval by the Academic Council. But when the proposal was put up to the latter it was out-voted. One could easily make out that a few vested interests of the conventionalists had ganged themselves against the Directorate. How could they tolerate that a course of that novel nature and having so vast a potential should be taken up ( of all the Departments) by the Directorate!

Equally eye-opening was the case of the proposal made to the Directorate of Correspondence Courses, Panjab University, by the Chandigarh College of Nursing to institute with their collaboration a diploma course on nursing through correspondence. They assured that they would extend to the Directorate all types of assistance (faculty, technical, institutional and even monetary) needed to put that proposal into effect. The higher-level authorities of the University, conventionally oriented as they have always been , did not see kindly to that proposal. Two years later when the Nursing Council of India made that very proposal to the IGNOU, it jumped over it. Today, that course is in strides.

It is thus amply evident that the conventionalists do not want, willy nilly, that these Institutes should break new grounds on academic horizons. It is a nation-wide complaint that these university dons have frustrated innumerable plans of these Institutes to expand their academic activities in many new directions. Whenever a request is made to them to allow these Institutes to run a certain existing class-room-based course through the distance mode, they turn down the request on the pretext that the well-maintained high standards would be drastically eroded once these courses are passed on to these Institutes. And in case the proposal pertains to a non-conventional type of a course, their argument is that the Institute would not be able to muster up the resources needed to run that course. Obviously, academic climate so much vitiated by mistrust and (even) hostility would make these Institutes confine themselves indefinitely to a handful of beaten track degree-level courses in arts and (at best) commerce. Thus, they have been deliberately crippled and declared incapable to render real service to the nation in alleviating the rigours of such of its ailments as unemployment, mal-administration of public services, redeployment of skills, inservice training to the technical and professional personnel, etc. etc. Indeed, this was one of the laudable objectives behind the institution of this new system of education. But unfortunately our conventionalists did not allow these Institutes to go ahead in this direction — partly out of their ignorance of the potentialities of this system, and partly out of their jealousy as well as apprehension that this system might overtake them.

The third model in the series is the Autonomous Institutes Model. Shaped on the lines of autonomous colleges, this model grants autonomy to the Institute in all such matters as academic, administrative, financial and the like. Without narrating its details (for that might mean repetition of what has already been said earlier) suffice it to say that this model resembles, by and large, the college model in so far as the administrative and financial dimensions of its autonomous character are concerned. As regards its academic aspect, this model grants to the Institute perfect autonomy to launch any course it likes. The parent university will not have any objection whatsoever. The role of the latter will be confined only to the award of degrees and diplomas, and also to provide necessary financial and administrative support that the Institute would need from time to time. In order to develop courses and curricula thereof, the Autonomous Institute will set up its own Boards of Studies, Faculties and the Academic Council which will be composed of the Institute's faculty only. Thus, this model combines in it the merits of the earlier two models, namely administrative and financial autonomy of the college model and faculty's active involvement in the enactment and introduction of the new courses and curricula, of the departmental model. It should therefore, commend itself to everyone.

However, it is an open secret that the concept of the autonomous colleges could not sell well in India. The college teachers feel apprehensive that once a college is given autonomy and the restraining hand of the universities is relaxed a bit, the private managements and, for that matter, even the government, would spare no effort to economise on the academic staff as much as it can. Besides, their service conditions would also be tampered with. The Institute's faculty will also feel no less concerned on this account. Moreover, the idea of their having no longer anything to do with the academic bodies of the university will also be equally repugnant to them. For, they are obsessed with the impression that their destinies are inseparably intertwined with those of the general faculty of the university. They want to sit in the 'benign' shadow of the latter, rather than carve out an independent place for themselves by their own hard work. Having lived in the company of the conventionalists for far too long, they do not appear to have developed confidence in themselves or in their own system. Thus, total separation of the two systems (conventional and distance) from each other can alone mitigate this deep sense of dependence from the minds of the distance teachers, as also release distance education from the stranglehold of the conventionalists. We dilate upon this suggestion a little later in this chapter.

## III

As hinted above, the conversion of the Institute from a college to a department has undoubtedlly benefited its faculty quite considerably. For it has mitigated their main grievance of a share in academic decision-making at par with the others. In turn, this has washed off much of the humiliation which it had to suffer at the hands of the latter. But for this gain, the Institute has been a loser in every other respect. It had to forgo the benefit of the services of two of its very valuable institutions, namely a permanent director and its governing council. The loss of these two institutions is irreparable in the literal sense of the term.

These losses notwithstanding, the Institute by no stretch of imagination, can be equated with a typical university teaching department. Both may be important in their own right, but they are certainly different from each other. The difference between the two lies, firstly, in the nature of the work that they perform. The functions of the Department are limited only to class-room teaching and research. The courses that the Department gives are limited and fixed. Similarly, each faculty member's area of specialisation is well-defined and he is allotted teaching accordingly. He performs his work round the year in a manner that he determines for himself without any outside direction or interference. As for research, it is the students who select their own field and the topic thereof. The nature of the field automatically brings them into the lap of their supervisor. How a researcher further proceeds with his work, it is a mutual affair between him and his guide. The scope of external interference in research is thus all the more limited. Occasionally, the faculty may meet and exchange notes regarding their common problems, if any. The chairman presides over them. Thus the academic aspect of the Department is highly limited in nature, though profound in significance. It is tuned on autonomous and individualistic functioning of the faculty which provides for but very little external direction, co-ordination and control.

As regards the administrative dimensions of the Department, its small office comprising a superintendent, a few clerks-cum-typists, one or two librarians, and a couple of class four personnel — handles the administrative work of a small body of students (whose number hardly exceeds 150 including the research scholars) and a handful of faculty members. To spell out the nature of this work, it relates to the student admission, correspondence with the university office and external examiners; conduct of the terminal examination and evaluation of the answer books thereof: preparation of the salary bills and the bills of certain purchases; convening of the meeting of the Boards of Studies, and such like other small jobs. The management of all these administrative operations is so simple and non-technical in nature that whatever little of supervision and control that they entail, can be performed by any faculty member. Hence it hardly matters whether the chairman's tenure is limited to a few years or is life-long in nature. In fact, he is there more to co-ordinate the activities of his colleagues and the others and less to control and direct them. To bind down an academic permanently to this trivial work of a co-ordinating and supervisory nature is to waste his talent. In such a situation, the system of rotation is ideal.

In contradistinction to the Department, the Institute is a mammoth organisation, comprising about 75 to 100 faculty members, 150 administrative officials, a huge library, an educational media centre, a computer unit, a number of technicians, a lesson production unit, etc.etc. Its physical size apart, the administrative operations that the Institute is required to perform are not only varied but highly elaborate and subtle in nature. Though these functions have been exhaustively highlighted in the preceding chapter, some of them need to be briefly emphasised again. Firstly, the printing of more than 1,100 lesson units in itself is a gigantic operation. Besides, it involves the continuous contact and dealings with innumerable private printing presses. Secondly, the purchase of tons of paper for the printing of lessons, a large number of books for the library, numerous types of stationery articles and various other things of wear and tear. Thirdly, administration and accounts-keeping of the huge establishment. Fourthly, innumerable students' problems. Not only does the annual enrollment run into thousands but the non-contiguous nature of its students adds tremendously to the publicity of the work. Every aspect of this particular area of Institute's administration demands continuous watch lest the students at the other end are not put to any unnecessary hardship. This task thus becomes both taxing and time-consuming.

In this way, we find that the Institute's office is as elaborate and organisationally as complex as the Registrar's Office. The time-bound nature of many of its operations adds another dimension to its functioning. It must work efficiently so that all operations are gone through in time and its goals are effectively achieved. Though there are the assistant and deputy registrars to ensure expeditious discharge of the administrative activities, the Director head (which office is necessitated partly by the educational nature of the Institute and partly by the presence of a large-sized faculty) must also exercise on his own close supervision on each and every aspect of the Institute's office, exercise an effective control on it and must also seek continuous feedback from it. Any laxity on this account would make a mess of the whole administration. To exercise an effective control on such a vast and complex organisation, we need a person who has a close insight into, and tight grip on, this machine. A slight ignorance of, or even unfamiliarity with, any aspect of its details may seriously erode the level of his control. Obviously, only that person would qualify to be its head who is appointed strictly for this purpose and enjoys a permanent tenure. If, on the contrary, a person comes to this office by virtue of rotation and that too for a limited period of, say, three years, his newness to the chair, his lack of familiarity with the detailed structure of the Institute's office and the subtlety of its operations, and , above all, his orientation more to books and studies than to office administration and control, would seriously hamper the effective discharge of his responsibilities vis-a-vis the Institute's administration. Moreover, his fear to revert to the ranks at the end of his tenure would make him avoid hard decisions and evade his duties.

There is yet another dimension of the Director's responsibilities. He is the head of a large faculty. The nature of the work of the faculty is quite different from that of the Department's faculty. The Institute's teachers are required to write and vet lessons, evaluate response sheets and teach in the PCP. As mentioned earlier, the nature of this work is such that it leaves a vast scope for truancy. The absence of any in-built mechanism of the teachers' accountability to their students further widens the nature of this scope. Such a situation warrants the Director to be a hard task master. He should not hesitate to pull up a teacher if he does not discharge his duties properly. A rotating head ill-qualifies for this unpleasant task. For one who is not one amongst them but above and distinct from them, alone can be an effective head of the Institute's administration.

The system of the rotation of heads of the university Departments has been adversely commented upon by a number of well-meaning persons, including some of those who adorn the chairs of high academic eminence. It is often pointed out that the system has led to laxity of control, decline in academic activities and consequent dwarfing of the stature of the Departments. If such a system which is already under so much of public criticism, is extended to the Institutes of Distance Education, it will do an irreparable harm to them. These Institutes which have hardly anything in common with the Departments, need to be differently structured and differently attuned. The Director who is the kingpin of this structure, must be kept outside the pail of the system of rotation, even if the scheme of democratisation (rotation being a part of which) is to be extended to these Institutes. This valuable institution of the Director thus needs to be effectively protected against the emotionally surcharged cry of importing democracy to educational administration.

Another valuable institution is the Governing Council of the Institute. As repeatedly emphasised earlier, this institution provides to the Institute the rare benefit of a close scrutiny and fostering care at the hands of all those persons who command the destinies of the university—Vice-Chancellor, Deans, Syndics, Registrar and Finance Officer. No other department is privileged enough to be overseen by such a high level body. Our experience shows that many a time decisions of vital importance flow out of the deliberations of the governing council which otherwise are not possible if decision-making were to rest with an authority of a lesser stature as generally happens under the departmental model. Besides the tangible benefits of these decisions, the presence of a few eminent educationists endows a new orientation to the deliberations of this body. The Institute's functioning is reviewed in the wider perspective of the latest thinking and developments in the realm of distance education which, again is not possible but for this body. Thus, there is a very strong case in favour of the retention of this body.

## IV

To come to the issue of the relationship of these Institutes with their parent universities. While discussing this issue in the course of a national level workshop organised by the NIEPA (National Institute of Educational Planning and Administration) a few years ago a participant very aptly compared this relationship with the one that subsists between a coloniser and the colony, (Workshop Report, 1987). There is absolutely no exaggeration in this remark that these universities treat their Institutes of Distance Education in no way better than their colonies. As in the hey-day of imperialism, the entire policy making vests with the university authorities, the Institutes are the mere recipients and faithful implementors of these policy decisions. If a certain study programme is to be introduced, the decision is to be taken by the Academic Council, if the syllabus of an existing course is to be or not to be modified, the Board of Studies decides the issue; if an office functionary is to be transferred to or from the Institute, it is the Registrar who decides it in his absolute discretion; if paper is to be purchased, a high level committee, comprising such officials as Registrar, Finance Officer, Secretary, Publication Bureau and the Director (head of the Institute) steps in to handle the operation, and so on. If a certain development grant is given by the U.G.C., say, for the strengthening of the faculty or library stock, every Department of the university would get a share but not the Institute. The argument that is advanced in justification thereof is that these grants are generally meant for the conventional system. If, on the contrary, the budget of an Institute shows some surplus (as is the case with such Institutes as Madras, Tirupati, Madurai or Rohtak, the surplus budget of which is a normal feature), the university would take away the entire surplus. At that time, the distinction between the conventional and the distance systems is deliberately overlooked.

Thus, we find that "the present university structure exhibits a kind of asymmetry," wherein the entire decision-making vests in the hands of the conventionalists, while those who have a stake in the system stand virtually marginalised. (Ruddar Datt, 1982). More deploringly, those who take decisions for distance-education system constitute a lot of the highly unconcerned and indifferent persons. Having no stake in the system, they evince but little interest in its development. Rather, their decisions exhibit an element of bias, and even of hostility, against the system. What would thus be the fate of this system when its destinies are governed by persons who neither want to surrender this role nor do they want to play it well, protecting and advancing its interests.

When these Institutes were started about a quarter of century back, there was some justification for their being tagged with the conventional system. For the concept of distance education was then new and thus enjoyed but little credibility with the public at large. Obviously, it needed some crutches to stand upon which the existing university system could alone provide. But that does not by any means imply that it should be permanently tied to its apron strings, creating problems both for the universities and the Institutes. The former feel unnecessarily burdened by its weight (as the British once used to describe their colonies as White Man's Burden), while the Institutes nurse the grievance that their growth is stunted by the university. Now when distance education has carved out for itself an independent place of its own, there is little reason for their being tagged to the conventional system any longer. It needs more of flexibility in its approach and greater innovation. But unfortunately this system has failed to attain both flexibility and innovation largely because of its having been put in the shadow of the conventional system. Compared to these Institutes, the Open Universities which are completely free from the encumbrances of the conventional universities, have shown a remarkable degree of flexibility as well as innovation. Highlighting this fact in a more pungent way, Ruddar Datt, 1982 says, "Discussions (in conventional universities) go on whether a particular course is amenable through correspondence medium, while discussion in Open University centres round the innovations to be made so that every kind of knowledge can be transmitted through distance education medium." (p.26). If under such a situation distance education continues to play a subservient role to the traditional universities, then it will remain a poor relation of the latter, its wings of innovation completely clipped off and would thus become impossible for it to break new grounds and to give purposeful direction to our education.(Bakshish Singh, 1982).

The incongruence of the two systems (conventional and distance) in their overall objectives and orientations apart, the administrative models (college and the departmental) that the traditional university system has to offer to the Institute's organisational pattern – ill-serve its needs and requirements. If the former model subjects the faculty to a humiliating situation, the latter robs the Institute of its administrative and fiscal autonomy.

The linking of the Institute with the traditional university system further provides an immense scope for the Registrar's office to unduly interfere in the Institute's administration. To cite a case of this unwarranted interference. Recently (1992-93) the Panjab University faced an extraordinary financial stringency. To overcome it, it put a general cut of 10 per cent on all items of expenditure. The finance department of the university extended that cut even to the printing of lessons without realising that it is such a vital component of the budget where economy is neither possible nor desirable. Incidentally, the enrollment of students in that very year had far exceeded the budgetary estimates necessitating the Institute to print a larger number of lessons. No amount of pleading would make the finance department budge from its illogical stand. At long last, the Vice-Chancellor had to be approached to get the cut restored.

Making a parallel complaint, Jose Chander (1982) says, that while advertising courses and disseminating information about them through wide publicity is crucial for the well-being of the Institute, the top management of the University is generally reluctant to make necessary budget allotment for it. Further, even within the budget allotment they refuse to grant a free hand to the Director thus preventing him from applying foresight and imagination. (p.15).

Yet another drawback of the present system of organically linking distance education with the traditional system is the divided nature of the loyalty of the Institute's faculty. Having failed to identify themselves with the new system, these teachers always think in terms of shifting themselves over to the class-room based wings of their university. It is the duality in the system which lays before them a vast scope for comparing themselves with the others, that makes them clamour for a change. If the two systems are organically delinked from each other, the ground for unhappiness will then be pulled out from underneath their feet. Those who would then join this system would think twice before opting for it. In the absence of any alternative channel for diversion, they would work with a greater sense of dedication for the system, like those who are presently working in the open universities.

## V

Now what is the way out of this impasse? In the present situation, there are only two possible solutions. Either we may continue with the present dual model whereunder (to repeat) the conventional universities provide for both 'on-campus' and 'off-campus' education. Or alternatively, we discard this model altogether and convert all these Institutes into 'uni-instructional open universities', which do not have anything to do with their conventional brethren. Ruddar Datt (1993) a doyan among distance educators of this country, is a strong protagonist of the former proposal. In his keynote address to a seminar, organised by the Punjabi University in January, 1993, he made a passionate appeal to strengthen the dual mode in preference to Open Universities. He observed, "In an under-developed country like ours, it is not wise to immitate the high-cost U.K. model of Open University. It would be much better to utilize the infra-structure both in men and materials already developed in the dual mode and the single mode institutions to improve the quality of D.E.". In support of his thesis, Ruddar Datt (1993) advances three arguments. First, the dual mode as compared to the Open Universities, is a low cost model. Second, this mode can create conditions for improving the quality of instruction both in class-room and at a distance. Third, the teachers working in Open Universities are generally too much pre-occupied with "course designing, course preparation, interacting with technical consultants in the preparation of multi-media packages", with the result that "professional development in his or her own subject is relegated to a back seat." Such, however is not the case with the teachers working in the dual mode, for, this mode not only makes them interact with their class-room based counterparts more frequently but also provides to them the scope for a regular/occasional direct exposure to face-to-face teaching. Above all, he feels that the dual mode is much more effective than the single mode as measured in terms of the drop-out rate and the quality of student performance in terminal examinations.

On our part, we do not find much weight in all these arguments. It is an open secret (and Ruddar Datt also admits) that if distance education, as is provided by our Institutes today is far less costly than the one given, say, by the IGNOU, the secret is that they concentrate only on the correspondence medium. If they were also to supplement their instruction with audio-video media, the cost of their instruction too would escalate dramatically. Another factor that keeps the cost of their education at a comparatively low level is that they neither maintain well-equipped study centres nor do they employ the corporate approach to the preparation of their study material. Incidentally, the absence of both these things constitutes a major drawback of their functional methodology, seriously militating against the quality of their instruction. As for the argument that the teachers of the dual mode have a greater scope for closer interaction with their conventional counterparts, or for a regular exposure to face-to-face teaching, it is not supported by empirical evidence. Too overbearing an attitude of the conventionalists and the rigid casteism in the faculty rules out any such possibility. Above all, the way the conventional universities have been treating these Institutes over the years leaves little scope for the system of distance education to grow in a meaningful direction.

We honestly feel that so long as these Institutes are not delinked from the conventional system, they have but a bleak future ahead. They need to be put on an independent pedestal of their own. If that were to be the ideal solution then the Open University model commends itself the best. This model has already established its superiority over the dual mode by not only providing traditional education in a more open and flexible manner but also by opening the flood gates of distance education in many new and even unheard of directions. Thus, there is hardly any scope for more discussion on the comparative merits and demerits of the two models. The question that now needs to be suitably answered relates to the *modus operandi* of the change.

Assuming that all these Institutes are released from the limbo of the traditional university structure, would it then imply that all of them stand automatically converted into separate, independent open universities? That type of change would prove to be more counter-productive, for it would bring into existence a multitude of small open universities, with dilapidated financial structures and a highly frustrated faculty. The resources of the nation are too limited and precious to be squandered away on them. Their financing would add a new straw into the wind, making the centre-state relations further controversial. The change will therefore have to be imaginatively conceived and properly planned.

To us, the only viable alternative is that of the Regional Open Universities.(RUO) Let all these Institutes be clubbed together to form, say, half a dozen of regional open universities. In this respect, we may draw a leaf from the Australian book. Before we unfold the details of our plan, we may briefly relate the Australian experiment.

Australia had been seized of the problem of the hap-hazard growth of distance education in the country since the early seventies. In July, 1988 a policy statement was issued which set out 'efficiency', 'effectiveness', 'rationalisation' and 'amalgamation' as the main planks of the proposed reform. In pursuance thereof, the number of distance education institutions was reduced from 40 to 8. Only those institutions were given recognition and conferred the status of Distance Education Centres (DEC's) as had a sizeable strength of students on their rolls and had been renowned for quality instruction. Besides them, others too could exist, but they would neither get financial aid from the Government nor would they be allowed to give courses independently. At best they could adopt the courses of the DEC's. In this way, the Australian Government brought about the long-pending rationalisation of distance education in the country. (Refer to Livingston, 1990, and Seriven, 1990). We too can pick up courage in both hands and rationalise this system, thereby making it answer the national needs more effectively.

We propose that all the existing Institutes of Distance Education as also the Open Universities should be merged to form half a dozen or so of Regional Open Universities (ROU's). In order to ensure their proper functioning, free from the pulls and pressures of the local politics (which is one of the greatest banes of the Indian political system), all these

ROU's should be granted the status of Central Universities on the pattern of the IGNOU. To provide to them adequate financial support, there should be created a high level funding and coordinating authority on the lines of the U.G.C. It should be designated as Open Universities Grants Commission (OUGC) lest it should be eclipsed by the U.G.C. or by any other agency. The existing Parliamentary Statute of the IGNOU should be amended so that the role of developing, coordinating and funding of distance education which now vests with it, should be passed on to the OUGC. The creation of an independent agency, having no vested interests of its own, will alone ensure proper development of this new system of education.

Each one of these ROU's should be granted complete autonomy to institute courses. Conversely, their autonomy should neither be curbed by earmarking courses to them, nor should their geographical jurisdiction be limited to the narrow bounds of their respective regions. The idea behind this free play both with respect to the nature of the courses and their nation-wide jurisdiction is to make them freely and openly compete with one another so that the quest for academic excellence becomes sharper among them. Shutting them to the narrow confines either to a few courses or to their geographical boundaries would make them gloat with complacency, curb their urge to set high academic standards and, above all, make them foster their narrow regional interests. On the contrary, we want these universities to emerge as seats of academic excellence and also as national institutes of human resource development. Free and unhindered healthy competition among them can alone help them achieve that goal. A reference to some of the state-level open universities may not be out of place here. A few years back Rajasthan, for instance, set up an Open University with its head quarters at Kota. What the State Government did was to delink two of its existing Institutes of Distance Education (Jaipur and Udaipur) from their respective parent universities (Rajasthan and Udaipur) and merged them together to form one Open University. The change was confined only to their nomenclature and to the formal elevation of their status. Beyond that hardly anything worthwhile appears to have been done in order either to induct the spirit of openness and flexibility into their functioning or to the raising of the standards of their instruction. By and large, the two campuses of that university continue to function in the same old stereotyped manner.

In order to save the proposed Regional Open Universities from these typical pitfalls, we have already suggested that they should be kept out of the control of the State Governments and, instead, they should form a part of the responsibilities of human resource development of the Union Government. Further, they should be provided the benefit of the composite study centres, (as suggested earlier) so that they may not be hampered in their effort to disseminate their instruction as widely as they may choose. Above all, each one of them should develop its own courses and the study materials thereof. Having the benefit of a large faculty resulting from the merger of the faculty of all the Institutes of the region concerned, it would not be difficult for them to spare the senior faculty exclusively for the development of the study material. Centralisation, evolving from the merger of the various Institutes, would further facilitate the creation of the necessary infrastructure for the production of the audio and the video components of the study material. In this way, if requisite political will is forthcoming, these universities too can make a mark on the educational horizon of the nation in the same manner as the IGNOU has done.

## REFERENCES

Bakshish Singh, 'The Need for a National Institute/Open University for Distance Education'. Pandey, K.P. *et al.* (Eds.) *Distance Education: A Reappraisal.* (Papers of the Fourth National Seminar of the National Council for Distance Education). Shimla, H.P. University, 1982.

Chander, Jose. 'Problems of Management in Correspondence Education', in Chander, Jose (Ed.) *Distance Education in Indian Perspective.* (Papers of the Third National Seminar of the National Council for Distance Education). Trivandrum, Kerala University, 1982.

Datt, Ruddar, '*Planning and Development of Distance Education in India.*' Pandey, K.P. *et al. Op. Cit.*

Datt, Ruddar, 'Open Universities VRS Distance Education Directorates', *Keynote Address at the National Seminar* held on January 20-21, 1993, Punjabi University Patiala (Unpublished)

Livingston, K., 'The Shake-up in Australian Higher Education and its Impact on Distance Education', *I.C.D.E. Bulletin* No.24. (1990).

*Report of the NIEPA Workshop*, 1987.

Serivan. Bruce. 'Australia Restructures Distance Higher Education'. *I.C.D.E. Bulletin.* No. 22. (1990).

CHAPTER XII

# INTER-INSTITUTIONAL NETWORKING

IN this fast shrinking world, where cooperation among nations is the sole *mantra* of its existence, no institution or even an individual can afford to drive its/his lonely furrow. This is all the more true of distance education which depends for its quality on the collective wisdom of the many. Unlike the conventional system which is mainly a person-to-person instructional process, distance education needs to be pursued and promoted on a co-operative basis. If the Institutes tie up with one another in close fraternal bonds and draw upon one another's resources, they will not only assure quality of instruction but will also serve the nation more effectively and meaningfully. Thus, cooperation and not confrontation, mutual give and take and not isolation, should be the watchword of this instructional system. If most of our Institutes in India have, by and large, failed to make a mark of themselves, the main reason is that each one of them beats its own trumpet.

The network that the Institutes of Distance Education weave among themselves for purposes of mutual cooperation and collaboration may be limited to a few of them or may extend over to a region, nation or even the whole globe. Similarly, its scope may be restricted only to the bare use of one another's study material or may be pervasive enough so as to pool the resources for the preparation of the study material or for the management of other instructional services. Though the degree of closeness depends upon the individual Institute's vision of cooperation, the ideal situation would be that at the lower levels, the network is both closer and more dense/intense; as we move upwards, its density thins out while its coverage gets more pervasive. In the Indian context, a model of this type can alone make networking useful both for the Institutes and the system at large. We may examine this model at length.

## II

Based on the concept of concentric circles, the inner-most circle of this model consists of the regional network. As we open outwardly, the next circle we come across is that of the national network, while the outer-most circle comprises the international network. The possibility of a few more networks in between these circles cannot be ruled out depending upon the Institute's perception of the concept of cooperation. The Institutes may like to net together at the state level and, similarly, there may be developed international networks in between the national and the global networks. The Commonwealth of Learning, for instance, is undoubtedly an international network but it is certainly not global in character. Who knows the United Nations may set up tomorrow a world-wide network? Thus, this networking may assume any form and dimension. But the network that we propose should consist of three/four levels — rgional, national, Commonwealth-wide and global.

**Regional Network**

Region is a highly ambiguous term. It is generally interpreted in three different senses—the sub-state level (as for instance the Malwa or the Vidarbha regions), the supra-state level (the Northern/Southern regions) and the supra-national level (the Middle East or South Asian regions). In the context of this discussion, we refer to the region in its supra-state sense, the reason being that while the state is a small political entity, region is a large socio-cultural unit, hence making the educational needs and requirements of its people, more or less, uniform. Thus, there is a greater sense and scope for mutual give and take among the Institutes at the regional level rather than at the state level. However, it is not imperative that the Institutes must collaborate at the regional level. If they feel that there is a plenty of scope and advantages to network themselves at the state level, they may do so. It is therefore for the Institutes concerned to decide for themselves as to at which level would they like to network.

In the northern region of Punjab, Haryana and Himachal Pradesh which is culturally homogeneous there are four Institutes all of which, by and large, maintain the same type of study programmes. (The fifth Institute at Rohtak is one-dimensional in the sense that it provides for teacher's education only, hence having little in common with others.) Thus, there is an immense scope for regional networking among them. On the other hand, the State of Andhra Pradesh alone has 6 Institutes/ Open Universities. But for the Jawaharlal Nehru Technical University, all others make a provision for, more or less, identical type of study programmes. The number of these Institutes is so large that they may not have to go beyond the boundaries of their own State in order to derive the full benefit of networking. Thus, the situation may differ from region to region.

As for the nature and intensity of cooperation, networking at this level is useful only if it is closely-knit. Ideally all the collaborating Institutes should pool their resources together and develop the various services on a collective basis. The areas where networking can yield rich dividends are the preparation of the instructional materials and the development and maintenance of the study centres.

For purposes of illustration, we may refer to the Institutes of the Northern region, with respect to which this author had conducted in 1993 an indepth study and published a research paper thereon. All the institutes of this region, viz. Chandigarh, Shimla, Patiala and Kurukshetra, belong to their respective conventional universities and give study programmes of the conventional B.A. and M.A type. Most of these programmes are not only identical in name but are congruent with one another in so far as their courses and syllabi are concerned. As Table 12.1 highlights, out of the total number of 14 subjects that are taught at the B.A.level, 4 subjects (namely Political Science, Economics, History and English) are common among all the Institutes; 2 subjects (Public Administration and Hindi) are common among 3 Institutes; and 3 subjects (Commerce, Punjabi and Sanskrit) among 2 Institutes. In the same manner, most of the M.A.programmes are common;. 4 (namely Political Science, History, Economics and English) in all the four Institutes and 3 (Public Administration, Commerce and Punjabi) in 2 Institutes.

Not only is there a wide range of commonness in their study programmes but the courses and syllabi of most of these programmes are also identical. particularly their theoretical perspective which, incidentally constitutes a sizeable part of their syllabi because of the non-applied nature of most of them. To illustrate, the major areas of theoretical concern in the realm of Political Science are: Political Thought (Western and Indian), Modern Political Theory/Analysis, Comparative Politics and International Politics. These five areas constitute the main focus of study all over the world. In the Indian perspective, we must also study the Indian Political System/Indian Government and Politics. None can afford to ignore it. This type of commonness is not characteristic of Political Science alone, but is also true of Economics, Public Administration and the other social sciences.

Ironically, this commonness and congruity has not been taken advantage at all as each individual Institute prepares its own study

**TABLE 12.1: Study Programmes of the Four Institutes**

| *Study Programme* | B.A. | | | | M.A. | | | |
|---|---|---|---|---|---|---|---|---|
| | *PB* | *PBI* | *H.P.* | *KUK* | *PB* | *PBI* | *H.P.* | *KUK* |
| 1. Political Science | ✓ | ✓ | ✓ | ✓ | ✓ | ✓ | ✓ | ✓ |
| 2. Economics | ✓ | ✓ | ✓ | ✓ | ✓ | ✓ | ✓ | ✓ |
| 3. History | ✓ | ✓ | ✓ | ✓ | ✓ | ✓ | ✓ | ✓ |
| 4. Public Administration | ✓ | — | ✓ | ✓ | ✓ | — | ✓ | ✓ |
| 5. Commerce | ✓ | — | ✓ | — | — | ✓ | ✓ | ✓ |
| 6. Philosophy | ✓ | — | — | — | — | — | — | — |
| 7. Psychology | ✓ | — | — | — | — | — | — | — |
| 8. Geography | ✓ | — | — | — | — | — | — | — |
| 9. Hindi | ✓ | — | ✓ | ✓ | ✓ | — | — | — |
| 10. Punjabi | ✓ | ✓ | — | — | ✓ | ✓ | — | ✓ |
| 11. English | ✓ | ✓ | ✓ | ✓ | ✓ | ✓ | ✓ | ✓ |
| 12. Mathematics | ✓ | — | — | — | — | — | ✓ | — |
| 13. Sanskrit | — | — | — | — | — | — | — | — |
| 14. Education | — | — | ✓ | — | — | — | ✓ | — |

*Source*: Information Handbooks of the Institutes Concerned.

material. This policy of individualistic functioning further reinforced by the paucity of resources on their part, has rendered these Institutes incapable of providing either quality study material or its audio-video manifestations. It is this inadequacy on their part that earns an element of notoriety for these Institutes. If they pool all their resources together, they will more than make up their deficiency on these accounts. We may substantiate this fact with the help of the following illustration.

In the Chandigarh Institute, the 8-member Political Science faculty handles year after year 250 lesson-scripts of the B.A. and M.A. classes in English medium and another 90 each in Hindi and Punjabi Mediums (Table 12.2). This quantum of work, as highlighted in Chapter IV, is so large that the best part of the year of each teacher is spent on the vetting of these scripts. They are so much hard pressed by this work that the question of their attending to any other thing does not arise at all. If at any time, the syllabus of any class undergoes a change (wholly or partially) and they are required to rewrite a few lessons afresh, they would do so either at the cost of the effective vetting of other lesson scripts or get the

**TABLE 12.2: Showing Lesson Preparation Work-Load of Political Science Teachers in Chandigarh Institute**

| Class | Paper | No. of Classes | | | |
|---|---|---|---|---|---|
| | | English | Hindi | Punjabi | Total |
| M.A. I | I | 20 | — | — | 20 |
| | II | 20 | — | — | 20 |
| | III | 20 | — | — | 20 |
| | IV | 20 | — | — | 20 |
| M.A. I | I | 20 | — | — | 20 |
| | II | 20 | — | — | 20 |
| | III | 20 | — | — | 20 |
| | IV | 20 | — | — | 20 |
| B.A. I | I | 15 | 15 | 15 | 45 |
| | II | 15 | 15 | 15 | 45 |
| B.A. II | I | 15 | 15 | 15 | 45 |
| | II | 15 | 15 | 15 | 45 |
| B.A. III | I | 15 | 15 | 15 | 45 |
| | II | 15 | 15 | 15 | 45 |
| Grand Total | 14 | 250 | 90 | 90 | 430 |

*Source*: Institutes unpublished records.

new ones written from outside. Under such conditions of too tight a schedule of work, quality is bound to be the first casualty. This situation is not peculiar to the Chandigarh Institute only. It is, by and large, the same at Patiala, Shimla and Kurukshetra.

Imagine if the Political Science faculty of all the four Institutes combine together to do the 70 per cent of this work together (the common factor) how much relief that these teachers would get in order to attend to other things and how much collective wisdom that these Institutes would accumulate for qualitative improvement in this particular area of work. All these four Institutes have a total strength of 27 teachers on the faculty of Political Science. Assuming that the lesson preparation work is highly technical and difficult and hence not within the reach of every Tom, Dick and Harry, we exempt the 8 junior-most teachers (3 in each Institute) from this responsibility and instead detail them for the evaluation of response sheets and lecturing at the P.C.P. only. The rest of the teachers are exclusively set apart for the preparation of the study material, 12 (2 in each Institute) for the post graduate classes and the other 7 (2 in each Institute) for the under-graduate classes. The latter category of teachers being in-charge of the development of the study materials, will work in close liaison with their counterparts of the other Institutes in the manner as indicated below, while the junior teachers would function independently of their own.

The preparation of the lessons on a collective basis, as suggested above, would be undertaken by the senior teachers only. They would start this work by holding a plenary session of the faculty members of all the Institutes. In that session, the common areas of the syllabi of the various courses would be identified and the distribution of work among themselves would also be decided in accordance with the areas of their respective specialisation. After these preliminaries are over, the teachers specialising in various areas would then meet in separate groups in order to further distribute among themselves the lessons to be written in their respective areas, to formulate the detailed synopsis of each individual lesson and also to prepare a bibliography for the same. Thereafter, the teachers would retire to their rooms and sit down to write out the first draft of their lessons. When it is ready they would again meet and discuss the draft. In this way, they would try to hammer out the final script in stages. When that is ready, they would then hold consultations with the electronic technologists and would work on the audio and the video components of the written lesson.

This type of collaboration would prove to be highly beneficial to both the teachers and the Institutes. Once the teachers are entrusted with the exclusive responsibility of developing the study material in all its various manifestations, they would concentrate on this work. Since this work would relate to their area of specialisation, they would be too happy to do it. They would also naturally tend to keep themselves abreast with the day-to-day developments in their discipline. Collective deliberations with their counterparts and the human tendency not to cut a sorry figure in the presence of the others, would further goad them to self-study. Thus, they would be able to absolve themselves of the oft-repeated charge of distance teachers getting sluggish academically. They would be further benefited by learning the difficult art of preparing the audio and the video scripts.

As for the Institutes, they would have the advantage of making use of one an others' human resources and after these resources having been thus replenished, they would be able to effect radical improvement in the quality of their study materials and also to ensure its timely delivery. Above all, they would be in a position to make use of the modern electronic based instructional technologies. It may once again be pointed out that their inability to have access to these technologies thus far has denied to them a place in the coveted category of the Institutes of Distance Education. Networking would thus enable them to take a long stride toward the goal of distance education, *per se*.

Incidentally, the establishment of this type of a regional grid would rule out the need for the creation of audio-video hardware facilities at the level of each and every Institute. Instead, these can now be provided at any one central Institute of this network which would serve the needs of all others.

A closely-knit regional networking of this type would further facilitate these Institutes in their properly co-ordinated future development. Hitherto, the absence of any type of consultation much less collaboration and co-operation among the various Institutes had resulted into a good deal of overlapping and replication of courses and study programmes. To illustrate, the post-graduate courses in Political Science, Economics and History, are being offered, respectively, by 16, 15 and 13 Institutes (refer to Table 2.5, Chapter II).

It is further observed that whenever a certain new course is reported to be lucerative, it begins to be offered at once by a number of Institutes. While doing so, they do not care to assess either the potential need of a certain course in their region, or assess their own capabilities and resources to run it. Obviously, this unplanned, mushrooming growth results into the production of an endless number of half-baked graduates of that trade. In due course, a heavy glut is caused, and all employment channels get seriously choked. Thus, instead of helping the nation to alleviate the menace of unemployment, we in fact contribute to its perpetuation. The harm that these Institutes have done to the cause of teachers' training is an apt illustration of such a havoc. Thousands of ill-trained Bachelors in Education (B.Ed's) are roaming about the streets of our towns and villages.

Besides playing with the lives of the youngmen and youngwomen, we recklessly waste our precious little resources on the maintenance of these numerous unwanted study programmes. The need and logic behind the above-given regional networking scheme is to right these wrongs that have already been committed. Had some co-ordinated planning gone into the institution of these study programmes, much of the overlapping would not have taken place at all. Instead of the four Institutes of the region giving the same study programme, these programme could have been distributed mutually among themselves and would have thus managed them in a much better way than they do today.

Once this regional grid comes into existence, its various members may then co-ordinate themselves to work out their plans of future development. There is a vast scope for these institutes to supplement their existing study programmes with various new types of courses, particularly of the non-conventional nature. The fast-changing nature of our employment needs, arising out of the surging tide of the liberalisation of the economic policies all around, makes it incumbent on us to have these courses in order to train not only our youngmen and youngwomen but also those who need to be redeployed to new occupations/trades. What these Institutes need to do is, first, to identify the trades for which there is a scope in their respective regions and then distribute these new study programmes among themselves in accordance with their needs and capabilities. They may also then tie up with the industry in order to meet its requirements of the technical personnel and seek assistance from it in lieu thereof. This way the cut-throat competition among them and the resultant wastage of resources would be avoided, and perhaps the quality of instruction may also be maintained properly.

This concept of co-ordinated functioning can also be extended quite profitably to the existing study programmes. Given the requisite will, some of these Institutes may be persuaded to discontinue those study programmes that have turned unviable over the years. Thus, the regional grid can go a long way in streamlining both the existing and the future study programmes.

The other area where closely-knit network at the regional level can yield rich dividends is the collective development of the study centres. As highlighted in Chapter VII, every Institute does maintain a few study centres, but in most of these cases these are a mere apology of this concept. For, these are both ill-equipped and poorly maintained and hence of little use to the students. Many of the students are not even aware of their existence. Effective networking among the various institutes can go a long way in reinfusing life in them. Once the Institutes decide to pool their resources together, they can go ahead with the creation of composite study centres on the lines already suggested in Chapter VII.

To conclude, the benefits accruing from these closely-knit regional networks, are so profound in nature that those services (as for instance composite study centres or access to modern electronic technologies) which are presently beyond the reach of these Institutes, are made available to them at little or no cost. (Prakash Deshpande, 1985) More significant would be the image of enhanced respectability that they would reflect after having acquired the new capabilities. These Institutes would then be second to none in so far as the fulfilment of the various subtle requirements of distance education are concerned. Keeping in view such a far-reaching impact of regional networking, Mukhopadhyaya (1989) rightly emphasises that it is no longer a matter of choice for these Institutes. Instead, it has become a virtual necessity for them. The earlier this idea is put into operation, the better it is.

The question that now arise, if networking is so useful for the overall betterment of the Institutes, why has it not been given a trial so far anywhere in the country? Is it because the Institutes are not aware of the benefits that accrue from such a close collaborative arrangements? Or, is it because the Institutes and their parent universities shun such a give and take relationship? Indeed, it is the lack of awareness of the advantages as well as the unwillingness of the universities to bind themselves to any such quasi-compulsive network that lie at the root of this idea not getting mature. Until recently, it did not strike to anyone that this new system of education needed to be managed on lines different from the conventional system. On the contrary, the latter served as a model for it and, consequently, most of the Institutes of Distance Education have thus far been designed, staffed and managed on the lines of the conventional universities and colleges. Only lately, it has dawned upon our distance educationists that the needs and nuances of this system are different from the beaten track. Even this realisation has not become pervasive enough so as to catch the imagination of rank and file among them, with the result that the conventional university-run Institutes still continue to be modelled and managed on older lines.

The question arises, why do the conventional universities as well as the Institutes thereof hesitate to forge the ties of mutual co-operation with one another? The only roadblock in the way of the implementation of this idea is their functional autonomy. Today, they are quite free to command the destinies of these Institutes. Tomorrow when their Institutes enter into a regional network and commit themselves to prepare the study material, manage the study centres and do many other things on a collective basis, obviously the autonomy of these Institutes and their parent universities would suffer some erosion correspondingly. Instead of functioning independently without any outside interference, they will now have to work in collaboration with one another and as such each one of them shall have to show accommodation to another's viewpoint and act accordingly. In this whole game the biggest loser would naturally be the Director of the Institute. There is thus a danger that he might prove to be a villain of the peace. In India, no 'boss' wants to see his little empire invaded by anyone else and he thus spares no effort to fight out the 'aggression' and even to take pre-emptory steps if he apprehends at any time danger to his power and position.

But we must not overlook the fact that new developments and institutions when endear themselves to the rank and file of the population, do make a headway defying all opposition that obstructs their way and reach their destination ultimately. As for this type of networking, it is bound to come into being for the Institutes have been caught in such a situation that if they are to survive, they shall have no other way but to network themselves at the regional level and manage distance education in close collaboration with one another. The implementation of this idea is now a matter of time only.

## National Network

Next to the regional network comes the national network. It seeks to bring into its purview all the Institutes and Open Universities of the country, irrespective of the fact whether or not any Institute/Open University is a member of a regional network. In fact, the functional nature of the two networks is so different that hardly anything common is left between them. An Institute's partnership of a regional network encumbers it by no means from seeking the membership of the national network. In other words, the latter exists quite independently of the former which means that even if there is no regional level networking of the Institutes, the national network can still come into existence.

Unlike the regional network, the national network is a loose confederation/association of the various Institutes and Open Universities of the country. Its membership does not entail much of an obligation on individual Institutes, much less cause any erosion to their autonomy. It is a purely voluntary association which makes the members gain more than what they lose.

The national network is based on the consortium approach. As such, the members undertake to assist one another both directly and through the agency of the network. Since an experiment of this type has nowhere been conducted in India so far,(though it is quite common in Australia, Canada and Europe) nor are most of its exponents clear about the form that this network would assume in the long run, its functional nature cannot be spelled out clearly. Whatever little thinking has concretised thus far makes us infer that this network would primarily function as an information exchange agency. There would be set up one central information bank which would provide both to its members and the public at large all types of basic information about the state of distance education in the country. More than the public, it is the Institutes and Open Universities which feel utterly handicapped in the absence of any such source of information. If an institute, for instance, wants to introduce a certain new study programme, it would like to know as to which other Institutes/Open Universities already run that course so that it may either avoid its replication or seek help from others to run it effectively; it does not find any dependable source which may provide that information. In the same manner, if a person wants to pursue a certain course of study he too would feel handicapped, for he wants to know which of the Institutes/Open Universities are offering that particular course. Even this author had to face a good deal of difficulty in accumulating information regarding the courses of study and such other allied issues and if the information given in this book still remains incomplete despite the best of his efforts, the only reason is that no information store house has so far been built up. The national network would thus fill up this long-felt gap.

All Institutes and Open Universities of this country which would be brought into this network, would be required to feed the proposed National Information Bank of Distance Education (NIBDE). To begin with, they would provide to it such information as the study programmes that they offer, syllabi, duration, eligibility conditions thereof, the study material that they feed to their students, library, audio-visual and other facilities that they maintain and so on and so forth. Later on, whenever they institute a new study programme, they would transmit the relevant information thereon. In this way, they will help in NBIDE to up-date its information from time to time. On its part, the NBIDE would systematically process that information and would properly store it to be retrieved in times of need. In order to make this information available to the Institutes and the others, it would bring out publications and up-date them from time to time.

The information that will thus be available readily to the Institutes/ Open Universities will be of immense use to them. It will help them, *inter alia*, to suitably tie them up with one another for varied purposes. As suggested earlier, those falling within the geographical bounds of a region will set up a regional network for purposes of preparing the study materials for their various common study programmes, collective development and management of study centres and the like. Why must such an arrangement remain confined geographically? A few Institutes situated across the country may like to collaborate with one another for the limited purpose of the administration of only one common study programme. Hypothetically, there may emerge a host of such bilateral or multilateral collaborations in which four institute tie up with one another for the efficient administration of , say, Hotel Management Course, another four for Population Education Course and so on. Or, one Institute tying up with one set of three Institutes for one course, and with another four for another course, and with yet another three for the third course. In this away, the various ties of mutual collaboration may criss cross the country. The advantages accruing from this type of collaboration have already been explained at length.

The second important function that can profitably be assigned to the care of the national network is the accredition of courses of study that the various Institutes of Distance Education administer. Today, these Institutes offer an endless number of courses. But for those that are conventional B.A. and M.A. degree-oriented, the others are not recognised by one another. Obviously, their students are put to good many difficulties. They cannot for instance switch over/migrate from one Institute to another. In the same manner, a person who completes one level of a certain course from one Institute (say, the Diploma) wants to pursue it at its higher level (degree) which the Institute concerned does not provide for, he cannot go in for the higher course with another Institute unless he once again clears the lower level course with the Institute he now wants to join. The National Network can conveniently perform the role of accredition of those courses. It can call from the various Institutes exhaustive information regarding such aspects of their courses as their detailed syllabi, the duration of their completion, the study material that is given to the students, etc. On the basis of that information, it can extend recognition to those Institutes/courses which meet the standards laid down by it whereas those Institutes which fail to satisfy those standards may be refused this privilege. The study programmes thus nationally recognised will be open for admission/migration to every person. This accredition would further elevate these courses in the eyes of those employers who need the services of the personnel trained by these Institutes.

This accredition will thus go a long way in raising the quality of distance instruction in the country. For, in order to project a good image of itself, every Institute would like to gain national accredition for the courses of study that it offers. To that end, it would strive hard to maintain them at a certain universally-recognised level of efficiency. On its part, the national network can also work out the absolute standards that it would expect the Institutes to maintain in order to gain recognition at its hands. These standards can be prescribed in such terms as the quality of the study materials, the number of response sheets that a student should submit and the percentage of marks that one obtains, the number of PCP's to be given and attended by a student and so on. To further assure a certain reasonable quality of the lessons, the Institute may prepare national panels of subject specialists in various disciplines whose services they may requisition for purposes of the writing, vetting and reviewing of its lesson scripts. It may also work out the rates of remuneration for the various types of academic assignments to the teachers. In this way, it can help the Institutes maintain themselves and their courses of study at a certain nationally determined level of efficiency. If the national network assumes to itself this onerous responsibility and discharges it efficiently and objectively the distance education system of this country will then pull itself out of the dirty waters that have badly stained its reputation. Its social credibility will get a boost.

It may not be out of place to mention here that the British have already set up since 1969 a Council for the Accredition of Correspondence Colleges of their own country. Its principal objects are:

(a) "To promote education by setting standards for all aspects of tuition, education or training carried out wholly or in part by post, to investigate the manner in which such activities are carried out and to grant where appropriate, the award of accredition stating that the activities of the college so investigated conform to such standards.

(b) "To make known requirements of standards set by the Council from time to time . . . .

(c) "To give effect to the standards with a view to raising standards of postal tuition, to furthering its development on sound and progressive lines, to improving existing methods and introducing new techniques in postal tuition and to linking, where appropriate, correspondence courses with other forms of education.

(d) "To protect the interests of students and colleges having regard to the distinctive characteristics traditions and needs of both" (Quoted by Deshpande in *Indian Journal of Open Learning*, p.3).

As proposed above, our National Network can function on the lines of the British Council for Accredition of Correspondence Courses and thereby render substantial service to this nascent system.

Besides reflecting the correct state of health of this system, it will help it right many of its wrongs. This type of networking is, therefore, a national necessity. The earlier it is constituted the better it is.

## International Network

In this world where information plays a very dominant role in the lives of all of us, we need to be fully informed about what is going on around the globe concerning all those things that touch us directly or even indirectly. It is therefore highly imperative that our system of distance education should also be suitably linked with other parallel systems of the world. Unfortunately, today no such linkage exists. As a result, we are totally in the dark as to what type of courses are being given by the various Institutes the world over. Not to speak of the courses, we do not know even the names and nature of the Institutes that function in various countries. This information gap needs to be bridged at the earliest, only then can we think in terms of borrowing something from one another. It is here that we need international networking.

Like the National Network, the International Network can also serve as an ideal institution for the mutual exchange of information among the countries. Based thereon, the various Institutes across the world may then think of tying up themselves with one another for the joint administration of certain programmes, or may even consider the possibility of adopting wholesale those study programmes that are given by a few institutes. Another very important task that it can perform is the exchange of teachers among one another or to arrange for their short-term visits. Thus, this network can help distance educators draw closer to one another and thereby enrich their knowledge and experience.

Keeping in view such a wide range of advantages that would accrue from networking, International Networks have already been established at various levels. We may make a mention to two of them and explain their composition, objects and functions at some length. They are the DERRC (the Regional Resource Centre for Distance Education in Asia and the Pacific) and the Commonwealth of Learning.

*The Regional Resource Centre for Distance Education (DERRC) :* In November, 1989 two international meetings of distance educators were organised by the Asian Development Bank at the Allama Iqbal Open University (Pakistan) at Islamabad. The main theme of those conferences was how to forge closer ties of understanding among the various Institutes of Distance Education of the Asian and the Pacific Region. It is out of the deliberations of those conferences that the Regional Resource Centre for Distance Education for Asia and Pacific (DERRC) was born. It is located at the Sukhothai Thammathirat Open University (STOU) of Thailand, Bangkok.

The aims and objects of the DERRC then enlisted are as follow:

> "—the establishment and maintenance of a database containing information about member institutions' programmes, materials, personnel, etc;
> "—the collection and classification of print and non-print materials and their translation where necessary;
> "—the establishment and facilitation of a support information and communication network between participating institutions;
> "—the facilitation of co-operative production and use of distance teaching resources;
> "—the arrangement of training programmes and conferences;
> "—the organisation of co-operative research programmes".

The membership of DERRC extends to India, Pakistan, Nepal, Sri Lanka, Bhutan, Thailand, Indonesia, Japan, Korea and China (Ronnie Carr, 1990).

## The Commonwealth of Learning (COL)

The idea of sharing Commonwealth resources for the advancement of distance learning traces its origin to the growing concern of Commonwealth leaders about sharp reduction in student mobility due to the escalation of fees in certain countries. Commonwealth Heads of Government meeting at Nasau in 1985 requested the Secretary-General "to explore the scope for new Commonwealth initiatives in the field of distance education." The ensuing report, *Towards a Commonwealth of Learning*, recommended the establishment of an institution which should aim at "to widen access to education, to share resources, to raise educational quality and to support the mobility of ideas, of teaching, of relevant research and people" by harnessing in particular the advantages of new communication technology in the field of distance education. In 1987, when the Commonwealth Heads of Government again met for their conference at Vancouver, they recommended the creation of a Commonwealth institution to promote co-operation in the field of distance education. On the 1st of September, 1988, Commonwealth Governments formally agreed through a Memorandum of Understanding to establish the Commonwealth of Learning (COL) in Vancouver (Canada). It became operational in January, 1989 when the founding President, Professor James A Maraj assumed office (*Comlearn*, Vol.3, No.1).

The functions and objectives of the Commonwealth of Learning include:

(a) assisting the creation and development of institutional capacity in distance education in member countries;
(b) facilitating the channelling of resources to projects and programmes in distance education;
(c) providing information and consultancy services on any aspect of distance education including the selection of appropriate technology;
(d) undertaking and supporting staff training in the techniques and management of distance education;
(e) facilitating inter-institutional communication links;
(f) understanding and supporting evaluation and applied research in distance education;
(g) assisting the acquisition and delivery of teaching materials and more generally facilitating access to them;
(h) commissioning and promoting the adaptation and development of

academic credit;

(i) establishing and maintaining procedures for the recognition of academic credit;

(j) assisting in the development of local support services to students;

(k) stimulating and supporting any other activities that fall within the Agency's areas of interest by such means as may be approved by the Boards of Governors (*COL, Annual Report*, 1990, p.4).

In pursuit of these objectives, COL has initiated action in six different areas, namely Training in Distance Education Techniques; Materials Acquisition and Development; Technologies and Telecommunications; Information and Consultancy Services; Continuing Professional Education; Women in Development and Environment.

*1. Training in Distance Education Techniques:* With a view to developing training facilities on the techniques of distance education, a Round Table was organised at Vancouver, in 1990. In that meeting an action plan was drawn and, accordingly, three pronged action was initiated: training of trainers and key resource persons in each region of the Commonwealth, training the staff of national institutions in association with COL projects; and support for training initiatives by way of provision of training resources. During the second half of 1990 COL sponsored workshops, one in each of the four regions. These were held at Swaziland (Africa), Vannatu (Pacific region), IGNOU (South Asia) and Barbados (Caribbean region). In 1992, the second Pacific Region Training Workshop was held in Sydney (Australia) and similarly a four-day workshop, for the South Asian Region was organised by the COL at the IGNOU in July, 1994. The latter was attended by distance educators from India, Pakistan, Maldives, Sri Lanka, Bhutan, Nepal.

COL has also undertaken in collaboration with the Open Learning Agency of British Columbia the development of multi-media training packages on the use of technology in distance education. In this way, COL has taken various steps to promote training techniques in distance education in the developing half of the Commonwealth of Nations.

Yet another mechanism developed by COL to promote training facilities is the institution of COL Fellowship. In co-operation with the Government of British Columbia, COL has instituted 10 Fellowships for distance educators from developing countries. These educators spend one year on the campus of the British Columbia University and learn new things. In April, 1994, Rajiv Gandhi Foundation instituted in collaboration of COL Rajiv Gandhi Fellowships. Under the Scheme scholars from all over the Commonwealth will be awarded fellowships to pursue post-graduate studies through distance mode. In the first phase, 100 fellowships will be awarded for the study of distance education from the IGNOU. The applicants will be nominated by their respective countries. COL also promoted exchange of distance educators.

2. *Materials Acquisition and Development* : In collaboration with the UNESCO, COL has initiated a programme to develop learning material in engineering sciences at the under-graduate and the post-graduate levels. Materials have already been produced in such engineering fields as Applied Mechanics, Strength of Materials, Electrical Principles and Environmental Engineering. Study materials have also been produced for a post-graduate programme in management.

Recognising sports as an important area for furthering international understanding and the need to assure that all member countries of the Commonwealth have access to scientific training techniques, the Commonwealth Games Association of Canada and the Coaching Association of Canada have agreed to co-operate in providing audio-visual material for use in the training of athletes and sports coaches within the Commonwealth. Thus, COL has been making strenuous efforts to develop study materials in areas where there is a deficiency of them.

3. *Information and Consultancy*: With a view to providing information about the courses, institutions and literature in distance education, COL has built up a massive database. Till the end of 1991, this database contained detailed description of over 14,000 courses and programmes offered by institutions throughout the Commonwealth. The database also contains more than 300 institutional descriptions and in excess of 3,000 entries relating to distance education literature, research and study. The institutional and literature sections are world-wide in scope.

This database is located at the International Centre for Distance Learning (ICDL) of the British Open University. It is available both on-line and on CD-ROM (Compact Disc Read Only Memory). It is accessible to everyone, both individuals and institutions. The ICDL staff undertakes searches and answers enquiries on behalf of those who are not in a position to make use of either of these two means of access.

4. *Technologies and Telecommunications* : One of the important

concerns of COL is to develop modern educational technologies in all countries and institutions thereof. The first step that it took in this direction was to examine the existing state of these technologies in various regions and countries and then to explore the ways how to upgrade them. With these ends in view, it conducted indepth studies in various regions of the Commonwealth and consequent thereupon it helped a number of countries to acquire new technologies. In the African region, for instance, it commissioned a study on the status of TV/Radio network and rural communications infrastructure, covering 12 Commonwealth countries. Later on, COL entered upon an agreement with the Volunteers of Technical Assistance to make use of the Low Power Satellite System of the latter to strengthen communication links among the four West African Commonwealth countries.

In the same manner, COL's main contribution in the Caribbean Region has been to supply and install communications equipment to establish inter-institutional links within distance education infrastructure. It provided to the University of Guyana with a communication/word processing/desk top publishing centre for the development of study materials.

More significantly, COL has developed at the Indira Gandhi National Open University, New Delhi, the Commonwealth Educational Media Centre for Asia with view to promoting cooperation and co-ordination in the use of communicational media resource for distance education in Asia and South East Asia. This Centre became operational in July, 1994. Equally significant is the effort of the COL toward the establishment of a satellite-based global television service with a view to providing "an effective vehicle for North-South communications and for expressing and reflecting the cultural diversity of the world community as a whole". It has entered into an agreement with the Canadian International Development Research Centre for this purpose. Yet another significant development is the acquisition of video-conferencing capability for COL Brunie Centre for Professional and Continuing Education. It is hoped that as technologies advance and transmission costs decline, video-conferencing will become a major vehicle for communications sooner than later.

*5. Continuing Professional Education:* Promotion and upgradation of training facilities for the technical personnel forms another important area of operation of the COL. In 1990, it identified five broad areas in this respect. These are:

(a) Health Sciences (Medical, Nursing, allied health services, Medical technology and population/demographic studies),
(b) Law, Law related and Public Administration,
(c) Management, Accounting, Finance,
(d) Resource Management (Surveying, Planning, Land Economy and Engineering), and
(e) Support Services (Libraries, Archives, Journalism, Parliamentary Services).

Later on, another area, namely distance education to train unqualified and under-qualified teachers, was also identified. In 1991, COL entered into an agreement with the Ministry of Education, Jamaica, on the nature and scope of assistance that it would advance to the latter in the training of 800 primary school teachers. In 1990, COL sponsored a visit by six officials from Sieria Leone and the Gambia to the National Teachers' Institute in Nigeria to study the operation of distance education programmes for unqualified and under-qualified teachers. COL has also collaborated with the Commonwealth Secretariat in the production of a collection of case studies, demonstrating the use of distance education mode in teacher training and upgrading programmes.

In the field of health education, COL co-operated with the Malaysian Health Ministry in the creation of distance education network for health training. In 1993, an audio-graphics teleconferencing system was installed at the Malaysian University Faculty of Medicines. This network is being used to provide the delivery of a training programme in family medicine, continuing medical education, post-basic nursing, health services education, amd community education services.

As regards continuing judicial education, COL has undertaken two projects on the use of distance education and modern communications in this field. In 1992, a symposium on judicial education by distance education medium was organised at Trinidad. Thus, we find that COL is assisting many nations in the development and upgradation of training facilities in various fields of technical nature, which facilities are difficult as well as costly to create and manage by various individual Commonwealth members.

6. *Women and Development:* To promote the role of women in development, COL convened in New Delhi in November, 1990 a Conference of Women Vice-Chancellors and the others. "The conference affirmed the important role of distance education in extending access to

education to more women, and recommended that COL should play a central role in the dissemination of information on women's studies and legislation concerning women's status, as well as addressing training related to economic development as a priority for women." These recommendations formed the basis of an action plan on women in development. Some follow-up action was also initiated. Priority is being given to improve access to education by such sections of the women who must acquire skills to support their families and also to those who want to re-enter the workforce or become community leaders.

**REFERENCES**

Annual Report (1990), *Commonwealth of Learning*. COMLEARN. Vol. 3, No. 1; Vol. 4, No. 1; and Vol. 5, No. 1.

Deshpande, Prakash M., 'Validation of Programmes and Courses: Offered by the Indian Open Universities'. *Indian Journal of Open Learning*. (New Delhi), Vol. 2, No. 2

Deshpande, Prakash M., 'Student Support Services in Dual-Mode Correspondence/Distance Institutions', in Bakshish Singh (Ed.) *New Horizons in Distance Education*. New Delhi, Uppal. 1995.

Mukhopadyay, M., 'Networking in Distance Education', *Indian Journal of Distance Education*. Vol. III (1989).

CHAPTER XIII

# LOOKING AHEAD

AFTER having traversed a long course of history, distance education appears to have come of age. Multi-faceted objectives, methodological innovations and the dynamics of its operations have accorded to it, more or less, an independent place of its own, away and separate from the conventional system. Untrammelled by the constraints of time and space, it seeks to provide education to people as per their needs, requirements and convenience. It also equips them with work-skills of a varied nature. In an industrial society where hard competition for jobs pushes people into the employment market at a comparatively younger age and where incessant urge to better one's lot (professionally, economically and socially) goads them to an unending process of educational/work-skill improvements—distance education alone provides an avenue to fulfil their aspirations. The new electronic-based communication technologies and the remarkable manner these have been harnessed by distance education, have made it tread even the most difficult terrains of educational/work-skill development. Older fears about the capability of this system to manage technical education or anything of the sort have long since been allayed and the system is now fully geared to meet any challenge of educational development. Its having demolished the narrow walls of the school/university and also (thus) having acquired for itself the capacity to impart instruction on a mammoth scale has further equipped it to meet the challenge of the mass industrial society of the 20th and the 21st centuries.

Thus distance education has distanced itself pretty away from the conventional system. That both the systems are basically educational in nature should no longer mislead us that their objectives are identical and that they should continue to be clubbed together. Though both of them have thus far been functioning together with hands in gloves with each other not only in India but almost everywhere else in the world (the dual mode), distance education has been evolving itself slowly and gradually into an independent system of its own. The Open University model, an outcome of this quest, has caught the imagination of the people the world over. Unhampered by the constraints of the conventional system and (more specifically) of its managers, open universities freely innovate as well as undertake ventures in all domains of human resource development, thereby enhancing their capability to face the challenges of modern industrial societies. Marvellous success achieved in this direction by the British Open University, on the one hand, and the IGNOU, on the other, have proved the efficacy of this model beyond doubt.

The two systems—conventional and distance, even though different from each other, are by no means locked in competition against each other. Both of them have their own respective roles to play. While the conventional system is engaged in imparting education and skill-development to the youngsters, distance education provides to the grown-up adults second-chance education, thereby fulfilling their life-long ambition for higher education as also enhancing their competitive capability and helping them redeploy themselves from one occupation/employment to another. Thus having two different sets of people to cater and two different instructional technologies to operate, they should be kept separate from each other. This is all the more desirable in the Indian context where the overbearing attitude of the conventionalists have reduced these Institutes to their personal fiefdoms, thereby stunting their growth badly.

Their distinctness from the conventional system with respect to their domain and methodology of instruction as also the raw deal that the latter gives to it, impel us to suggest that the distance system should be delinked from its conventional counterpart. The dual mode as it operates today should be given an early burial and all the Institutes of Distance Education as well as Open Universities should be merged together to form half a dozen of Regional Open Universities. The existing duality in the system (somewhere there are Institutes and somewhere Open Universities) should be completely done away, making place for the unidimensional model of the open universities. Each one of these Regional Open Universities should be conceded full freedom to operate at a nation-wide scale and also to offer any type of courses that it may deem fit. This type of freedom would assure to them, on the one hand, congenial environment for healthy competition among them and immunity against the interference of the state level petty politicians, on the other.

In order to meet the monetary needs of these Open Universities, both capital and recurring, there should be constituted a new separate funding agency which may be designated as Open University Grants Commission (OUGC). It should be furnished with sizeable allocation of funds for their onward distribution among the National as well as Regional Open Universities, lest financial stringency on their part should tell upon the standards of their instruction as is the case today. The present policy of leaving these institutions to fend for themselves shall have to be discarded in the larger interests of human resource development of the nation. These institutions deserve to be given a treatment identical to the institutions of the conventional system.

That all the Institutes of Distance Education and the Open Universities (with the sole exception of the IGNOU) should be, first, delinked from their parent conventional universities and then merged with one another to form half a dozen of Regional Open Universities, that the latter should be treated as Central Universities and be conceded nation-wide functional jurisdiction, and that their funding be taken away from both the U.G.C. and the IGNOU and, instead, be entrusted to a new body Open University Grants Commission (OUGC) are too bold suggestions to be accepted easily by the powers that be. For, they would give a jolt to many a vested interest which is too formidable to be disarmed easily. To name a few of these interests. They are, first, the parent universities of these Institutes. Howsoever loudly they may decry distance education and the Institutes thereof, they would certainly not cherish the idea of their being deprived of these Institutes. Not to speak of those universities whose Institutes earn for them fabulous profits, even the others too would feel quite sore over the loss of the vast patronage that they exercise on them. Equally true would be the case of those State Governments which would also be deprived of control over their Open Universities. Further, they would also not cherish the idea of the Regional Universities being put under the purview of the Central Government. In these days of ultra-chauvinistic state politics any such move is bound to create a new spur in the already controversial centre-state relationship. Teachers working in these Institutes would constitute another roadblock. As mentioned earlier, they who identify themselves less with the Institute they serve and more with their counterparts working in the conventional wings of their parent universities with whom they consider their interests inextricably intertwined, would also not like the existing arrangement to be disturbed. Yet another interest to be affected is the IGNOU which is on the threshold of assuming to itself the total responsibility of developing, co-ordinating, controlling and funding of distance education in the country.

These vested interests apart, the proposed suggestions, embodying fundamental reforms in the realm of human resource development as they do, would evoke wide-ranging reaction, thereby precipitating the gravity of the challenge. To push these reform through may therefore become difficult. But at the same time, the urgency involved in streamlining the structural mechanism of the system so as to meet the growingly-complex challenge of human resource development can neither be overlooked nor delayed. It may be emphasised that day by day our dependence on distance education is increasing, the reason being certain inherent limitations of the conventional system and the resource constraint to stretch its network too wide.

The phenomenon of the growing dependence on distance education, coupled with the not-so-favourable an attitude of the conventionalists and, above all, the boldness of the suggestions made above, impel us to propose that it would be in the fitness of the situation if the Government of India gets the whole issue thoroughly examined through a high-power committee before it undertakes these reforms. In this respect, we can draw a leaf from the Australian book. The Government of that country has shown a remarkable degree of courage and far-sightedness in streamlining the system in all its various dimensions, thereby arresting the state of drift that had crept into it. Why cannot we also pick up courage in both hands and do it ?

In continuation of our above-given suggestion to delink distance education from conventional education, we feel that the former should concentrate increasingly on technical type of education and provide skill-development to the people. By doing so, it would not only meet the aspirations of the grown-up adults but would also share with the conventional system the responsibilities of furnishing to the nation with large cadres of such well-trained technical personnel as accountants, managers, teachers, doctors, engineers, computer scientists and the like, which task the latter would not be able to perform on its own. The delinking of the two systems would further imply that distance education should not undertake instruction in general education. Let the latter remain the exclusive privilege of the conventional system. Such a compartmentalisation would obviously raise the question of the fate of those youngsters who when fail to find accommodation in conventional colleges and universities, make their way to the Institutes of Distance Education. Generally, it is the lure of general education of B.A. and M.A. that pushes them to this system. There is no denying the fact that the nation cannot afford to set up more of conventional type of institutions for them and distance education shall have to absorb this overflow. However, we must not at the same time overlook the fact that a fast-developing industrial society like India needs more of technicians than graduates in liberal arts, languages and humanities. Moreover, the youngsters who come to distance education are mostly those persons who, hailing from the economically and socially depressed sections of society, are not well-exposed to the harsher realities of the every-day world. Hence they are in greater need of both educational guidance and the job. Distance education system would do well by helping them divert themselves from the beaten-track unproductive courses to the more employment-oriented technical courses. However, in the initial stages, distance education system may design courses having a good mix of both the general and the technical education. Such courses would provide due incentive to these youngsters, on the one hand, and help meet the requirements of the nation, on the other.

Distance education needs to be further rescued from the traditional criteria of its evaluation. Today, the success and failure of an educational institution (those of distance education including) is judged, quantitatively, in terms of the rate of the drop-outs and the percentage of the successful candidates in the terminal examinations, and, qualitatively, by the number of merit positions and first divisions that an institution bags, again, in the terminal examination. As mentioned earlier these criteria are misplaced in so far as this system is concerned. To measure its success objectively we need to devise new criteria which may take due cognizance of such factors as the nature of students who come to this system, the constraints they suffer from and the objectives they seek to achieve. We feel that the value of an Institute of Distance Education can be assessed better in respect of the effectiveness of its study programmes as measured in terms of (a) securing employment to its students, (b) re-deploying them from one job to another, and (c) helping the in-service personal to keep themselves abreast with the day-to-day developments in their respective disciplines/trades. On the top of it, how do its students acquit themselves at their work-places both professionally and morally. It may also be observed that distance learners are so highly motivated that they hardly need to be told to be serious in their studies. They themselves spare no effort to successfully accomplish the task they have undertaken. If anyone of them fails to do so, it must be due to some unavoidable reason.

However, the quest for the new criteria and the discarding of the older ones must not make the distance education providers oblivious of the standards of their instruction, may be out of sheer indifference or a sense of complacency. They must ensure at all costs that the study materials that they issue forth in any form—written, audio, video, computer-mediated, etc. etc., is by no means inferior in quality. Before these materials are sent out to the students, they must be properly pre-tested on a select sample of students, carefully reviewed by the experts, meticulously up-dated, suitably illustrated, impressively brought out and thereby assured of its quality in every possible way. Likewise, the PCP that they hold, are handled competently by seasoned and committed teachers. In the same manner, the response sheets that students submit (and they may be required to submit them as per the norms) are properly and promptly evaluated and returned to the students. In this way, care needs to be taken at every step so that distance education in general and the Institutes in particular are absolved of the oft-repeated charge of providing sub-standard education.

We feel that in case these Institutes take pains to keep their instructional services in top gear, they can bring about a radical improvement in our overall educational standards. For, compared to the conventional system, distance education commands to its service an educational technology which, if harnessed with a little bit of care and expertise, can furnish to the students a first-rate study material. It has been widely observed that some of the correspondence lessons, which bear an imprint of scholarship and hard work, have not only won the appreciation of the students as well as the teachers of the conventional system but have also furnished reference material to the text book writers. If such lessons are also backed up by audio and video support, they can galvanise the instructional system further. How to derive the full advantage of this technology depends upon the caliber of the teachers who are entrusted with the task of developing these study materials. In turn, it becomes imperative on the part of the Institutes that they recruit on their faculties well-qualified, seasoned and reputed teachers and must not compromise on this account under any circumstances. At this juncture we are reminded of Lord Perry, the first Vice Chancellor of the British Open University, who tells us that he had exercised utmost care and caution at the time of the recruitment of his faculty. Equally important is that the Institutes adopt the corporate approach in the development of the study materials. Seriousness shown on these accounts will go a long way in providing an edge to distance system over every other system.

To further ensure the standards of instruction, a suitable supra-institutional mechanism may also be evolved. As suggested earlier, this task may be entrusted to the national-level network of Distance Education Institutes/Open Universities. Basically designed to function as an Accredition Council for these institutions, this network would also work out standard norm which every Institute/Open University would be required to observe in order to gain accredition at its hands. Keen to maintain its reputation in the market as each Institute would naturally be, it dare not deviate from these standards. This national level council of the network, though a voluntary organisation, would thus act as a bulwark against the danger of the falling standards. Incidentally, this Council would also check the havoc that some Institutes are causing to such courses as the bachelor course in education.

## II

The foregoing part symbolises the ideal. To translate it into practice would require massive political will which, in turn, would be generated only if the various vested interests are suitably reconciled, which indeed is a difficult and time-consuming task. It is therefore but obvious that reforms would take a long time to mature. Till this task is accomplished successfully, numerous measures of an interim nature are urgently called for in order to stem the rot.

At the outset attention needs to be paid towards those ugly tendencies on the part of the Institutes which fetch a bad name not only to them but also to the system at large. One such tendency relates to the reckless extension of the admission dates by some Institutes. It is observed that though the last date for admission (even with late fee) generally expires in late September or early October, these Institutes go on admitting students, under one pretext or another, till the following February. They do so in order to boost their enrolment which, in turn, means greater income. Late admissions imply that with the terminal examination scheduled for April, the Institute's student's get hardly two months for studies. In comparison to them, their counterparts, enrolled with conventional colleges and university departments, who too are governed by the same courses and syllabi of studies and who too are to take the examination along with the Institute's students, study for nine months—July to March. Evidently, such a practice of unduly late admissions would make a mockery of the system of distance education and put the Institutes to public ridicule.

Another equally deplorable tendency is that the Institutes consider that their academic responsibility to their students is confined to the servicing of the lessons only (written scripts). As a result, such other aspects of the system as response sheets, PCP and counselling are badly neglected. It is not that they do not provide for these academic adjuncts. But they do not take them seriously. Take the case of response sheets.

Detailed rules and regulations regarding their number and the timings of their submission are laid down by all these Institutes. But in practice, they do not bother whether or not any student has submitted the required minimum number of response sheets and if any one has not done so (in fact there are lots and lots of them) they would not care to take due cognizance of this defaulter and detain him from taking the terminal examination. Further, they also do not properly attend to the task of effective and timely evaluation of response sheets. In so far as the PCP is concerned, it too is conducted neither at as many places as needed nor by competent and committed teachers. Obviously many students find it listless and devoid of any utility.

These two tendencies when combine together make the system of distance education abut of public criticism. The conventionalists who decry it as an institutionalised contrivance to sell the eligibility of the university examination, cannot be rebutted. It is therefore highly desirable that these Institutes must be made to strictly adhere to the official dates of admission. If admissions to regular colleges/university departments close, say, by the end of July, the Institutes can legitimately prolong them by another two months in view of the flexibility in the system both with regard to the mode of study/instruction and the size in enrolment. But the September-end should be the outer-most limit. No extension, regular or clandestine, should be allowed under any pretext. This is quite certain that once it becomes clear that an Institute is not going to relent in matters of admission, all those candidates who are desirous of seeking admission to it, would do it in time.

In the same manner, the Institutes should also be equally firm with regard to the response sheets. To overcome the problem of non-compliance of the stipulated requirement of the submission of a minimum number of response sheets, the Institutes of a region should develop a common policy not to admit one another's rejectees. Once they firmly implement that policy they can go ahead without any fear or hesitation in taking full cognizance of those cases where the said condition is not satisfied. When they harden their posture, the students would dare not defy that condition. After all, the Open Universities too get this condition discharged from their students. At the same time, the Institutes should also streamline the mechanism of effective evaluation and quick disposal of the response sheets lest the students have a grouse to grumble.

Another tendency which too needs to be curbed relates to the rat-race among the Institutes toward the introduction of new study programmes. Whenever an institute finds a certain study programme a bit lucrative, it adopts it without any proper planning or preparation and also without the least consideration for either its managerial capability or the absorption capacity of the market. In due course of time, the others also follow suit. All of them appear to be led away by the rich revenue potential of the course concerned.. Why would it not yield huge piles of money for the Instituten especially when it admits students in tens of thousands? There is nothing wrong in admitting a large number of students to a course. In fact, economies of scale demand so, provided the Institute has the requisite wherewithal as well as the will to provide quality instruction to all those who are admitted. But unfortunately most of our Institutes have badly failed on this account. The B.Ed. course provides the best illustration of both the lust for money on the part of the Institutes and the poor quality of their instruction. The cumulative impact of this rat-race is that the market gets flooded with half-baked graduates of that particular discipline or trade, inflating the ranks of the unemployed, on the one hand, and further lowering the performance-standards of the public servants, on the other. Distance education thus gets another blow at the hands of the public. Tragically, the UGC does not possess any power to dissuade or forbid them from entering into that mad race. The plain truth is that when these courses fetch fabulous incomes for these Institutes, they care a fig either for the U.G.C. or for its grants. To curb this tendency, it is essential that the U.G.C. should be provided teeth so that it may be able to put an effective curb on the erring Institutes. Side by side, serious efforts should be made to set up the National Network of the Institutes and the Open Universities. As alluded above, the national level Council of this Network would put an effective check on such reckless tendencies of the member Institutes. Besides making them adhere to the prescribed academic standards for the various study programmes, this Council would put a moral pressure on them with regard to the introduction of new courses. It hardly needs to be emphasised that where everything else fails, moral pressure and the fear of the public opinion alone succeeds.

Steps also need to be urgently taken with regard to the networking of the Institutes and the Open Universities at the regional level. As discussed in Chapter XII, the Regional Network would enable the member-Institutes to pool their resources, among other things, for the preparation and production of the study materials on a collaborative basis. Not only will the Institutes be able to improve the quality of their lesson-scripts but would also bring them out in their various new electronics manifestations. A major shortcoming on their part would then be removed, thereby qualifying them for enlistment in the coveted category of the Institutes of

Distance Education, *per se*. It is not necessary that networking should remain confined to one geographical region only. For purposes of the management of different types of study programmes, the Institutes may tie up with one another across the length and breadth of the country in bilateral and multi-lateral collaborative relationships. These ties that would criss-cross one another like airways, would facilitate the task of the member-Institutes in proliferating their study programmes in a more meaningful and constructive manner than what has been the case thus far. Incidentally, this arrangement would also avoid the colossal wastage of resources, arising from the current practice of unplanned multiplication of these study programmes.

Staffing pattern constitutes another area of serious discord among the Institutes. Some of them do not maintain any faculty at all, some support a skeleton faculty of a few teachers only, while some go in for a full-fledged faculty of professors, readers and lecturers. Each one of the Institutes commends the model that it adopts. But objective assessment does not approve of anyone of them. Every model has its own strong and weak aspects, which land it into various types of different problems. If the non-faculty Institutes put their reliance exclusively on outside teachers for the administration of their instructional programme, the full-fledged faculty Institutes are confronted with such problems as arise from the sagging morale of their teachers, their trade-union activities and the inelasticity of mobilisation. On the top of it, both these models do not provide a scope, for the introduction of the corporate approach in the preparation of the study materials. The whole issue thus needs to be comprehensively looked into with a view to developing the norms for the staffing pattern of the Institutes of Distance Education. While working out the norms, care should be taken to ensure (a) that the Institute should not be left completely at the mercy of either the outside faculty or the internal faculty of its own, (b) that sufficient academic support is available from within the Institute so as to provide effective guidance to the students as also to meet the emergencies arising out of the delay in lesson-preparation; (c) that the work of the preparation of the study materials is undertaken in a corporate (as distinguished from the individual) manner; and (d) the faculty does not suffer from the sense of alienation.

Howsoever well-managed an Institute may be, it cannot ever hope to be fully self-sufficient in its faculty requirements. There are a number of academic needs which being seasonal in nature, cannot be fully coped with internally. To employ a very large whole time internal faculty for these things would not be either academically sound or administratively prudent. Every Institute must therefore depend to a small or a large extent on the guest faculty from outside. Keeping in view the critical role that the latter performs in the overall functioning of the Institute, it is very important that the Institute recruits them on semi-permanent basis implying thereby that teachers once selected would be seldom removed unless their conduct or work is not satisfactory. If they are to work year after year on a semi-permanent basis and perform such academically crucial functions as evaluation of response sheets, conducting of the PCP and even the writing of lessons, it is imperative that they are selected carefully and then given an orientation course so as to induct them into the new system in a proper manner. Random selection of such a personnel on contract to contract basis and without any regard to one's familiarity with (much less expertise in) distance education, is yet another cause of the poor performance/image of this system. Staff training and development not only for the internal faculty of the Institute but (perhaps more importantly) for the guest faculty is an essential input of the system. How ironical it is that those conventional teachers who derive various type of the benefits from distance education, turn out to be its arch critics. More often than not their criticism/animosity emanates from their ignorance of the nuances of the system. It is therefore all the more important that they are properly educated about the system and imparted training in the performance of the various duties that are entrusted to their care.

Non-contiguous nature of distance education and, concomitantly, the postal and tele-communicative mode of reaching the students put an extra-ordinary burden on the administrative wing of the Institute. As a matter of fact, administration is the central arch upon which the whole edifice of the Institute rests. The success of the system, therefore depends to a very great extent upon the efficient conduct of this particular branch of the Institute. But it is observed that most of the Institutes and Open Universities do not take pains to make their administration as efficient as the system demands of them. Being a product of the general ethos of the society, they too tend to take the things in a casual and indifferent manner. That sense of earnestness to serve and satisfy the manifold requirements of distance students is somehow lacking on their part. Quite often, the lessons do not get ready in time and when they are ready, they are despatched late or even wrongly. Public inquries are not seriously attended to. Students' difficulties and letters written in connection thereof are not redressed and replied promptly. In this way, their administrative functioning presents a dismal picture. By and large, this is true of every Institute. In order to streamline the administrative wing of the Institute, it is important that the functioning of each branch/cell should be made target-bound. The targets should be defined more in terms of time than in numbers. More importantly, the targets, once determined, should be strictly adhered to and those who show sluggishness on this account should be duly punished. Mere enunciation of policy will not do, unless its strict enforcement is ensured. The possibility of introducing a system of punishment and reward may also be explored.

Another method of inducting efficiency in administration is to computerise its various operations. It is an open secret that machines are far more efficient and accurate than men. There are a number of areas in the Institute's administration where a computer can really do wonders. These are : printing and production of lessons, maintenance of the records of students fees, response sheets, periodic progress, accounts-keeping, library, etc. etc. It hardly needs to be empahsised that it is on account of its poor performance in these specific areas that the Institute's reputation suffers. Computer can thus help it to rehabilitate itself, administratively.

Students' complaint redressal is yet another aspect of the administration which needs to be taken due care. Ironically, where this particular administrative area is so vitally important for the overall well-being of the administration, it generally tends to be ignored. In an Institute of Distance Education, where the clientele is physically situated away from the scene of action, it is but natural that the number of complaints is larger than in the case of those institutions where there is a direct face-to-face interaction between the clientele and the administration. This is all the more so because of the generally low level of administrative responsiveness of the Institutes. The complaint redressal mechanism needs to be suitably geared up so as to ensure prompt disposal of the complaints and grievances. It will help the Institute to gain students' confidence and the goodwill of the public at large. The main objective of the overall reforms of the administration is to see that the recipients of the system who cannot come to the Institute every now and then for the receipt of the lessons or the payment of the fees and the like, are promptly entertained to. Their satisfaction and goodwill constitutes the barometer of the success of the Institute as well as of the system.

## III

The ultimate goal of distance education is to provide an alternative channel of education so that whoever has not been able to derive the benefit from the conventional system, may get his aspirations of educational development fulfilled through it. This goal can be achieved only if this system is delinked from the conventional system and is completely freed from all such pre-conditions of time and space as are characteristic of the former. In other words, it should be made as open and flexible as possible. The emerging theory of education that one is neither to be forced for education nor debarred from it; one may have as much of it as one likes and can absorb, further makes a case for openness and flexibility. Conversely, if such conditions as entry qualifications for the various distance study programmes, ceiling the limit on enrolment of students, attendance in PCP, and the like, are not dispensed away innumerable aspirants of education/skill development who suffer from one constraint or another would not be able to derive the benefit of even this system. But once it is released from all such pre-conditions, it would revolutionise the whole gamut of educational opportunities. People would no longer feel handicapped. They will have access to every type of educational and skill improvements whenever and wherever they may like to have it. In this age of competition and economic hardship the common man is prepared to go to any extent in order to better his lot. He wants to enhance his capabilities by means of hard work and even by acquiring new skills and educational qualifications. The pursuit of excellence has become the watchword with everyone. It is therefore incumbent on society that it must throw open the floodgates of all educational institutions and more specifically those of distance education, so that it provides congeniality of opportunity to all. It may be added that after the battle for social and political equality has been successfully concluded, the task ahead is to demorcatise educational opportunities. The conventional system cannot be democratised beyond a certain point, because of the inherent limitations in it. Distance education, being free from those systemic constraints, needs to be thrown open for all so that everyone, irrespective of one's age, sex, place of residence, occupation, education and the like may be able to derive benefit from it and thereby enhance his competitive capabilities, if he so desires, or meet his aspirations, whatever these may be. Distance education must therefore rise to the occasion and discharge the responsibilities that democracy and development has put on it.

## IV

In the end, it may be observed that the times ahead are going to be highly challenging. Fast-spreading urbo-industrial culture and the impressive success of the massive literacy campaigns (that we have initiated of late) combine together to infuse among the rank and file of the people a passion for education. Those who are without education want to have it while those who already have it want to have more and more of it. Obviously, the number of the education seekers is increasing with a geometrical progression. At the other end of the continuum, inelasticity inherent in the conventional system inhibits it to cope with this ever-inflating demand. As a result no less than one-tenth of the higher education students have already gone over to the Institutes and Open Universities. This is the state of affairs when only one-third of our population is literate and the youth have not so far been stung by the bug of the modern civilization of running amuck with materialistic pursuit of jobs and jobs (one after another) in order to acquire economic prosperity and status in society. Imagine the magnitude of pressure that would be mounted on distance education when the literacy rate is doubled (if not trebled) and those who are presently living in the rugged country-side are also exposed to the modern cult of consumerism and competition. Everyone would then be driven mad for distance education in order to find in it a suitable passport both for a better station in life and a good pastime to while away their boredom at home and in the later years of their life.

When distance education is going to sell at such a higher premium, the question arises, is it suitably conditioned to meet this colossal challenge? The answer is, obviously no. The reforms proposed in the foregoing pages thus become all the more urgent and imperative in view of the demands that are going to be made in the 21st century. Everyone—educationists (distance as well as conventionalists), administrators and planners —must take this work seriously and apply his mind imaginatively in tandem with one another so that the highly crucial task of human resource development is tackled in an effective manner, thereby securing the future of the nation.

# INDEX